GH00359676

HARPER & ROW SERIES IN ACCOUNTING AND FI

Consulting Editor: Michael J. Sherer

The aim of this series is to publish lively and readable te
polytechnic and professional students, and important, up-to-date reference books
for researchers, managers and practising accountants. All the authors have been
commissioned because of their specialist knowledge of their subjects and their
established reputations as lecturers and researchers. All the major topics in accounting and finance will be included, but the series will give special emphasis to recent
developments in the subjects and to issues of continuing debate and controversy.

THE PRICING DECISION: ECONOMIC THEORY AND BUSINESS PRACTICE

Neil Dorward is Pro-Rector at the Polytechnic of Central London. Previously he held the posts of Dean of the Business School, and Head of Accounting and Administrative Studies, at the Polytechnic of North London; Visiting Fellow in Business Economics at the University of La Trobe, Australia; and Senior Lecturer in Economics at the City of London Polytechnic. Since gaining a Ph.D at the London School of Economics, he has published over twenty-five articles and research papers in a wide range of journals, including the *Journal of Industrial Economics*, *Applied Economics*, *Accounting and Business Research*, *Managerial and Decision Economics*, *The Manchester School* and *Accountancy*. He has extensive CNAA experience both as an external examiner on degrees in business studies and economics and as a board and committee member.

THE PRICING DECISION: ECONOMIC THEORY AND BUSINESS PRACTICE

NEIL DORWARD
Polytechnic of Central London

Harper & Row, Publishers
London

Cambridge
Mexico City
New York
Philadelphia

San Francisco
São Paulo
Singapore
Sydney

First published 1987

Harper & Row Ltd
28 Tavistock Street
London WC2E 7PN

British Library Cataloguing in Publication Data
Dorward, Neil
   The pricing decision: economic theory and business practice.
   1. Price policy
   I. Title
   658.8'16   HF5416.5

ISBN 0-06-318369-2

Typeset by Mathematical Composition Setters Ltd, Salisbury
Printed and bound by Butler & Tanner Ltd, Frome and London

To my father

Contents

Series Editor's Foreword

Price is the most important element in a company's marketing mix, and hence the pricing decision is often crucial to a company's entire marketing strategy. The price of a product or service performs a number of roles, both inside and outside the company. The price of the final output represents the financial sacrifice that a consumer needs to make in order to consume the product on offer; that price also provides information to competitors and potential new entrants about the returns that can be earned from selling a particular product. Inside the company, the price of a department's products will affect its profits and, perhaps, the remuneration of the departmental manager. Consequently, although economic theory can identify the correct pricing policies a company should follow, these policies may not always be appropriate for the actual long term objectives of the company, and economic principle may at times have to be compromised in order, for example, to induce the right kind of behaviour from department managers. Therefore, business practice rarely conforms exactly to the behaviour predicted by economic theory.

In his original and highly readable book, Neil Dorward compares what economic theory says about pricing with what accountants say and with what businessmen do. He has produced one of the most thorough and extensive reviews of the empirical evidence on the pricing decisions in British firms in recent years. One conclusion that emerges from the book is that many of the rules of thumb used by businessmen in their pricing decisions are often reasonably good proxies for the technically correct rules derived from economic theory.

This book will be particularly valuable to accounting students since most of the conventional accounting books give a very summary treatment to the pricing decision. In addition, business studies and economics students will benefit from a textbook which puts pricing policies firmly within the context of marketing management, and which recognises the contribution that accounting academics are making to the problem of measuring the appropriate costs for pricing decisions.

Neil Dorward has previously written many articles on pricing in academic, professional and management journals, and he has now produced a textbook which combines a thorough and comprehensible analysis of economic pricing theory with an extensive survey of pricing in practice. I am delighted that "The Pricing Decision" is one of the first books in the new Harper and Row Series on Accounting and Finance.

Michael Sherer

Preface

I have sought to present, within the same text, the main economic theories of pricing and the evidence on business pricing practices and, in so doing, examine the nature and extent of the gulf that is supposed to exist between theory and practice. Although this is a subject which occupies an important place on most undergraduate courses in managerial economics, industrial economics and applied economics, there is currently a lack of a suitable up-to-date undergraduate text devoted to a detailed discussion and review of pricing issues. While there are plenty of texts which present the economic theory of the pricing decision, they tend either to ignore or to skip briefly over the empirical evidence. This text attempts to fill this gap in the market.

The intended readership is primarily second and final year undergraduates studying for degrees in the fields of business studies, economics and accounting. It should also serve as a useful supplementary text for first year graduates of industrial economics and accounting, as well as for students on MBA programmes. The reader is assumed to have taken an introductory course in the theory of the firm and to have an elementary understanding of the basic quantitative techniques used by economists, including the ability to read a regression equation. While I have tried to use a non-mathematical approach whenever possible, many economic pricing models cannot be presented concisely and intelligibly without some minimal use of equations and differential calculus. However, those without a formal training in mathematical and statistical methods need not be put off as a supporting verbal and diagrammatic exposition is used wherever necessary.

This book is envisaged as a supplementary text, complementing the main textbooks used on courses in managerial economics, industrial economics and applied economics. However, the subject-matter covered by the term managerial economics is rather ill-defined and readers will find that this book covers most of what are generally regarded to be the core areas of the subject. In fact, the only areas featuring on most managerial economics courses which are not covered in depth are linear programming; competition policy; public sector pricing; and the location decision. On the other hand, this book offers the additional topics of overhead allocation and joint costing; marketing strategy; the interrelationship between the pricing, advertising and investment decisions; as well as a range of specialist pricing topics.

The scope of the book

The book is basically designed in four parts. First, Chapters 1 and 2 provide an introduction to the pricing decision and a review of the main theories of the firm, with the emphasis on their respective contributions to the analysis of pricing. Second, Chapters 3, 4 and 5 review costing in theory and practice to provide an understanding of the costing base used for making pricing decisions. Third, Chapters 6, 7, 8 and 9 consider general pricing issues including the traditional profit-maximizing pricing model, the effect of oligopolistic competition, the theory of full-cost pricing, demand estimation, and the empirical evidence on business pricing practice. Then finally, Chapters 10 to 14 consider a number of special pricing topics, including the pricing of new products, product bundling, price discrimination, transfer pricing, pricing and the advertising to sales ratio, and target rate of return pricing.

Throughout the book, there is an emphasis on the results of empirical research. Chapters 4 and 9 and much of Chapter 6 are exclusively devoted to an analysis of the empirical evidence on costing and pricing. With the exception of the main theoretical chapters – 3, 7 and 8 – all the remaining chapters include summaries of the empirical evidence and consider its theoretical implications. While I have given a strong British orientation to my selection of studies of pricing practice, I have also summarized, or made reference to, the main studies emanating from the United States, Canada, Western Europe and Australia.

Acknowledgements

In many ways this book has grown out of the intellectual stimulus I have received from the many colleagues with whom I have worked at different times over the past twenty years, particularly John Curran, Howard Davies, Norman Foot, Peter Franklin and Len Stafford. I would like most of all to thank my wife, Lynn, for all her help, encouragement and forbearance as well as for undertaking most of the typing. My special thanks also to Mavis Robinson who helped with typing the final manuscript.

1 An Introduction to the Pricing Decision

THE COMPLEX NATURE OF THE PRICING DECISION

Studies of actual pricing decisions taken by businessmen have revealed a very complex decision process. Much of the complexity results from the multi-dimensional nature of pricing decisions. They usually incorporate many variables, of which the number, composition, and relative importance, together with the form of their interrelationships, can vary between different pricing situations within the same company. Further complexity is added by observations showing that the pricing decision is made in different ways in different companies with many varying procedures to be followed. Hague (1971) found that the way managers analysed the information used to determine price varied with the size of the group involved in taking the decision. Indeed, with large group pricing there was so much informal discussion going on between several levels of management outside the formal meetings, that he found it difficult to know where, and by whom, the final decision was made. Hague (1971) also discovered that management's freedom to fix prices was constrained by the company's own pricing objectives; the pressures of market competition; and by the human and organizational relationships and pressures within the company.

At this stage it is as well to point out three further complications affecting the analysis of the pricing decision. First, although price is often regarded as being the most important decision variable in a company's marketing strategy, its effect on the other marketing decision variables, such as advertising, sales promotion and product differentiation, cannot be ignored. While all marketing decision variables, including price, have their own independent effects on sales revenue, they can also interrelate with each other. Such interrelationships imply not only the need to estimate the trade-offs between the marketing decision variables but also an approach to decision-making in which the key marketing variables are considered simultaneously.

A second complication is that 'the price' can mean different things in different market situations. While 'the price' of a packet of biscuits in a supermarket can be unambiguously read from its price label, the price sticker on a popular brand of motor car normally indicates only the maximum price likely to be paid. The actual price paid is usually the outcome of confidential negotiations between customer and dealer involving either cash discounts on the sticker price or 'special' trade-in values on the customer's existing car. The price of hiring a car for the weekend is normally in two parts; a fixed rental plus a rate per mile. The transfer price for a promising young soccer player can be in three parts; for example, £50,000 on transfer, a further £50,000 after a specified number of first-team appearances for his new club, and another £100,000 if he plays for his country. In this case, both buyer and seller are uncertain of the 'final price' at the time of the agreed transaction. As a final example, the price of electric windows in a new BMW motor car is different when bought separately than when bundled together with other optional extras in a one-price luxury pack.

Third, for some product groups the price set today may have considerable implications for future demand, cost and competition. For example, a 'skimming strategy' of charging an initially high price which is then progressively reduced over time should take full account of the effect of that initially high price on the market entry of new competitors, as the rate of new entry can affect the steepness of the downward price path. In these circumstances, the pricing decision should be considered in a dynamic context as prices today will affect prices tomorrow. This should require the discounting of future revenues and profits to express them at present value so that alternative pricing strategies can be properly compared and evaluated.

MODELLING THE PRICING DECISION

Faced with such complexity, management has developed various methods of simplifying the process of taking pricing decisions. These tend to be based on the common problem-solving procedure of looking at the various parts of the problem sequentially rather than simultaneously (see Hague, 1971). Simplification is also achieved by concentrating only on what management regards as the key pricing variables. It seems that management has approached complex pricing decisions by stripping the problem down to its bare essentials and including only the most important factors affecting price. More formally this procedure is known as modelling. In many companies, the 'models' remain informal and appear to operate in the form of custom and practice. In others, they take the form of fully documented procedures concerning detailed costings and demand estimates. However, an increasing minority is building fairly complex computerized models similar to those used by economists and which have the potential for a more sophisticated and simultaneous approach to the price decision.

It is in the area of modelling that economics can make its most effective contribution in helping management resolve its complex pricing problems. Microeconomic price theory provides an extensive toolkit of economic principles and assumptions which can be used in various ways to model the price decision.

Most economic pricing models have been largely concerned with predicting the effect of changes in model parameters on the direction and amount of price change needed to bring the system back to equilibrium. In so doing, they have developed methods of identifying relationships between the pricing decision and a number of important explanatory environmental variables (or constraints), including the number and size distribution of sellers (competitors); barriers to new competition; new technology; and utility-maximizing consumer behaviour. Consequently, economic price theory has much to contribute to the solution of the practical business problem of selecting the most appropriate pricing strategy for a particular economic environment or market situation.

While stressing the important contribution that economic models can make to business pricing decisions, it is equally helpful to point out their limitations. Otherwise, as Nagle (1984, p. 3) stated, 'if one approaches economics expecting too much, one may well come away with too little'. Models are intended to take the complexity of real-world situations and reduce them to something manageable. A pricing model should provide a highly simplified, or abstract, representation of a real-world pricing situation. It should not attempt to describe realistically in every detail how management comes to make a pricing decision. The purpose of modelling is to eliminate as many of the real-world variables as possible leaving only that minimum number necessary to convey an accurate representation of the fundamental relationships dominating a pricing process. Consequently, with so much detail stripped out, the resulting model cannot be directly applied to produce a complete and satisfactory resolution of a practical real-world pricing problem. Its use is limited to providing a good understanding of the principles at work in any given pricing situation. The practical decision still has to be taken by the businessman applying common sense and hunch to whatever detailed information is available. The value of the modelling approach is that it should result in better pricing decisions than relying on pure hunch alone.

Regrettably, many businessmen become disillusioned with economic models because they find them to be oversimplified and too remote from reality. Much of the problem lies in their misunderstanding of the role of assumptions in economic analysis. The purpose of assumptions is to simplify the problem by restricting its behavioural possibilities so that it can be abstracted sufficiently from reality to permit analysis and solution. For this purpose, the assumption need not be completely realistic. An example is the frequently criticized assumption that the firm seeks to maximize its profits. While most businessmen admit to setting profit targets, many deny any attempt at maximizing profit. However, in a pricing model the relevant test should be not whether profit maximization is a realistic assumption, but whether its inclusion makes the model more effective in explaining price-setting behaviour or in predicting future price movements.

The failure of most businessmen to appreciate the role of assumptions in simplifying complex pricing problems down to easily manageable proportions has resulted in their unfortunate tendency to construct pricing models which are either too informal or too detailed to ensure that their decisions meet their own corporate objectives. Informal models are not documented, the assumptions remain obscure and, as a consequence, pricing decisions can veer towards inconsistency. Excessively detailed models lack sufficient assumptions to be operationally efficient and, in extreme cases, different managers within the same company can make different assumptions when attempting to solve their own separate parts of a sequential price decision. By contrast, a careful selection of assumptions can provide a useful modelling framework with which to construct appropriate pricing strategies on which detailed pricing decisions can be based. Without well constructed pricing models, management is more likely to select the wrong strategies and in so doing risks making a series of inconsistent and sub-optimal pricing decisions.

OPTIMIZATION, UNCERTAINTY AND RULES OF THUMB

The traditional economic model of the firm and all the managerial economic models of corporate behaviour assume that management seeks to maximize an objective function. Although they differ in respect of the content of that objective function – the traditional model including only a single profit variable while the managerial models include one or more variables other than profit – they can all be classified as models of optimizing behaviour. This means that decisions (a form of behaviour) can be evaluated in terms of whether or not they are optimal – meaning they result in outcomes which maximize the objective function of the particular model being applied. For example, an optimal pricing decision under the profit-maximization assumption would determine a volume of sales which would maximize the difference between the firm's total revenue and total cost. For this to be possible, we must also assume that the decision-maker has *complete knowledge* of the firm's demand function, production function and factor costs.

One major problem in applying maximization models of the firm to an analysis of decision-making in business is that businessmen have to operate with *incomplete knowledge*, or *uncertainty*. Instead of each price generating a unique revenue outcome, it will have a range of possible revenues, of which some may be more probable than others. In the case of complete uncertainty, all possible outcomes would be equally probable. Consequently, businessmen have to make their pricing decisions with a paucity of information, more of which can be acquired only by incurring additional research costs. With uncertainty, therefore, information takes on the characteristics of a scarce resource.

It would appear from the management literature (see, for example, Ansoff, 1965) that the typical management response to decision-making under uncertainty is to abandon any quest for a maximand. Instead of maximizing an objective function, management specifies a set of *minimum performance targets* or goal thresholds, including such targets as a rate of profit, a market share and a rate of growth. In these circumstances, decisions tend to be based on rules of thumb, each of which incorporates one of the targets. Typical pricing rules of thumb would include pricing to earn a target rate of return; full-cost pricing, where a target gross profit margin is added to unit variable cost; and the price-matching of competitors' price in an attempt to maintain market share.

However, it is possible that under conditions of imperfect information the joint specification of performance targets and simple decision rules of thumb could be used as a route towards the maximization of those targets. Baumol and Quandt (1964, p. 23) went so far as to argue that 'rules of thumb are among the most efficient pieces of equipment of optimal decision-making'. We will consider the optimality potential of targets and rules of thumb separately.

Performance targets and long-term optimization

Although management performance targets tend to be loosely specified, with little known about their interdependences, Loasby (1976) considered this to be an advantage in that it permits a more flexible management response to the many new promising opportunities made available by an ever changing environment. Indeed, one could go one step further and suggest that the flexibility made possible by loosely specified targets could in itself be regarded as an objective for a long-run objective function. Dorward and Wiedemann (1981) more or less did this when they specified *robustness* as an appropriate maximand for a management facing uncertainty, where maximizing robustness means taking only that decision which retains the maximum number of *desirable* and *attainable* options from those existing prior to the decision (note that it is the nature of a decision to foreclose at least one option). By defining robustness only in terms of preferred courses of action, it becomes the *dynamic* instrument by which management can manoeuvre the firm into a position of being able to make decisions which could optimize its performance targets over the long run. Therefore, optimality and uncertainty are not incongruous when placed in a dynamic framework.

Rules of thumb and optimal decision-making

Simple rules of thumb can offer a rational and consistent approach to decision-making when faced with either unknown or partially known demand and cost functions. As information is imperfect and therefore costly, an efficient management will stop acquiring it when the incremental cost of additional research is equal to its anticipated incremental gross yield. (One would like to substitute marginal for incremental but this might be inappropriate in conditions of uncertainty.) Therefore, the amount of information considered by management to be worth acquiring will frequently be inadequate for the direct application of maximization decision rules such as 'marginal cost equals marginal revenue'. With the amount of information for direct maximization being too costly, management is forced back to the second best of using cruder, though more cost-efficient, rules of thumb based on performance targets.

In a simulation study using different cost and demand functions, Baumol and Quandt (1964) found that three of their six pricing rules of thumb could on average get within 75 and 95 per cent of the maximum profit. They also found that the simplest rule outperformed the more sophisticated. Therefore, in business practice, where the profit-maximizing price will always be unknown in advance of the decision, the popular target rate of return and full-cost pricing rules of thumb could provide the basis for alternative routes to profit maximization. However, their implementation could only be regarded as approximating profit-maximizing behaviour if the rate of return and profit margin were adjusted in accordance with significant changes in demand and variable costs. A failure to make such price adjustments would suggest non-profit maximizing behaviour.

DECISION RULES FOR SUBJECTIVE RISK

An alternative route to maximizing an objective function when faced with uncertainty, and one which is theoretically more acceptable than the rule of thumb approach, is to establish a 'probability' framework for the pricing decision. This is possible when the businessman has some intuitive feeling as to the probabilities of different revenues materializing from a particular price decision. As the assigned probabilities are based on the subjective assessment of the decision-maker, the decision framework is referred to as one of *subjective risk*. We will look at two decision rules based on subjective risk which in certain circumstances may be applicable to the pricing decision, namely 'expected value' and 'certainty equivalents'.

Expected value

This decision rule assumes that businessmen are indifferent towards risk (risk-neutral). If a businessman were to estimate five possible revenues, R_i, expected from charging price P_j, and then assign probabilities p_i to the revenues such that

$$\sum_{i=1}^{5} p_i = 1 \qquad\qquad 1.1$$

the expected value of the revenue from charging P_j would be calculated as

$$E_j = \sum_{i=1}^{5} p_i R_i; \text{ where } j = 1, \ldots, m \qquad\qquad 1.2$$

In other words, so long as the probabilities of the estimated revenues sum to 1.0, each estimate can be weighted by its probability of occurrence and the results summed to give the expected value of the revenue to be received from charging price P_j. Obviously, different prices give different expected values. From a range of m possible prices, management can calculate a distribution of expected values, E_j, sufficient to construct a revenue schedule from which the profit-maximizing price (or the price optimizing some other function) can be estimated in the usual way. The maximization procedure has been made possible by substituting expected values for the unknown certainty values.

 Statistically, this decision rule is based on the *law of large numbers* which requires the subjective probabilities to be derived from a number of successive and independent trials. Unfortunately, these conditions are rarely satisfied in business practice. Not only do environmental conditions tend to change, particularly consumer preferences and competitive forces, but managers tend to learn from their experiences. Therefore, it is difficult to get observations on a series of revenue outcomes which are both independent and subject to identical environmental conditions.

A more fundamental objection to the expected value decision rule is that it does not take account of the fact that decision-makers may have positive or negative attitudes to risk. Rather than being indifferent to risk, some managers have been observed to enjoy risk-taking, while the vast majority are often assumed to be risk-averse.

Certainty equivalents

This decision rule is based on the widely accepted assumption that managers are risk-averse. This means that when confronted by two or more revenue distributions, each having the same expected value, the typical manager is assumed to prefer that distribution characterized by the lowest amount of risk exposure. Given uncertainty, all expected values will contain an element of risk in the form of a dispersal of estimated revenues so that the risk-averse manager will need to adjust each expected value downwards by his or her degree of aversion to risk.

What is assumed to happen is that each manager applies a risk-adjustment factor to convert a risk-exposed expected value, E_j, into a lower certainty equivalent value, C_j. The difference between the two values can be expressed as a risk premium which would have to be paid to the manager to make him or her indifferent between them.

The certainty equivalent decision rule can be expressed as

$$C_j = \alpha E_j \text{ where } 0 < \alpha \leq 1 \qquad\qquad 1.3$$

The certainty equivalent adjustment factor, α, is inversely related to the manager's expectation of, and aversion to, the degree of risk such that it will become infinitely small at very high levels of risk exposure. Consequently, as with expected value, the certainty equivalents can be substituted for the unknown revenue values and the profit-maximizing price estimated in the usual way.

There are at least two significant drawbacks in trying to apply certainty equivalents. The first is that, other than in risk-oriented activities such as insurance, management will find the estimation of α to be too complicated and expensive. Useful estimates of the α function will require an exact specification between α and those coefficients used to measure risk. This requires not only estimates of the variance or standard deviation of a dispersal of estimated revenues but also estimates of its skewness; the degree to which there is a greater or lesser probability of high revenues rather than low revenues. The more a distribution is skewed towards high revenues the less the assumed risk. Normally, management's revenue estimates will not provide a data set of sufficient detail or quality to generate meaningful risk coefficients.

Second, the assumption of total risk aversion may be rather too strong. It precludes consideration of the fact that managers may change their attitudes to risk as circumstances change. It could be that they are risk-averse when expected values are relatively low but then adopt positive attitudes to risk when expected values are relatively high.

PRICING IN PRACTICE

There seems little doubt that a profit-oriented management would adopt the *marginal revenue equals marginal cost* rule of pricing if its decision-making scenarios were as well specified as those of the abstract models of economic theory. In practice, pricing decisions have to be made in economic environments characterized by uncertainty, where the available information is usually too sketchy for the direct application of those marginalist principles that form the basis of economic maximization models. Although the economic analysis of subjective risk provides a theoretically acceptable way of generating estimated values for inclusion in applied versions of economic pricing models, we have seen that such estimates could be both costly to produce and in violation of the statistical theory on which they are based.

Business management has tended to take the more practical and lower cost route to optimal decision-making by employing pricing rules of thumb which it can adapt to suit the prevailing market conditions. The dominant pricing rule of thumb in business practice is full-cost pricing. Most managements tend to use this cost-based price to provide an initial estimate of the unknown demand function. However, as we shall see time and time again in the later chapters dealing with the theory and practice of pricing, this initial demand estimate (the full-cost price) will be subsequently adjusted in the light of experience and a series of more directly demand-oriented prices will follow. Circumstances causing revisions to be made in the full-cost price include rising order books; increases in unused production capacity; changes in competitors' prices; and changes in variable costs. (For a brief case study of such an application of full-cost pricing to the Jaguar XJ12, see Harrison and Wilkes, 1973.)

By using a full-cost pricing model which incorporates, either formally or informally, a demand adjustment term, marketing managers can set prices which form a practical analogue to those that would be predicted from a profit-maximizing pricing model when subject to the same informational constraints of unknown demand functions and non-marginalist accounting cost data (Dorward, 1986). The emphasis throughout this text will be on comparing pricing decisions as observed in business practice with those suggested by the profit-maximizing model. On balance, the evidence suggests that most firms set prices which correspond with the qualitative predictions of the profit-maximizing model.

REFERENCES AND FURTHER READING

Ansoff, H. I. (1965) *Corporate Strategy*, McGraw-Hill.
Baumol, W. J. and Quandt, R. E. (1964) Rules of thumb and optimally imperfect decisions, *American Economic Review*, Vol. 54 pp. 23–46.

Dorward, N. (1986) Overhead allocations and 'optimal' pricing rules of thumb in oligopolistic markets, *Accounting and Business Research*, Vol. 16, pp. 309–17.

Dorward, N. and Wiedemann, P. (1981) Robustness as a corporate objective under uncertainty, *Managerial and Decision Economics*, Vol. 2, pp. 186–91.

Hague, D. C. (1971) *Pricing in Business*, George Allen & Unwin.

Harrison, R. and Wilkes, F. M. (1973) A note on Jaguar's pricing policy, *European Journal of Marketing*, Vol. 3, pp. 242–6.

Loasby, B. J. (1976) *Choice, Complexity and Ignorance*, Cambridge University Press.

Nagle, T. (1984) Economic foundations for pricing, *Journal of Business*, Vol. 57, pp. 3–26.

2 Corporate Objective Functions and Pricing

PROFIT MAXIMIZATION

The traditional theory of the firm assumes that the firm has an objective function containing only one variable, namely profit, which it seeks to maximize in the short run. It also assumes that the firm makes its decisions on output and price with a complete and certain knowledge of future costs and revenues. Given these two simplifying assumptions, the theory has the advantage of predicting a unique and easily interpretable price and output for any given set of market conditions.

Essentially, the profit-maximizing assumption is an abstraction from reality. It is not designed as a precise and realistic description of what motivates management within real firms in the everyday world. Rather, it represents a simplification or distillation of the complexity of motives and their trade-offs which exist within real-life business organizations. It states not that real firms *are* profit maximizers, but only that the profit-maximizing assumption provides a meaningful abstraction by which to predict the pricing and output behaviour of real firms when reacting to given changes in the conditions determining costs and revenues.

As Friedman (1953) argued, the test of a good theory is whether it can accurately predict aggregate behaviour, not whether its assumptions are real. And the predictive record of the profit-maximizing objective is reasonably good. While, in general, firms may not actually set out to maximize profits when setting prices, the evidence seems to indicate that they often appear to behave as if they do. Certainly, no alternative specification of the objective function has yet been able to come within reach of its ability to predict price levels and price changes.

Short-run profit maximization and price prediction

If total revenue is denoted by R and total costs by C, the total profit of a firm is given by

$$\pi = R - C \qquad\qquad 2.1$$

Maximum profits are determined by selecting an output, Q, where marginal revenue, $\delta R/\delta Q$, equals marginal cost, $\delta C/\delta Q$. This profit-maximizing output can be found by differentiating equation 2.1 with respect to Q to give marginal profit and then setting this equal to zero before solving for Q

$$\frac{\delta \pi}{\delta Q} = \frac{\delta R}{\delta Q} - \frac{\delta C}{\delta Q} = 0 \qquad\qquad 2.2$$

Interestingly, equation 2.2 provides us with the conditions for predicting changes in output and price. As marginal revenue and marginal cost define the slopes of the total revenue and total cost curves respectively, we can see that the only factors of change which will affect the profit-maximizing price or output will be those affecting the rate of change of total revenue and total cost in respect of changing output. Therefore, we can make the following predictions:

(i)   an increase in demand will increase $\delta R/\delta Q$ and so *increase* output and price;
(ii) an increase in variable costs will increase $\delta C/\delta Q$ and so *decrease* output and *increase* price;
(iii) an increase in fixed costs (or a lump-sum tax) will not affect $\delta C/\delta Q$ and so output and price will remain *unchanged*;
(iv) an increase in the rate of profits tax will not affect $\delta R/\delta Q$ or $\delta C/\delta Q$ and so output and prices remain *unchanged*.

Despite its widespread acceptance among academic economists, the profit-maximization assumption has been subjected to three major criticisms. First, as a static theory it ignores the dynamic nature of business behaviour, such as when charging relatively high prices in the short run could lead to an influx of new competitors causing relatively low prices to be charged in the long run. Second, if the certainty assumption is dropped, there will no longer be an objectively based unique price–output prediction, but many possible prices, each dependent on the subjective risk attitude of individual managers. Third, it fails to take account of circumstances where managers are determined to maximize some other objective such as current sales or growth. Such alternative motivational assumptions will result in different pricing predictions from those given above. These criticisms will be taken up in the following sections.

LONG-RUN PROFIT MAXIMIZATION AND UNCERTAINTY

A dynamic approach to profit maximization requires the firm to maximize the aggregate difference between all future revenues and costs up to some time horizon. Profits are now envisaged as a stream, or flow, running through time which must be discounted back to a present value in order to evaluate alternative long-run pricing strategies comparatively. That strategy offering the highest present value will be selected for implementation.

The purpose of discounting is to convert future expected profits to a current or present value. The logic of this procedure is that £1 today is worth more than £1 in, say, two years time as current money can be invested to earn interest. For example, at the end of two years our £1 would be valued at £1$(1 + i)(1 + i) =$ £1$(1 + i)^2$, where i is the rate of interest. Therefore, the present value (PV) of a stream of future profits, π_t, is given by

$$PV_\pi = \sum_{t=1}^{n} \frac{R_t - C_t}{(1 + i)^t}$$
2.3

where n is the time horizon. Equation 2.3 defines the long-run profit function. When capital markets are perfect, the maximization of equation 2.3 will maximize the market value, or corporate wealth, of the firm.

Unfortunately, there are two problems with the dynamic approach to profit maximization. The first is that it implies a pricing strategy rather than a specific price. Although some pricing strategies contain a long-run base price, others frequently follow a price path in which price rises or falls over time (see Chapter 10 for a fuller discussion). Therefore, long-run pricing is more concerned with a direction of price movement than a particular price at a given point of time. In addition, a particular base price or price path may be chosen as part of the strategic decision in the knowledge that it will be accompanied by a series of short-run tactical price decisions, an example of which would be price discounting (Rao, 1984). Consequently, the long-run profit-maximizing model, while placing current pricing in the context of its effect on future profits, may not always be helpful in predicting an optimal tactical price for the short run.

The second problem derives from the fact that one cannot sensibly discuss long-run pricing without taking into account the uncertainty affecting future revenues and costs. For example, a skimming price strategy of charging high prices now to those with immediate needs and low prices later to those who can afford to wait may have to be abandoned either because of unexpected price cutting by new competitors or intervention by the Monopolies and Mergers Commission. Although the statistical techniques for handling uncertainty (as outlined in Chapter 1) can be used to compute expected values or certainty equivalent profits, for substitution into equation 2.3, the resultant present value of profit has become dependent on the assumed risk attitude of management. In other words, an objective present value criterion is transformed into one of subjective evaluation. As a result, the important characteristic of making generally applicable price predictions for a given point in time has been lost. Given uncertainty, the long-run model is only usefully applicable to the selection of a rather generalized and somewhat subjectively based pricing strategy.

The direct effect of uncertainty on the selection of a pricing strategy can be seen in the context of the time horizon, the value given to n in equation 2.3. The longer the time horizon, the greater the uncertainty affecting more distant revenues and costs. As uncertainty devalues longer-term profits, a strategy of charging relatively low prices to improve market penetration will have a higher probability of being rejected the longer it takes to build up a dominant and profitable market share.

MANAGERIAL OBJECTIVE FUNCTIONS

Since Berle and Means (1932) claimed that a separation of ownership and managerial control tended to occur in large organizations, there have been many instances of such organizations enjoying positions of market power. This has led many writers to suggest that the combination of these two conditions allows management sufficient discretion to pursue its own motivations at the expense of the owners' profit objective. Management motivations are variously described but can be summarized as power, prestige, salary, and security from takeover (Marris, 1964, ch. 2). However, these motives are difficult to evaluate in terms of the conventional theory of the firm as they do not easily translate into recognizable variables such as profit, sales, output or growth.

The most popular view is that managerial utility is most readily satisfied through larger firm size. Roberts (1956), McGuire, Chui and Elbing (1962) and Marris (1964) all found significant correlations between executive income and corporate sales. This empirical work and a large number of detailed studies of actual business organizations have inspired the development of a number of managerial models of the firm based on the maximization of an objective function in which profit features as a constraint rather than as an objective. Baumol's (1959) sales-maximization model, Williamson's (1963) model of managerial discretion and Marris's (1964) growth model are prime examples. We will go on to review these in terms of the differences between their pricing predictions and those of profit maximization.

However, more recent research into the relationships between executive income, corporate size and profitability has cast some doubt on the motivational validity of managerial objective functions. Meeks and Whittington (1975), while confirming previous research that executive income was more closely correlated with sales than profitability, also found that changes in profitability will have more effect on income than changes in size. A stronger defence of the role of profits was provided by Lewellyn and Huntsman (1970) who found executive income to be correlated with profit but not with sales.

Baumol's sales revenue maximization model

Baumol (1959) argued that managers of large corporations seek to maximize total revenues rather than total profits. He presented static and dynamic versions of his model and suggested that short-run revenue maximization might be consistent with long-run profit maximization. We will only be concerned with the single-period model. The one constraint on sales revenue maximization is for profits, $\pi(Q)$, to be at least equal to $\pi(Z)$, a minimum level determined by the capital market.

The model can be presented with the help of Figure 2.1. The firm will maximize sales revenue when marginal revenue is zero. Therefore, assuming positive marginal costs, the associated output Q_R will exceed the profit-maximizing level Q^* as long as $\pi(Q_R) > \pi(Z)$. In this case, the profit constraint, $\pi(Z)$, will be

Figure 2.1   Sales revenue maximization

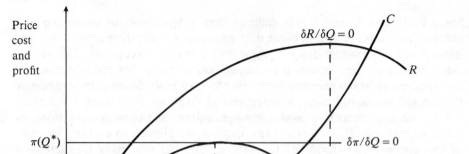

ineffective. However, should $\pi(Z)$ exceed $\pi(Q_R)$, say at $\pi(Z_1)$, the constraint will become effective and the firm will be forced to restrict output to Q_1. Yet this new output still exceeds Q^* and, as long as $\pi(Z)$ is less than the level of maximum profits, $\pi(Q^*)$, the sales revenue maximizer will produce at a point where marginal revenue is less than marginal cost. As a result, it will always produce a larger output than a profit-maximizing firm and, assuming a downward-sloping demand curve, it will always sell at a lower price.

Obviously, the price predictions derived from this model depend on whether or not the profit constraint is effective in restricting output to a level either at or below that required for maximizing sales revenue. Baumol (1959) argued that as short-run revenue maximization was compatible with long-run revenue maximization, the firm would spend all profits in excess of $\pi(Z)$ on advertising so as to increase sales for any given price level. As a consequence, actual profits will always be kept equal to the profit constraint which will be effective over all future single time periods.

Assuming that the profit constraint is effective, any change in costs, fixed or variable, and any change in taxation by affecting profits will result in a change in price and output. Whenever $\pi(Q) < \pi(Z)$, output will have to be reduced in order to bring profits back up to the minimum $\pi(Z)$. This results in the following differences in price prediction from those given by the profit-maximization model:

(i)   an increase in fixed costs (or a lump-sum tax) will reduce profits and lead to a decrease in output and an *increase* in price;
(ii) an increase in the rate of profits tax will reduce profits and lead to a reduction in output and an *increase* in price.

In both these cases, prices would have remained unchanged under profit maximization.

A major difficulty in evaluating managerial models is that their predictions depend as much on the specification of the constraint as on the content of the objective function. This was effectively demonstrated by Yarrow (1976) when respecifying the constraint in the Baumol (1959) model as

$$\pi(Q) \geq \pi(Q^*) - c \qquad 2.4$$

where c is a fixed cost borne by wealth-maximizing shareholders and takeover bidders when seeking to compel management to revert to profit-maximizing behaviour. The cost of compulsion includes the costs of forming a shareholder coalition, of proxy fights and of changing the management team. Therefore, inequality 2.4 shows that the amount of management discretion in allowing profits to fall below the profit-maximizing level, $\pi(Q^*)$, is limited to the size of the compulsion cost, c.

If we respecify the Baumol (1959) model by using inequality 2.4 rather than his constraint, $\pi(Z)$, and assume that it is fully effective, we get price predictions different from those given by him. For example, if fixed costs increase by F (or a lump-sum tax of T is imposed), the profit curve moves downwards by the same amount, F (or T), at all rates of output. It follows that when the constraint is effective, $\pi(Q) - F = \pi(Q^*) - c - F$ and, therefore, the intersection of the constraint and the reduced profit function must occur at the same output level as before. Consequently, by simply respecifying the constraint, the price prediction for a sales revenue maximizer faced with an increase in fixed costs has been altered from an increase to one of no change. While in this particular case the price prediction is identical with that for profit maximization, in other situations it can be different.

Wiliamson's model of managerial discretion

Most managerial motives are prevented from being directly incorporated into models of corporate behaviour because they cannot be measured in monetary terms. Williamson (1963) attempted to get round this difficulty by arguing that managerial motives tend to be realized in the form of *expense preference* behaviour. He identified three types of managerially preferred expenses. The first type is staffing expenditure (S) which is approximated by administrative and selling expenses. A larger staff provides greater authority and opens up promotional opportunities. The second type is emoluments (E) which take the form of payments in excess of that required to retain the services of managers, such as expense accounts and executive office suites. The third type is discretionary investment expenditure (I_D) which is over and above that undertaken by a profit-maximizing management.

Williamson (1963) incorporated the three types of expense preference into a utility function (U) which management seeks to maximize as

$$U = U(S, E, I_D) \qquad 2.5$$

Maximization is subject to a profit constraint whereby the reported after-tax profit $(\pi_r(Q) - T)$ must either equal or exceed a minimum profit, $\pi(Z)$, demanded by shareholders. Management always plans to exceed the profit constraint as the excess profit (discretionary profit) is required to fund discretionary investment.

An essential condition for utility maximization is that the optimal output is determined by equating marginal revenue with the marginal cost of production. Although this is identical to the profit-maximizing condition, it does not imply that the output levels are the same. The reason for this is that in both models marginal revenue is an implicit function of selling expenses (part of S) and the utility maximizer, unlike the profit maximizer, has a positive preference for expenditure on S. To the extent that the utility maximizer's relatively higher S expenditures are devoted to selling activities, he will be on a higher demand curve and enjoy a higher marginal revenue than the profit maximizer. Therefore, there is a tendency for the utility maximizer to produce a greater output and sell at a higher price. However, there remains some ambiguity about this outcome as it depends on the utility management gains through selling expenses as against that gained from other items in S.

The Williamson (1963) model predicts the following differences in price reactions from those given by profit maximization:

(i)   An increase in fixed costs (or a lump-sum tax) will enforce the profit constraint and the firm will have to generate more pre-tax profits by reducing expenditure on S and E. To the extent that this cuts selling expenditures, the demand curve will shift to the left causing a *reduction* in both output and price.

(ii)   An increase in the rate of profits tax will encourage the firm to reduce its tax burden by reducing discretionary profits through increasing expenditure on S and E. To the extent that this increases selling expenditures, the demand curve will shift to the right causing an *increase* in both output and price.

As in the case of the Baumol (1959) model, these results are dependent on the specification of the profit constraint. For example, if the Yarrow (1976) specification of the constraint was applied, the predicted price reaction to a change in fixed costs would again revert to one of no change as in profit maximization.

The Marris growth model

Within the Marris (1964) model, the motivations of managers are realized by maximizing the rate of growth of the firm. However, growth has to be funded via a capital market which acts to constrain those financial policies it finds unacceptable, such as low liquidity ratios, high profit retentions and high gearing ratios (the ratio of debt finance to the total of debt plus equity). The capital market constraint can be measured either as a minimum valuation ratio (the ratio of the market value of the firm to the book value of its net assets) or by some profit index such as a minimum rate of profit. Effectively, the constraint is that

Figure 2.2   The Marris (1964) growth model

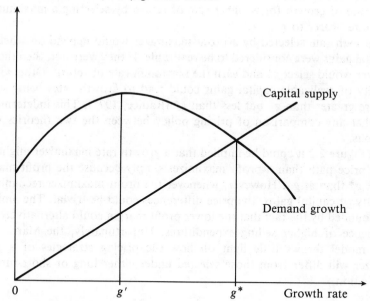

level of financial security at which present management feels safe from the threat of takeover and insolvency.

In maximizing its objective function, management must seek to balance the growth of demand with the growth of the supply of capital. This is because the model assumes *steady-state growth* in which all corporate variables, including assets, sales and profits, grow at the same constant exponential rate for ever. A failure to achieve balanced growth would result in a permanently growing excess capacity or excess demand. Any decision to change the rate of balanced growth would cause the firm to shift to a new steady-state growth path.

The trade-off between growth and profitability that is available to management is illustrated in Figure 2.2. The growth of demand curve shows the maximum rate consistent with the rate of profit. Increasing the rate of demand growth from zero will initially improve profitability as the firm is enabled to exploit more new product opportunities and enjoy any associated monopoly profit, but eventually still higher growth will require lower prices and higher marketing expenditures causing the profit margin and hence the rate of profit to fall. The supply of capital curve is a straight line through the origin and shows the maximum sustainable rate of growth in capacity at each rate of profit. Its slope is determined by the financial security constraint; a tighter constraint, say in the form of a higher rate of profit, causing a steeper slope. The intersection of the growth of demand and supply curves at g^* determines the maximum 'safe' steady-state balanced growth path. Any growth rate in excess of g^* would breach the constraint and would be unsafe. Although all rates of growth to the left of g^* are safe and sustainable, the growth maximizer would only be interested in reaching g^*. The analysis underlying Figure 2.2 portrays the financial security constraint as a minimum profitability constraint, with a more security conscious management trading off a lower rate of growth for a higher rate of return by selecting a maximum safe growth rate nearer to g'.

The growth rate selected by a profit maximizer would depend on whether or not capital gains were considered to be realizable. If they were not, then the profit maximizer would select g' and earn the maximum rate of return. Otherwise, the possibility of realizable capital gains could lead to growth rates being selected which are greater than g' but less than $g*$ (Radice, 1971). This indeterminancy means that any comparison of pricing policy between the two theories will be ambiguous.

From Figure 2.2 it could be implied that a growth rate maximizer might be on a lower price path than a profit maximizer simply because the profit margin is lower at $g*$ than at g'. However, whenever the profit maximizer recognizes the possibility of capital gains, the price differences could be trivial. The ambiguity is compounded by the fact that the lower profit margin could alternatively be the consequence of higher selling expenditures. Unfortunately, the Marris (1964) growth model throws little light on how the pricing strategies of a growth maximizer will differ from those selected under either long or short-run profit maximization.

PRICING OBJECTIVES IN PRACTICE

In a recent study of the pricing objectives of 728 British manufacturing firms, Shipley (1981) found that while most firms had more than one pricing goal, two-thirds specified a target profit or return on capital as their principal objective. The next most popular goals were 'prices fair to the firm and customers'; 'price similarity with competitors'; and 'target sales revenue'. Nearly one-half of the firms included one of these three non-profit based goals in their set of pricing objectives, although only around one in ten specified any of them as a principal objective. Lanzillotti (1958) in a study of twenty large US companies also found profit, in the form of a target return on capital, to be the most popular objective. Other frequently cited pricing objectives were 'stable price and margin'; 'target market share'; and 'matching the competition'. Although target market share got relatively poor support in Shipley's (1981) study, it was one of the most popular objectives, along with profit, in Hague's (1971) study of thirteen UK manufacturing firms.

The importance of profit as a pricing objective is not really surprising given that it features so prominently as either an objective or a constraint in most theories of the firm. However, this is not the same as profit maximization. While nearly one-half of Shipley's (1981) sample claimed to be motivated by profit maximization, only one-sixth were classified as 'true maximum profit motivated firms' in that their profit objective was held to be of overriding importance. Also, three-fifths of Shipley's (1981) sample had a long-term profit preference as against only one-fifth preferring short-term profits. Although most of the firms in the Lanzillotti (1958) study which had a profit target actually exceeded their targets over the 1947–55 period, he did not consider their behaviour gave strong support for long-run profit maximization. Perhaps the strongest support for profit maximization comes from the Hague (1971) study where five of his thirteen firms attempted to maximize profits when taking the pricing decision.

The Baumol (1959) revenue-maximization hypothesis gets even less support. In the Shipley (1981) study, only one in twenty firms cited revenue as the principal goal with profit as the secondary target, while one in ten had profit as the principal goal with revenue as the secondary target. Unfortunately, the utility-maximizing and growth-maximizing theories are very difficult to identify in terms of the published evidence on firms' declared pricing objectives. The problem lies in that, unlike profit maximization, they are not theories of price determination and, when applied to pricing problems, their predictions can be the subject of some ambiguity.

A RETURN TO PROFIT MAXIMIZATION

The three managerial models we have just reviewed have a number of weaknesses which cast serious doubts on their ability to contribute more to our understanding of price determination than simple profit maximization. First, we have seen that the price predictions derived from the Baumol (1959) and Williamson (1963) models are just as dependent on the specification of the profit constraint as they are on the content of the objective function. For example, when the Yarrow (1976) specification of the profit constraint was imposed, a change in fixed cost left prices unchanged, just as with profit maximization.

Second, some of their price predictions are ambiguous. This is particularly the case with the Williamson (1963) and Marris (1964) models. For example, Williamson (1963) himself admitted that his predicted output response to a change in the rate of profits tax was subject to ambiguity. Under his specification of the profit constraint, an increase in the rate of profits tax would result in a negative income (discretionary profit) effect and a positive substitution (shift to S and E) effect. The consequent change in output would depend on the balance of these two effects. Williamson (1963) assumed the balance would be positive and predicted an increase in output. However, whenever the profit constraint was biting really hard, the balance could be negative and output would drop. As we are talking about demand shifts – price is implied to change in the same direction as output – we get different price predictions depending on whether management enjoys much monopoly power (a weak profit constraint) or suffers much competition (a biting constraint). (This ambiguity disappears under the Yarrow (1976) constraint.)

Third, there is yet no clear evidence that the maximization of growth will result in significantly different pricing strategies from the maximization of profit. Solow (1971) suggested that their qualitative reactions to events such as tax changes and changes in capital costs would be very similar.

It would appear that profit maximization provides a more consistent model for analysing the price decision that any of the managerial objective functions. Much of its predictive power derives from its concern with price determination in a variety of competitive conditions. Also, the survey results on pricing objectives suggest that it could be a more realistic explanation of behaviour than the so-called 'realistic' managerial models. Consequently, profit maximization will be retained in this book as the basic assumption in the analysis of pricing behaviour. We will see that in most circumstances it is a reasonably good predictor of business behaviour.

REFERENCES AND FURTHER READING

Baumol, W. J. (1959) *Business Behaviour, Value and Growth*, Macmillan.
Berle, A. and Means, G. (1932) *The Modern Corporation and Private Property*, Macmillan.
Friedman, M. (1953) *Essays in Positive Economics*, University of Chicago Press.
Hague, D. C. (1971) *Pricing in Business*, George Allen & Unwin.
Lanzillotti, R. F. (1958) Pricing objectives in large companies, *American Economic Review*, Vol. 48, pp. 921–40.
Lewellyn, W. G. and Huntsman, B. (1970) Managerial pay and corporate performance, *American Economic Review*, Vol. 60, pp. 710–20.
Marris, R. (1964) *The Economic Theory of 'Managerial' Capitalism*, Macmillan.
McGuire, J. W., Chui, J. S. Y. and Elbing, A. O. (1962) Executive income, sales and profits, *American Economic Review*, Vol. 52, pp. 753–61.
Meeks, G. and Whittington, G. (1975) Directors' pay, growth and profitability, *Journal of Industrial Economics*, Vol. 24, pp. 1–14.
Radice, H. K. (1971) Control type, profitability and growth in large firms, *Economic Journal*, Vol. 81, pp. 547–62.
Rao, V. R. (1984) Pricing research in marketing: the state of the art, *Journal of Business*, Vol. 57, pp. 39–59.
Roberts, D. (1956) A general theory of executive compensation based on statistically tested propositions, *Quarterly Journal of Economics*, Vol. 70.
Shipley, D. D. (1981) Pricing objectives in British manufacturing industry, *Journal of Industrial Economics*, Vol. 29, pp. 429–43.
Solow, R. (1971) Some implications of alternative criteria for the firm, in R. Marris and A. Woods (eds.) *The Corporate Economy*, Macmillan, pp. 318–42.
Williamson, O. E. (1963) Managerial discretion and business behaviour, *American Economic Review*, Vol. 53, pp. 1032–57.
Yarrow, G. K. (1976) On the predictions of managerial theories of the firm, *Journal of Industrial Economics*, Vol. 24, pp. 267–79.

3 Theory of Production and Costs

RELEVANT COSTS FOR MANAGEMENT DECISIONS

There are a large number of costing conventions used in practice which when applied to the costing of production give different estimates of the unit cost of a particular product. However, for optimal decision-making, economic theory gives very clear guidance as to the type of cost information which is relevant. The *relevant cost information* is that which is affected by the decision. Relevant costs are based on three clearly defined principles.

The first principle is that only *future costs* are relevant. Decisions can only be *ex ante* to the affected costs. Production decisions should be based on information concerning those costs expected to be incurred as a result of taking the decision. The time perspective is forward looking. As a result, costs incurred prior to the taking of the decision and costs to be incurred yet contracted prior to the taking of the decision are irrelevant and should not form part of the planning data. These past and committed costs are the result of earlier decisions, not the one currently being considered.

The second principle is that they should include only *differential* or *incremental costs*, those costs which vary between the alternative opportunity choices available to the decision-maker. In terms of the production decision, the relevant costs would be those which vary between the different outputs being considered. In this case the only relevant costs are those variable costs which are mathematically differentiable with respect to output. Fixed costs are unaffected by the changes in the level of output within a fixed capacity and so are irrelevant. Therefore, the leasing costs of machines already leased before the production decision is made and the straight-line depreciation costs of already owned machines are unaffected by the alternative production decisions and so are irrelevant.

The third principle is that the relevant cost assigned to a factor of production is the *market opportunity cost*. The cost of employing the factor is its value in the best alternative use. This can be easily found where, as a result of a production decision, the firm purchases a factor of production in the open market. The cost is the market price which results from the firm bidding the resource away from alternative users. It is more difficult to calculate the opportunity cost of factors which have already been purchased to the extent that free markets may not readily be available for providing estimates of current or future value. Where those markets do exist, the opportunity cost would be either the cost of replacement or the revenue from disposing of the resources currently held in stock. In some cases the best alternative use might be in substituting for a more expensive material used on another product or contract within the firm.

Essentially the opportunity cost principle equates the cost with realizable value in the market. In this sense, cost is conceptualized in cash terms. The cost of purchasing an additional factor of production is the money payment, or cash outflow, necessary to make the acquisition. The relevant cost of previously acquired factors is the best price that could be gained, or the highest cash inflow, from their disposal. Therefore, the opportunity cost principle implies that the relevant costs are those which affect the cash flows within the timescale of the decision.

This means that relevant cost information for production decisions should be concerned only with costs incurred *ex post* the decision, which are differential between output choices and relate directly to future cash flows. This provides an approach to business decision-making which is entirely compatible with the economic theory of costs which we shall now go on to explore in detail.

THE PRODUCTION FUNCTION

The traditional economic approach to the theory of the firm is based on a hypothetical production function which describes a production process by specifying the maximum output of a given product which can be obtained from combinations of productive inputs, otherwise known as methods of production. Given the state of current technology, the theory assumes that the firm can choose from an infinite variety of technically efficient methods of production.

In business practice life is somewhat more constrained. Instead of having an infinite number of efficient methods of production, the choice is restricted to the limited number of feasible methods which have been discovered by production engineers. Thus, in practice any given decision to adopt a method of production is restricted to a very few, and maybe only two, choices. However, the theory can easily be adapted to incorporate this restricted choice.

Traditionally, the production function is defined as a relationship between one output, Q, and two factor inputs, L and K, representing labour and capital respectively. The general form of the function is given as

$$Q = f(L, K) \qquad\qquad 3.1$$

Each combination of L and K defines an efficient method of production which can only be changed by substituting between the factor inputs. Where there is an infinite number of production methods, the production function is based on the possibility of a continuous substitution of L and K in providing a given level of

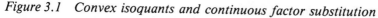

Figure 3.1 Convex isoquants and continuous factor substitution

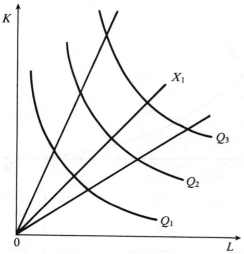

output, Q. Such a possibility is shown in Figure 3.1 where a given level of output, Q_1, can be provided by continuously substituting L and K as given by the convex isoquant, Q_1. The isoquant Q_1 forms the locus of all technically efficient methods of producing that level of output. Given the current state of technology, it is possible to produce larger outputs such as Q_2 and Q_3 by increasing the inputs of L and K. The effect of applying more inputs to the technically efficient methods of production is shown by the intersection of the isoquants with rays or isoclines drawn from the origin. Each isocline, such as X_1, represents one method of production. Thus output can be increased along X_1 by applying more L and K in the same fixed proportion given by the slope of X_1.

The fundamental importance of the production function to costing is that it shows the direct relationship between individual factor inputs and the output of a particular product. It relates the rate of change in factor inputs necessary to achieve a rate of change in output. When factor prices are constant with respect to output, production costs can be derived directly by multiplying the factor inputs by their respective market prices and then aggregating across factor inputs.

One of the most important economic concepts derived from the production function is that of the law of variable proportions, otherwise known as the law of diminishing returns. The law of variable proportions is said to operate when one factor (normally capital) is held constant while the other factors remain variable. In our case, holding capital constant allows us to see how output changes with variations in the labour input. This relationship is known as the total product of labour.

The derivation of the total product of labour from the production function is shown in Figure 3.2. If the production function is homogeneous (the isoclines are straight lines from the origin) with constant returns to scale (the isoquants will be equidistant apart along any isocline such as Q_1 to Q_4 along isocline X) then the returns to a variable factor will be diminishing wherever one factor is fixed. This can be demonstrated by holding capital constant at $\bar{K}$ and doubling the input

Figure 3.2   The law of diminishing returns

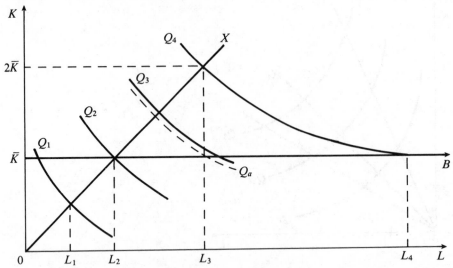

of labour from L_2 to L_3. This only gives an increase in output from Q_2 to Q_a which is less than the 50 per cent increase to Q_3 while if K had also been doubled output would have doubled to Q_4. Therefore, to double output when K is held constant at $\bar{K}$ requires the incremental input of labour to much more than double from L_2 to L_4. With the incremental increase in output requiring more than a proportional increase in the input of the variable factor(s) means that the latter suffers from diminishing returns.

The line $\bar{K}B$ represents the *product line* when K is fixed at $\bar{K}$ and shows the physical movement from one isoquant to another as labour input is changed. As we follow the product line $\bar{K}B$ from $\bar{K}$ we can see that the distance between each of the isoquants increases as output is increased. Therefore, the product of each additional input of the variable factor progressively decreases. Or in the language of economists, the variable factor exhibits decreasing marginal productivity.

The cost-minimizing method of production

The cost of using a given method of production to produce a target output volume will be governed by the relative prices of the factor inputs. The least-cost method minimizes the total cost of inputs, subject to the state of current technology. This can be written as

Minimize $C_1 = (w)(L) + (r)(K)$
subject to $Q_1 = f(L,K)$ 3.2

where w is the wage rate, r is the price of capital and Q_1 is the target output.

Equation 3.2 defines an isocost line forming the locus of all combinations of factors which the firm can purchase with the fixed budget C_1. The slope of the isocost line is the ratio of the prices of the factors of production which in this case equals w/r. Such an isocost line, C_1C_1, is shown in Figure 3.3. Given the

Figure 3.3   Optimal short and long-run expansion paths

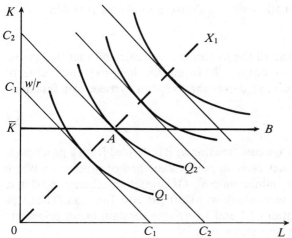

budget, C_1, and the target output, Q_1, the firm will produce Q_1 at minimum cost C_1 when the isocost line C_1C_1 is tangential to the isoquant Q_1. Again, the higher output, Q_2, is produced at minimum cost when its isoquant is tangential to C_2C_2. These points of tangency denote the minimum-cost combinations of the factors K and L, which in turn define the least-cost method of production X_1.

With the slope of the isoquant being given by the ratio of the marginal product of labour to that to capital, MP_L/MP_K, the first condition of equilibrium becomes

$$\frac{w}{r} = \frac{MP_L}{MP_K} \qquad\qquad 3.3$$

The minimum-cost method of production is where the ratio of the prices of the factor inputs equals the ratio of the marginal products of the same factor inputs. The second condition of equilibrium is that the isoquants must be convex to the origin.

Equation 3.3 can be rewritten as

$$\frac{MP_L}{w} = \frac{MP_K}{r} \qquad\qquad 3.4$$

This means that the minimum-cost method of production requires the marginal productivity of the last £1 spent on labour to equal the marginal productivity of the last £1 spent on capital. In disequilibrium, the marginal product of labour (or capital) for an additional £1 spent might exceed that of capital (or labour). Equilibrium can be restored by spending less on capital (or labour) and more on labour (or capital) until the condition of equation 3.4 is met.

The derivation of cost functions

From Figure 3.3 we can seen that by increasing output along X_1 the firm can produce a series of outputs at a corresponding series of minimum costs. Thus for each output Q_i, $i = 1, \ldots, n$, there is a corresponding level of cost C_i, $i = 1, \ldots, n$. From this information we can derive a total cost function

$$C = f(Q) \qquad\qquad 3.5$$

This cost function assumes that all the factors are variable and that there is no limitation to the expansion of output. It forms the long-run cost curve of economic theory. From this we can derive the long-run average cost function

$$\frac{C}{Q} = \frac{f(Q)}{Q} \qquad\qquad 3.6$$

It forms the most efficient average cost function as it is derived from a production function where the firm produces each output by a method of production which uses best practice techniques at minimum cost. Of course, any change in relative factor prices and production technology will shift the cost function. Thus, the cost functions defined by equations 3.5 and 3.6 assume constant factor prices and an unchanged state of production technology.

When capital is fixed, we have the short-run condition where output can only be varied along a product line parallel with the axis of the variable factor. Such a product line $\bar{K}B$ is reproduced in Figure 3.3. As the only optimal expansion path is $0X_1$, any expansion in output from Q_2 along $\bar{K}B$ would suffer from diminishing returns. Therefore, given $\bar{K}$, the only minimum-cost factor combination is at A, producing Q_2. Any expansion or contraction of output from A would cause the average cost of production to rise. This is illustrated by the isoquants veering away from and above the isocost lines for any move away from isocline $0X_1$. Therefore, from the production function and the constant prices of the factor inputs we can derive the U-shaped average cost curve, where the bottom of the 'U' would correspond with an output of Q_2, which is normally referred to as minimum average cost.

As the capital factor is constrained, the short-run cost function is specified with a fixed cost element. From the information basic to Figure 3.3 we can derive the short-run total cost function as

$$C = f(Q) + k \qquad\qquad 3.7$$

where k is constant fixed cost (noting that k is not a function of output). Consequently, the short-run average cost function becomes

$$\frac{C}{Q} = \frac{f(Q) + k}{Q} \qquad\qquad 3.8$$

where k/Q is average fixed cost and $f(Q)/Q$ is average variable cost.

Returns to scale

Returns to scale can be considered by examining the effect on output of changing all the input factors by the same proportion. There are three possibilities. First, if the proportionate change in output is equal to the proportionate change in all factor inputs, we have *constant returns* to scale. Second, if the proportionate change in output is greater than the proportionate change in all factor inputs, we

Figure 3.4   Returns to scale

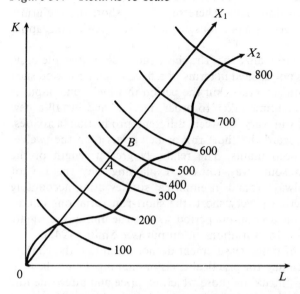

have *increasing returns* to scale. Finally, if the proportionate change in output is less than the proportionate change in all factor inputs, we have *decreasing returns* to scale.

Increasing, constant and decreasing returns to scale are shown in Figure 3.4 along the isocline X_1. The capital to labour ratio is fixed and is given by the slope of X_1. Where the successive isoquants become closer together we have increasing returns, as between the origin and point A. This is followed by constant returns between A and B as the isoquants are equidistant apart. After B the successive isoquants get further apart so exhibiting decreasing returns.

Generally, economic theory is concerned only with homogeneous production functions. That given by isocline X_1 in Figure 3.4 is homogeneous as it forms a straight line through the origin and so the proportion of labour applied to capital remains constant along the isocline. In the case of non-homogeneous production functions, the isoclines will form curves with the capital to labour ratio varying along the isocline as in the case of X_2. Such functions are very difficult to analyse and so homogeneity is normally assumed in empirical work. However, there is no reason to suggest that production functions are necessarily homogeneous in the real world. The lack of knowledge of the mathematical characteristics of the actual production functions must increase the uncertainty faced by businessmen when deciding on the scale of the production plant and the production cost implications of that decision.

SHORT-RUN COST FUNCTIONS

The short run is that period during which some inputs are fixed and at least one input is variable. Output can be varied by adjusting the input of the variable factor(s) up to some limit determined by the maximum output possible from applying variable factors to the fixed factor(s). This limit is generally given as the physical capacity of the production plant. Therefore, in the short run the firm's production decision is constrained by a previous or 'historical' decision on capital expenditure.

It is important at this stage to realize that the short run is defined as the basic unit of economic period. It is not defined in terms of a fixed calendar period such as a specific number of months or years, but the period in which some input is fixed. As it is dependent on the time taken to order, receive, and install a new unit of the fixed factor, it will vary between different production activities. However, most economists regard the short run as being less than the twelve-month period reported by accountants. The relatively greater length of the accounting period could go some way towards explaining why the law of diminishing returns is not always found in empirical studies using accounting data. When the economic period is very short, the short-run variations in cost would be averaged out over the accounting period so that the unit cost estimate would be shown as a constant for variations in output (see Smith, 1942).

These empirical problems of time measurement do not mean that the concept of the short run has little meaning for practical decision-making. Quite the contrary. All operating decisions, including those which fix price and affect the rate of capacity utilization, essentially relate to that period during which at least some of the firm's productive equipment is fixed in supply. Therefore, any decision which is not primarily concerned with long-range planning is concerned with the short run. The short-run total and average cost functions were specified in equations 3.7 and 3.8 and were shown to derive from a production function subject to the law of diminishing returns. With the fixed cost of capital remaining constant for changes in output, changes in short-run total costs will be a function of changes in variable cost. These characteristics are as illustrated in Figure 3.5a where variable cost increases at a decreasing rate up to Q_1 and at an increasing rate beyond Q_1. The positive intercept on the total cost curve is equal to k, the level of fixed cost.

The corresponding average cost and marginal cost functions are illustrated in Figure 3.5b. As k is constant, average fixed costs, AFC, form a rectangular hyperbola. Average variable costs, AVC, exhibit the expected U-shape, falling initially as the productivity of labour rises, reaching a minimum when the optimal combination of fixed and variable factors is achieved, and then rising beyond that point, reflecting the law of diminishing returns. Average total costs, ATC, are also U-shaped as they are partially determined by average variable costs.

One of the most important cost concepts for business decision-making is that of marginal costs. It represents the rates of change in total costs as output changes by one unit and mathematically forms the first derivative of total cost with respect to output. It is written as

$$MC = \frac{\delta C}{\delta Q} \qquad\qquad 3.9$$

Marginal costs also correspond with a U-shaped function so long as the production function is subject to diminishing returns. As they measure the changing

Figure 3.5a   Short-run total costs

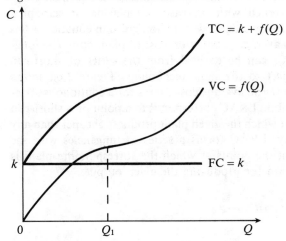

Figure 3.5b   Short-run unit costs

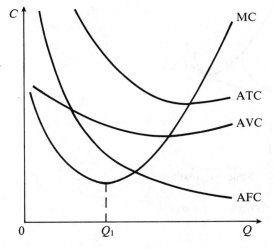

slope of the total cost curve, their minimum point corresponds with the inflexion point on the total cost curve at Q_1. Economic theory is concerned mainly with that output range where marginal costs are rising, corresponding to a diminishing marginal product of labour, as this is where the profit-maximizing equilibrium is attainable.

LONG-RUN COST FUNCTIONS

The long-run cost curve is generally referred to as the *planning curve*, that which guides the businessman in selecting his future production strategy. Long-run production planning is largely concerned with deciding on the optimal plant size given the expected growth, or decline, in market demand. Consequently, long-run output decisions are concerned with increasing, replacing or scrapping production capacity. The long-run average cost function given in equation 3.6 is really a scale curve as it relates average production cost to plant size. The long-run average cost curve, LRAC, can be derived from the series of short-run average cost curves when subject to the same technology. Figure 3.6a shows LRAC as an envelope of the short-run average cost curves for a continuous series of production plants. Each point on LRAC corresponds to a point on a short-run cost curve specifying that output which the given plant produces cheaper than any other plant scale. Consequently, LRAC forms a series of tangencies with the short-run average cost curves at the points at which the corresponding plant is the most efficient planning option for producing the given output.

Figure 3.6a   Long-run average cost curve

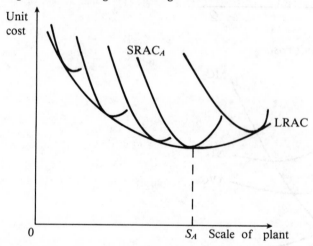

Figure 3.6b   L-shaped long-run average cost curve

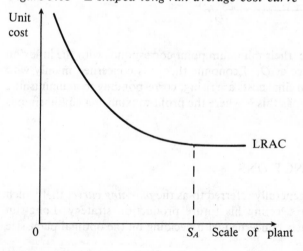

The minimum cost output S_A in Figure 3.6a signifies the minimum efficient scale and represents the point at which economies of scale are maximized. The U-shape of LRAC results from the cost effect of the returns to scale discussed above. The unit costs of production decrease as plant size increases up to S_A owing to the effect of increasing returns. Beyond S_A unit costs progressively rise as decreasing returns set in. The decreasing returns, or diseconomies of scale, are attributed to management's progressive loss of effective control leading to proportionately greater inputs being required for a given increase in output.

There is a considerable dispute in economic theory over the existence of diseconomies of scale. A number of writers, including Andrews (1949), Bain (1956) and Koutsoyiannis (1979), argue that average production costs fall continuously with increases in plant size, although there is a tendency for some levelling out at the upper end of the plant-scale curve. While these writers appear to accept that some management costs will rise at an increasing rate at very large scales of output, they are not expected to rise sufficiently to offset the continuing fall in average production costs. At worst, these two opposing cost trends will offset each other beyond the minimum efficient scale giving a constant LRAC after S_A. What results is an approximation to the L-shaped LRAC curve shown in Figure 3.6b.

The theory of the L-shaped LRAC curve is based on the dominance of production economies of scale at all plant scales. These economies have a number of sources including indivisibilities of capital equipment, increased dimensions, specialization, massed resources and the organization of production (see Pratten and Dean, 1965). Indivisibilities occur when certain items of equipment are only available in a limited number of capacities so that increasing the scale of output allows increasing returns from spreading such discontinuities over large output volumes.

Economies of scale arising from increasing the dimensions of capital equipment depend on a geometric relationship existing between the material required in constructing the equipment and the physical capacity of the equipment. This relationship is generally expressed by the exponential function

$$C = aQ^b \qquad\qquad\qquad 3.10$$

where b is the scale coefficient. In engineering design there is a rule of thumb that b equals 0.6. This means that a 100 per cent increase in the scale of the unit of equipment results in a 60 per cent increase in cost. Using industrial equipment catalogues, Haldi and Whitcomb (1967) found 42 per cent of their estimates gave a value of b between 0.5 and 0.69.

Economies of specialization generally derive from the division of labour and the automation of the production process. Economies of massed resources derive from the fact that stocks of raw materials and the required working capital do not increase in proportion to output. Finally, larger-scale plants permit superior techniques of organizing production which can give savings in supervisory and management costs and so hold in check any tendency for managerial control loss diseconomies to increase.

The dispute over whether the LRAC curve is U-shaped or L-shaped remains unresolved. Empirically, there have been very few studies which can conclusively reject the hypothesis of a U-shaped LRAC curve. The problem is the lack of availability of suitable data to test the hypothesis. Administrative costs disaggregated at plant level are not generally available as multi-plant firms do not tend to undertake such cost allocations. Even if they did, the allocation base would be arbitrary. Again, single-plant firms do not tend to be the largest plants in an industry. And as Walters (1963, p. 52) stated, 'why should any competitive entrepreneur expand and stay on the rising part of the cost curve?'

LINEAR COST FUNCTIONS AND ECONOMIC THEORY

Short-run linear cost functions are exhibited in Figures 3.7a and 3.7b. The total-cost curve shows a linear relationship with output (the slope is constant) with variable costs being drawn as a straight line through the origin. Consequently, marginal costs are constant and equal to average variable costs. With input prices assumed to be invariant with quantity purchased, constant marginal cost implies a constant marginal product of labour. It follows that the law of variable proportions does not apply and that the fixed and variable factors are combined in such a way as to ensure minimum variable and marginal costs at all levels of output up to the limit of full capacity.

Most business decision-making techniques are based on linear cost functions, with some of the most common uses being in breakeven analysis, the breakeven output being where a linear total-cost curve intersects a linear total-revenue curve (TR in Figure 3.7a). The linear assumption is also basic to standard costing which provides the accounting costs used for budgeting. Despite linear costing being the most popular assumption in business practice, 'There has been no attempt to show how this form of short-run cost function is a necessary consequence of some set of fundamental and self-evident postulates.' (Walters, 1963, p. 40.) This most popular costing practice exists in a theoretical vacuum. It is not derived from any alternative theory of production. Its defence is based entirely on empiricism, the proposition being simply that this is how businessmen consider costs (see Andrews, 1949; Eiteman and Guthrie, 1952).

As cost functions are derived from production functions, it seems appropriate to consider the implications of linear costing for the theory of production. Linear cost functions would appear to imply one of three possible types of production function. First, that the production isoquants are negative sloping and linear. Second, that there are substantial returns to scale sufficient to offset the occurrence of diminishing returns. Third, that the fixed factor is so physically divisible into homogeneous units that it can be introduced or withdrawn in fixed proportion to changes in the labour factor. We will look at each of these three possibilities in turn.

Linear isoquants assume either perfect substitutability of factor inputs or limited substitutability. In the latter case, there are just a very few methods of production and direct substitution between labour and capital can take place only

Figure 3.7a   Short-run linear cost functions

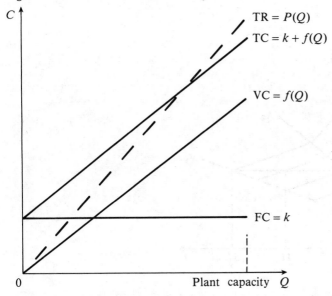

Figure 3.7b   Linear cost functions

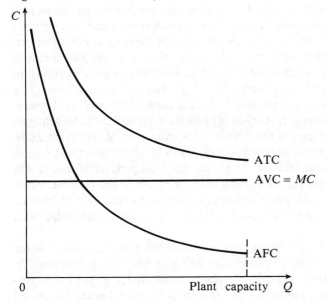

with a change in the method of production as represented by the kinks in the linear isoquants. An example is shown in Figure 3.8 with direct factor substitution taking place along X_2. Between the kinks, on the straight sections of the isoquants, a mix of the two adjacent methods of production can take place. Thus, while each homogeneous production method must retain fixed factor

Figure 3.8   Linear isoquants and diminishing returns

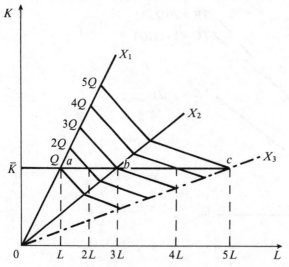

proportions, the mixing of methods of production between the kinks allows for a form of indirect factor substitution.

As limited substitutability is typical of engineering production functions and derives from linear programming applications, we will restrict our investigation to that case only. We will assume that the production function is homogeneous with constant returns everywhere and that initially there are only two methods of production, X_1 and X_2, each using K and L in fixed proportions as shown in Figure 3.8. With the capital input fixed at $\bar{K}$, output can be increased from Q by substituting the labour intensive method X_2 for the capital intensive X_1. Increasing output by equal increments from Q to $2Q$ and from $2Q$ to $3Q$ can be achieved by equal incremental increases in the labour input from L to $2L$ and from $2L$ to $3L$. Therefore, taking Q as the output base, increases in labour input and output will maintain a proportional relationship so that the total product of labour will be linear with respect to output. Assuming that the prices of the variable factor inputs remain constant for varying purchase quantities, the total cost of increasing output from the base at Q will also exhibit a proportional relationship with output.

While limited factor substitutability provides a theoretical explanation of linear cost functions, it is dependent on production being limited to only two possible methods. If a third method, X_3, existed, labour productivity would fall as one switched to using some of method X_3. This is seen in Figure 3.8 as the horizontal line from $\bar{K}$ intersects the isoquants at greater distances apart between b and c than between a and b. Thus, it takes a greater increment of labour to increase output from $3Q$ to $4Q$ than from $2Q$ to $3Q$. Productivity would fall and marginal cost would rise at outputs greater than $3Q$. Therefore, diminishing returns are present whenever the known methods of production exceed two.

While production engineers may only consider two alternative methods of production, they are likely to have selected them from a number of theoretical

Figure 3.9   Increasing returns to scale and no diminishing returns

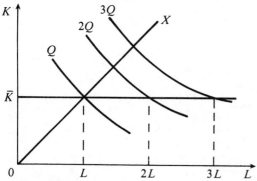

possibilities. If there are more than two theoretical possibilities, the case for constant marginal costs collapses. It would seem that the production condition restricting the discovery of production methods to only two would be an exceptional rather than a general occurrence. Such a break with orthodox theory where an infinite variety of production methods is assumed to be available requires some theoretical explanation. What has yet to be developed is an axiom covering the restriction on discovering more than two alternative factor input combinations.

The second possible explanation of linear cost functions concerns positive and substantive returns to scale sufficient to offset any diminishing marginal productivity of the variable factor. This condition is illustrated in Figure 3.9 for a homogeneous production function and convex isoquants. Doubling the labour input from L to $2L$ doubles output from Q to $2Q$, and trebling L to $3L$ effectively trebles Q to $3Q$. Note that the proportional relationship is maintained by the isoquant $3Q$ being nearer to $2Q$ than $2Q$ is to Q. The result is a linear cost output relationship. It is worth noting that in this case X is only one of an infinite number of possible methods of production.

The restricted generality of this second possible explanation is seen from its dependence on increasing and substantial returns to scale. This requirement will restrict its applicability to industries at the early stages of growth where plant size and economies of scale are restricted by low market demand. As firms expand their plant sizes towards the minimum optimum scale, the economy of scale compensatory factor for diminishing returns will weaken and become atypical.

The third possible explanation of cost linearity is novel in that it assumes only one method of production. The isocline for this method of production is given as X in Figure 3.10. The maximum output is at full capacity where X intersects the line from $\bar{K}$ at $3Q$. Horizontal product lines are debarred as they require variable proportions. This explanation assumes fixed factor proportions so that the fixed capital stock $\bar{K}$ must be disaggregated into employed and unemployed units. Thus, to produce Q units of output ab units of capital are unemployed as shown in Figure 3.10. As output expands up to $3Q$, the unemployed units are progressively put into employment until all are employed. The result is that equal increments of output require equal increments of labour and cost linearity prevails.

This explanation has been developed by Dean (1951) as the only theoretical

Figure 3.10   Infinitely divisible fixed factor and no diminishing returns

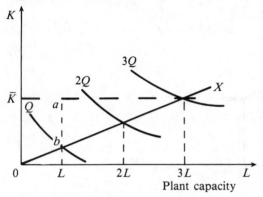

Plant capacity

attempt at a production analysis of the linear short-run cost function. This production condition requires that capital equipment has fixed relations with labour such that machines have constant unit labour inputs. This implies specialized machinery and a restriction to certain industries only. Capital equipment, such as blast furnaces or oil refineries, is not physically divisible into small homogeneous units and so cannot be adapted to provide constant labour productivity. Certain machine tools and most office equipment are adaptable in this way and would meet with this theoretical construct.

Again, the question has to be asked why output is restricted to only one method of production. It is impossible by definition to substitute capital for labour and so the short-run production decision is reduced almost to an irrelevance. If no other combination of inputs is possible, the method of production is not being determined by the relative prices of the factor inputs. It would simply be a chance event that w/r equals MP_L/MP_K for the given method of production. By being restricted to only one 'known' method, the firm would normally be unable to maximize its output at minimum cost and so the condition of equation 3.2 would not be met. It would appear, therefore, that this third explanation is again not generalizable. It is not surprising that most economic theorists have regarded the law of diminishing returns as the most promising hypothesis for building a general theory of production and cost.

As linear cost functions are so deeply embedded in business practice, they will be assumed in much of the succeeding analysis of pricing. However, throughout this analysis their shaky theoretical foundations will be borne in mind and frequent references will be made to *true costs* based on the assumption of diminishing returns. Where appropriate, true costs will be compared with accounting costs based on the linearity assumption in order to assess the implications of the latter for optimal decision-making.

REFERENCES AND FURTHER READING

Andrews, P. W. S. (1949) *Manufacturing Business*, Macmillan.
Bain, J. S. (1956) *Barriers to New Competition*, Harvard University Press.

Chenery, H. B. (1949) Engineering production functions, *Quarterly Journal of Economics*, Vol. 63, pp. 505–31.
Dean, J. (1951) *Managerial Economics*, Prentice-Hall.
Eiteman, W. J. and Guthrie, G. E. (1952) The shape of the average cost curve, *American Economic Review*, Vol. 42, pp. 832–8.
Haldi, J. and Whitcomb, D. (1967) Economies of scale in industrial plants, *Journal of Political Economy*, Vol. 75, pp. 373–85.
Koutsoyiannis, A. (1979) *Modern Microeconomics*, Macmillan.
Pratten, C. F. and Dean, R. M. (1965) *The Economies of Large Scale Production in British Industry*, Cambridge University Press.
Smith, C. A. (1942) The cost output relation for the US Steel Corporation, *Review of Economics and Statistics*, Vol. 24, pp. 166–76.
Walters, A. A. (1963) Production and cost functions: an econometric survey, *Econometrica*, Vol. 31, pp. 1–66.

4 Costing in Practice

STANDARD COSTING

In practice, costing for the price—output decision is typically based on the standard costs of the accountant's budgeting system. To the extent that standard costs are estimates of the relevant costs expected to be incurred at the budgeted output, they form the accountant's analogue to the costs of economic theory. Under best management practice this will tend to be the case.

Unfortunately, in most firms the standards are based on historical or current, and not future, data which are not subject to continual, and in many cases not even periodic, review. As such, they are irrelevant in that they have not been estimated from next period's plant layout, operational procedures or planned product mix. This implies that most managements expect the future to be little different from the past. To this extent, they ignore opportunity cost considerations whereby the cost of using a resource in a given activity equals the value of the best alternative opportunity forgone. Consequently, such standards are not applicable to efficient operating conditions.

Although the information used for setting standards is fundamentally of a technical nature, being provided by production engineers, work study experts and accountants, the actual setting of standards generally has a strong behavioural element, often provided through the influence of line management. This behavioural element is endemic within standard setting because realistic standards are required to be *attainable*. An attainable standard is based on a level of performance which can, with effort, be achieved and as such it forms a target which should motivate staff.

Material standards are based on technical and engineering specifications which allow for losses in production, expected levels of breakage, spillage, evaporation or rejections. The labour standards allow for normal breakdowns in machinery, maintenance and set-up time, sickness and idle time. After allowing for these technically sub-optimal conditions, a standard should embody a target which can be attained in normal operating conditions. However, considerations such as establishing what are normal conditions, trying to ensure that the standards relate to the production methods to be used in the budget period, and motivating staff, must in practical terms give a fairly wide range of tolerance within which a standard is actually set. This is particularly so when standards are negotiated between managers, each of whom has a different objective in relation to the standard set. It follows that a standard cost is not only dependent on a given production function and method of production but is also peculiar to the group setting the standard. Consequently, efficiency becomes a relative concept when applied to standard costing. Obviously, attainable standard costs are not the same thing as the economist's concept of costs, as the latter is based on a technically efficient standard which is removed from considerations of motivation and budgetary cost control.

One major problem of costing in practice is that the true cost function is unknown. Consequently, there is great uncertainty as to how costs vary with changes in the level of capacity utilization. Normally, management assumes that total costs are linear in respect of output in the short run, and this forms the basic assumption of the standard cost model. The assumption of linearity may appear to be reasonable where output changes are either abnormal or very minor in extent, and where output changes are frequently accompanied by changes in material quality, labour personnel, working conditions and significant environmental variables, making it difficult to isolate the effect of changing volume. Yet in situations where output changes within the budget period are a normal occurrence the pattern of actual cost outcomes should provide data sufficient for management to test statistically the validity of the linearity assumption. If the true cost function were instead to be curvilinear, then the differences between the budgeted and the actual material and labour costs occurring with output changes, and the consequential pendulum effect of favourable and unfavourable differences, should alert management to the non-linearity of cost. Of course, management's ability to identify the curvilinear nature of the true cost function would be dependent on fairly regular and reversible changes in output with other factors affecting costs remaining ineffective or being of infrequent and non-synchronized occurrence (see Dorward, 1985, for a detailed discussion).

The importance of testing the linearity assumption on which standard costing is based cannot be overemphasized. If standard costs are to be useful predictions of costs in the next budget period, they must form tolerably accurate estimates of the true, but unknown, cost function. Where the true cost function is non-linear, then the use of standard costing, by predicting a constant unit variable cost throughout the total range of plant capacity, will result in substantial differences between budgeted and actual costs whenever actual output differs significantly from budgeted output. These cost differences will occur with output deviations even though operations were actually conducted efficiently.

FIXED AND VARIABLE COSTS AND THE COST CLASSIFICATIONS OF ACCOUNTING PRACTICE

One of the most important accounting classifications of cost is the separation of costs into direct and indirect categories. When budgeting for the next accounting period these direct and indirect costs become the standard costs. *Direct costs* are those costs which can be *traced* to a particular area of operation such as a product or service, a department, or a division. There are three main categories of direct cost comprising direct materials used in the product, direct labour employed directly in production, and direct expenses incurred specifically for a particular product or service, such as the hire of machinery and the payment of royalties. Sometimes direct costs are referred to as *prime* costs.

Indirect costs are costs which cannot be traced to a product or service, etc. They are accumulated in a common pool either to be *allocated* to product in some *arbitrary* manner or not allocated and written off against the profits of the period in which they arise. Indirect costs are often referred to as overheads when they are allocated or as period costs when assigned to periods of time rather than to units of product. They include items such as fuel and power, supervisory staff, rent, rates, insurance, depreciation, management salaries and selling expenses.

While it is tempting to associate direct costs with variable costs and indirect costs with fixed costs, such an association would be superficial and incorrect. Direct costs are classified in terms of their *traceability* to product and not by their behaviour in the face of changing output. For example, when only one product is produced in the budget period a large number of conventional fixed costs, such as rent, depreciation and labour supervision, would be directly traceable to the product. In this special case they would all be reported as direct costs. Most of the non-variable elements in direct costs are included in the direct expense category, although some of them have semi-variable characteristics meaning that while they adjust to changes in output, they do so in discrete lumps rather than by continuous differentiation.

Likewise, there are a number of terms classified as indirect costs which behave in a variable manner with changing output, examples of which include power, most overtime and shift premiums, most indirect labour, and a number of sales and distribution expenses. Given the arbitrary nature of all schemes of overhead allocation there must be a temptation to shift as many costs as possible into the direct cost category. Such a shifting becomes easier the more product-specific the machinery, the supervisory and maintenance staff, and the materials not directly incorporated in the product such as grease, cleaning supplies and office supplies. Thus in single product departments many costs which would normally feature as indirect factory expenses can be classified as direct expenses.

These apparent difficulties in using internal management accounting data for economic analysis are further compounded by the fact that 'The term "variable costing" is not widely used in the United Kingdom and no definition appears in the Institute of Cost and Works Accountants' *Terminology of Cost Account-ancy*' (Sizer, 1971, p. 86). As Sizer correctly pointed out, making a distinction between fixed and variable costs cannot be accepted as evidence that the firms concerned used the variable costs in such a way as to determine the effects on costs and profit of changes in output. Thus, the result of Skinner's survey (1970) that 73 per cent of the 166 respondents analysed their costs into fixed and variable elements does not imply that they were concerned with the cost–volume relationship. It may just mean that the firms were separating out the fixed and variable elements 'as part of the process of establishing overhead recovery rates for calculating product costs necessary for cost-plus price calculations' (Sizer, 1971, p. 87).

These reservations regarding the use of accounting data to estimate a variable cost function are further strengthened when account is taken of the accountant's definition of marginal cost, which generally means direct cost plus variable overheads. As direct costs sometimes include some non-variable elements and as variable overheads are often semi-variable in behaviour, the accountant's definition is a rather messy version of marginal cost and will not usually provide a continuously differentiable cost function. Even worse, the direct costs for decision-making are the constant unit standard costs based on the linearity assumption and suffer from all the inherent difficulties of standard setting discussed above. Therefore, as the direct costs for decision-making are assumed to behave linearly in response to output changes, it is not surprising that accountants have shown little interest in 'variable costing' or 'marginal costing' whereby information is collected on the effect on costs and profits of changes in output in the short run. Thus, small wonder that Sizer (1966) found only 5 out of 21 firms using marginal cost as an analytical technique; that Howe (1962) found only 3 out of 28 firms using marginal costing; that Hart and Prusmann (1963) found only 6 out of 108 firms using marginal cost as a formalized system; and that Goodlad (1965) found only 2 firms out of 25 using marginal costing extensively. So long as accountants remain wedded to the linearity assumption of standard costing, differences between budgeted and actual costs resulting from output changes will concern them only as departures from efficient standards and not as a 'variable costing' relationship.

COST LINEARITY AND MARGINAL COSTING

The relevant range

Management accounting texts claim that cost linearity only occurs within the relevant range, 'a range in which the firm has had some recent experience' (Horngren, 1982, p. 48). In other words, linearity is held to apply over that range of capacity utilization in which the firm normally plans its budget. This does not necessarily deny the assumptions of the economist's theory of cost behaviour. The restriction of linearity to the relevant range implies non-linearity outside the range where the law of diminishing returns is presumed to apply. An economist's interpretation of the relevant range model is given in Figure 4.1. The average variable cost curve appears as a flat-bottomed U-shaped curve. Average variable costs, AVC, are assumed to be constant over the relevant range between outputs Q_1 and Q^* and are equal to marginal cost, MC. (An equivalence between the accountant's technique of measuring marginal cost and the economist's concept of marginal cost is assumed between Q_1 and Q^*.) The problem with the presentation of Figure 4.1 is that 'given that the law of diminishing returns is operative,

Figure 4.1   An economist's interpretation of the relevant range

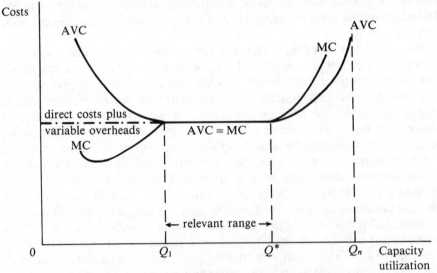

there is no a priori reason why constant returns (giving a constant variable cost) should occur within the range of normal operations' (Middleton, 1980, p. 265). Constant variable costs within the relevant range require some theoretical explanation of why the law of diminishing returns should be disbanded over that range. This is particularly important as the relevant range seems to cover such a large proportion of capacity. Sizer's (1965) inquiries showed that most cost accountants considered the relevant range to apply over some 30 to 40 per cent of capacity.

The conventional justification is that the relevant range corresponds with the *built-in reserve capacity* which is required for a flexible response to changing market conditions. Such flexibility is required to meet seasonal and cyclical fluctuations in demand and to respond quickly to long-term increases in demand for the product or service. The original idea came from Andrews (1949) who seems to have developed it as a justification for the constant unit direct costs of standard costing. Koutsoyiannis (1979) has gone even further and presented it as a basic assumption in her 'modern theory of costs'.

The trouble with these attempts at theorizing the relevant range is that they explicitly require the manufacturer to design plant and a supporting administrative and marketing organization which will be inefficient in current planned operating conditions. Quoting Koutsoyiannis (1979, p. 117), 'the businessman will not necessarily choose the plant which will give him *today* the lowest cost, but rather the equipment which will allow him the greatest possible flexibility'. By building in reserve capacity, management is indulging in the creation of organizational slack and productive inefficiency. Such behaviour has a central place in the organization theory of the firm, but it does not correspond with a theory of short-run profit maximization. Quoting Sizer (1965, p. 140), 'it is probable that constant marginal costs are an indication of underemployed capacity and possibly a failure to maximize short-run profits'. The built-in reserve capacity and the related relevant range explanations of constant variable costs are not only in conflict with the law of diminishing returns, but they also seem to be incompatible with the concept of efficiency.

Efficient practical capacity and rising marginal costs

Rather than trying to find sophisticated justifications for the relevant range, it would be preferable to adopt the more plausible explanation that linearity applies over the whole output range up to efficient practical capacity. Efficient practical capacity is given as Q^* in Figure 4.1 and is defined as the maximum level of output attainable at minimum variable cost. All output up to Q^* is assumed to be produced at constant unit direct cost plus variable overhead. The output Q^* can be exceeded in favourable demand conditions, but this output will be subject to increasing marginal cost. This follows from Q^* corresponding to the maximum efficient output for which the plant was designed. Output in excess of efficient practical capacity at Q^* will incur additional costs such as overtime, more frequent plant breakdowns, higher wear and tear, greater supervision and often the use of older, less efficient and previously 'mothballed' machinery; costs which although largely variable in nature are often lumped together by accountants and classified as indirect overheads. It is also the case that at outputs greater than Q^*, new costs will be incurred in the form of the degradation of central services in multi-divisional firms caused through the pressure of competing users (Zimmerman, 1979). Thus, diminishing returns through excessive use of central services occur after Q^* so causing increases in *true* average variable and marginal costs.

The restriction of these additional variable costs to outputs in excess of Q^* follows from such outputs being produced at plant operating levels in excess of those for which the plant was ideally designed. Marginal costs must rise at outputs in excess of the maximum efficient practical capacity by definition, and operation at such outputs will only be warranted to meet short-run shifts in demand. If the increase in demand continues into the long run, the plant will be extended to a higher level of efficient practical capacity to correspond with the new level of market demand.

Marginal costs of delay in waiting for central services, the degradation of their quality and the seeking of alternative more expensive external services when long queues develop for the internal central service, are being regarded as non-existent, or at least negligible, for outputs less than Q^*, and significant for outputs in excess of Q^*. Thus, the neutrality between joint products which held up to Q^* is relaxed to allow for the marginal joint costs which arise when products compete for a central service coming under intense demand pressure at levels of output beyond Q^*. This reversal in the costing of joint products and central services, from a fixed to a variable cost function which occurs at Q^*, is a consequence of moving from efficient to less efficient or, rather, inefficient operation. While operating efficiently the central services can cope with the flow of *potentially* competing demands. It is only after Q^* that the use of a central service by one user either hinders or prevents its use by other users, so giving rise to Zimmerman's (1979, p. 511) 'costly to observe non-zero opportunity costs associated with resource utilization within the firm'.

Differences between the marginal cost concepts of accounting and economics

We can conclude this account of linear cost functions and marginal cost by summarizing the discrepancies between the marginal cost concept of the economist and the marginal costs used by management. First, to the extent that the accountant's marginal costs are best practice in that they relate only to future expectations, are continuously differentiable, and are expressed in cash terms, they only provide a partial representation of the economist's cost function in that they largely ignore the effect of the law of diminishing returns on estimated cost. Second, even when the accountant's marginal costs are best practice, they will tend to underestimate the economist's marginal costs. This is because unit direct costs and unit variable overheads, as accounting variable costs, ignore the following: the increasing wear and tear per unit of output as machinery is run more frequently and faster; the additional stress on management as output rises towards Q_n; greater plant breakdown due to faster working; and the exclusion from variable costs of the variable components of some fixed overheads caused by the arbitrary nature by which semi-variable costs are separated between variable and fixed overheads.

In fact this last reason is likely to provide the largest source of discrepancy in normal circumstances. The division of indirect costs into variable and fixed overheads is a source of some contention in accounting as the variable elements have to be estimated from rather inadequate data, resulting in arbitrary cost categorization. Thus, the assumption underlying Figure 4.1 that the marginal costs of accounting and economics are equivalent is most unlikely to occur in practice.

Third, the economist's marginal costs relate to the short run within which at least one factor of production remains fixed. The determination of the short-run period in economic theory depends on the technical nature of production and cannot be generalized in terms of a fixed period of time. Each technique of production will have its own period and so the length of the short run is plant- and technique-specific. In practice, there is a given time period determined by the accounting convention. Normally it is one year. While the economist's short run is technologically determined, that of the accountant is determined by an arbitrary, yet standardized, division of time. For this reason alone there will be significant discrepancies in the determination of fixed and variable costs.

Fourth, the real minefield of discrepancy occurs when the marginal costs of business practice are not those of best practice. That is when standard costing departs from the future, differentiable, cash ideal. When they are based on historical costs and are not directly related to the planned output volume, any correspondence with the economist's concept of marginal cost has vanished out of the window.

ENGINEERING COST FUNCTIONS AS A BASIS
FOR RECONCILIATION

The cost functions used by production engineers provide one possible means of adapting standard costing to correspond with the rise in marginal costs which occurs when output progressively rises above efficient practical capacity. These cost functions assume fixed factor proportions for blocks of output in the short run, the proportions being adjusted between blocks of output. Under these conditions estimated marginal costs take the form of a step function (this is shown in Figure 4.3, below).

Engineering cost functions are based on engineering production functions which are derived from separate technical processes. In the analysis of production, the engineer is concerned with disaggregating the production process down into analytically convenient process units, often relating to particular pieces of production equipment. Here we have the first basic difference between an engineering production function and that of the economist. The economist takes the production methods as given and focuses instead on achieving the largest output possible from an infinite number of combinations of factor inputs. Not so the engineer, he is concerned with 'alternative methods of achieving a given production goal' (Chenery, 1949, p. 507) and so focuses primarily on alternative feasible production methods. Inevitably, this approach is limited to the analysis of the technical process and excludes non-technical considerations such as selling and administration. Thus the engineering approach is essentially practical, concerned only with the limited number of input combinations which are considered feasible.

A second basic difference between the approaches of the economist and the engineer is that the latter aggregates a production function by adding together the process units previously subject to detailed analysis. The engineer tries to exclude the interaction effects between processes by assuming each process unit to be independent. On the other hand, the economist is very concerned with these interactions, albeit at a theoretical level. The concern of the production engineer is one of measurement in a practical sense and multiplicative interaction effects are not often susceptible to practical measurement.

As a result of the differences in approach, it has proved difficult for economists to use engineering cost data for empirical analysis. However, Chenery (1949) and Ferguson (1951) developed economic production and cost functions based on engineering variables (for a recent empirical survey, see Goldschmid, 1974). In this way their cost functions approximated those of economic theory. As an approximation is possible, it seems potentially fruitful to attempt a closer correspondence between standard costing and the engineering cost function. Indeed, both engineers and cost accountants split up production into separate process units and the latter already relies on the former for factor input data. It is on this basis that we will proceed.

When applying the engineering concept of a production function to the analysis of efficient practical capacity discussed in the previous section, the estimated total variable cost curve would correspond to that illustrated in Figure

Figure 4.2 Total variable costs estimated from an engineering cost function

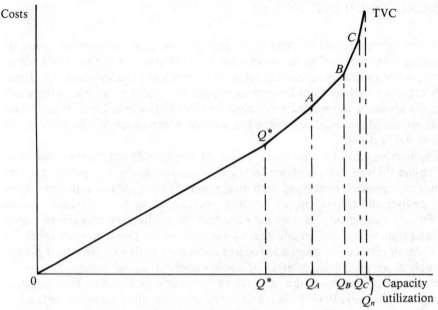

4.2. The estimated total variable cost curve, TVC, includes only short-run variable production costs, or direct costs plus variable overheads, and is made up of a number of linear slopes. The longest slope runs from zero output up to efficient practical capacity at Q^*. Beyond Q^* the factor proportions will have to be adjusted at given levels of output, such as Q^*, Q_A, Q_B and Q_C. The necessity for adjustment will be dictated by the requirement for a greater proportion of variable factors to be applied whenever there are further diminishing returns and externalities affecting further increases in output. Thus, we are assuming that TVC, which has been linear up to Q^*, retains its linearity, although only by increasing its slope at each point of adjustment to the factor proportions. It follows that TVC is formed from a number of linear segments, the second segment occurring after Q^*, and the number of additional segments depending on the necessity for adjusting the factor proportions.

Of course, the linear slopes of TVC represent the estimated marginal costs. As the linear slopes steepen along TVC, the corresponding marginal costs will increase in steps as shown in Figure 4.3. Between zero output and Q^*, marginal cost will equal average variable cost, but after Q^* marginal cost will progressively increase in a step-like manner and will exceed average variable cost, the steps getting larger as efficiency progressively decreases towards full capacity at Q_n. Average variable cost will rise as the irregular sloping curve AVC.

The marginal cost curve presented in Figure 4.3 indicates the way forward for a reconciliation between the accountant's standard costing and the economist's concept of marginal cost. While the best practice management accounting model of future, differentiable, cash-based standard costs would give a correspondence with constant marginal cost up to Q^*, it could be easily modified to estimate costs

Figure 4.3   Engineering marginal costs as unit cost standards

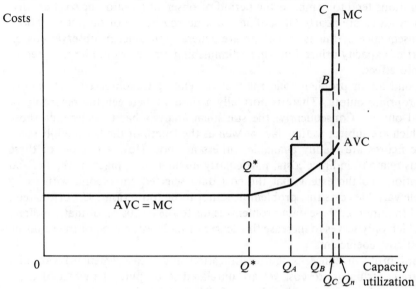

at outputs between Q^* and Q_n. All that is required is for the accountant to estimate the cost premiums to correspond with increases in marginal costs beyond Q^* which could then be added to the standard costs. The engineer's production function should provide the basic data for estimating the premiums, just as it provides the productivity data for standard setting. Thus, all that is required is a more complete integration of the engineering and accounting cost models. The result would be different cost standards for different blocks of output resembling the step-like marginal cost function of Figure 4.3. Such an approach would remove the theoretical objection that the accountant's cost–volume analysis ignores the law of diminishing returns and would reduce the accountant's underestimate of true marginal costs at high levels of capacity utilization. However, many of the practical problems of separating fixed and variable costs remain and the different concepts of the short run are difficult to resolve.

THE STATISTICAL ESTIMATION OF SHORT-RUN MARGINAL COSTS

Much of the empirical evidence is drawn from statistical estimates of cost functions. Ideally, the statistical cost function should relate costs to output after the elimination of the effect of all other influences upon them. To the extent that this can be done, it provides an empirical equivalent to the cost function of economic theory. Unfortunately, the problems of statistical estimation are unlikely to permit a close correspondence between the estimated and the true cost function. One major problem is that of finding a period in which the size of plant, the methods of production, the accounting system, the nature of the product, and the efficiency of management control all remained unchanged. Inevitably, these considerations tend to compress the period of observation into one so short that the observations are nearly all confined to a narrow range of output variation. One consequence of this is that there are generally insufficient observations on that part of capacity utilization where diminishing returns would be expected to come into effect.

A second major problem concerns that of relating the observed cost data to the appropriate output. There is normally a time lag between the recording of cost and output. Consequently, the statistical analysis has to determine those costs which are subject to time lags as well as the length of the lags. While some of these figures are readily available, others are not. However, most of these problems relate to indirect costs, particularly maintenance, machine repairs and depreciation. To the extent that the cost data selected correspond with easily separable variable costs this problem need not to be too serious. Unfortunately, the need to minimize these data problems leads to the exclusion of many indirect costs, which only serves to increase the degree of underestimation of the resulting marginal cost coefficients.

A third problem concerns the identification and measurement of variables which are contributors to cost yet are unrelated to output. The effect of these variables must be isolated so that the coefficient relating the change in cost to the change in output is an appropriate estimate of marginal cost. Unfortunately, many management information systems do not provide sufficiently detailed observations on variables such as the size and timing of production orders, the differing requirements of supervision and inspection when the product mix and the number of products change, the weather, the effect of labour disputes and variations in the quality of raw materials. As a result, the estimation equation is sometimes restricted to the following linear form

$$Y = a + bQ \qquad\qquad 4.1$$

where Y is total variable cost during the period of observation, Q is the quantity of output, and a and b are the parameters of the estimation model.

Despite the theoretical arguments which have raged over the shape of short-run marginal cost curves, less attention has been given to their estimation than to that of the long-run average cost curve. The empirical evidence on marginal cost is sparse in volume and rather historic.

Most of the pioneering empirical work was undertaken by Dean (1936, 1941a, 1941b, 1942) in a series of studies made during the 1930s. He applied the linear estimation equation to data from a furniture factory (1936), a leather belt factory (1941a) and a hosiery mill (1941b). In all cases the linear fit was significant, implying constant marginal costs. In his (1942) study of three departments in a large department store, he found evidence of constant marginal costs in the hosiery and shoe departments, but declining marginal costs in the coat department. However, cubic functions were also fitted and were found to be significant. Dean rejected the cubic form, because the curvatures were very slight.

As these four studies by Dean are the most satisfactory of the empirical studies of short-run cost functions from a theoretical standpoint they deserve some further comment. Although Dean claims that they all support the linear cost model, with the exception of the study of the coat department, we have to note that the cubic function could be fitted to all three departments in the study of the department store and that significantly increasing marginal costs could be found in the leather belt shop. Therefore, the evidence for constant marginal costs is far from overwhelming. Although maximum capacity was reached in the hosiery mill, and there were wide output, or sales transaction, variations for all the studies, Dean (1951) admitted that the studies were all made in the 1930s which meant that few observations were recorded at high capacity levels of output. 'Such flat curves indicate that there is some critical output level where marginal costs rise very steeply and that for a number of reasons these producers never pushed production to that critical level during the analysis period' (Dean, 1951, p. 292). When the depressed trading conditions in which the firms were operating are taken into account, the case against rising marginal costs beyond efficient practical capacity remains unproven. Of course, this does not deny Dean's substantial weight of evidence suggesting constant marginal costs at outputs less than efficient practical capacity.

Two early studies of the steel industry were undertaken by Yntema (1940) and Wylie and Ezekiel (1940). These two studies are less theoretically satisfactory than those of Dean as, first, they both used data for the late 1920s and 1930s during which steel demand was depressed and output rarely reached high rates of capacity utilization. Second, their long periods of observation using data which implied changes in available steel making capacity means that

> it is not clear whether the cost functions are approximations to short-run or long-run functions ... [the] variation [in capacity] strictly rules out the classification of the functions as short period; on the other hand, the variation in capacity is too small to justify much confidence in the view that an approximation to the long-run function has been obtained.
>
> (Johnston, 1960, p. 146)

While both studies provided satisfactory estimates of constant marginal costs, Wylie and Ezekiel also found evidence of declining marginal costs when using annual, instead of quarterly, data.

Most of the other evidence available is not based on statistical estimation and relies on either businessmen's responses to questionnaires or on discussions with businessmen. In the Eiteman and Guthrie (1952) survey of businessmen, 113 of the 366 respondents considered that their average cost curve declined rapidly, followed by a levelling out and then only a small upturn as full capacity was approached, while 203 thought their average cost curve declined continually through all levels of capacity utilization. The problem with this study is that it says very little about marginal costs. Troughton (1963, p. 114) concluded from his 'brief inquiry' that 'variable cost per unit tends to fall, slightly and unevenly, over the whole range of output'.

Steele and Gray (1982) used National Health Service data to test the relationship between output and cost in two types of maternity hospitals: specialist high technology hospitals providing the full range of services and small general practitioner units handling only routine non-complicated cases. Output was measured either in terms of the number of deliveries or occupied bed-days. Only the running costs were considered and the data were current cost estimates taken from their survey of hospitals. For both output measures the specialist hospitals were found to have a linear cost function and the smaller general practitioner units appeared to have a quadratic function which implied a downward-sloping marginal cost curve. However, the latter group seemed to have an average capacity utilization rate of some 30 per cent only.

All that can be drawn from the empirical evidence available suggests that marginal costs appear to be more or less constant over a substantial range of output. This conclusion has been heavily used by accountants to defend their assumption of constant direct costs over the relevant range. However, as Walters (1963, p. 51) concluded, 'the evidence in favour of constant marginal cost is not overwhelming'. With so few observations on outputs which exceed 80 per cent of full capacity, the empirical evidence remains silent on the law of diminishing returns.

REFERENCES AND FURTHER READING

Andrews, P. W. S. (1949) *Manufacturing Business*, Macmillan.

Chenery, H. B. (1949) Engineering production functions, *Quarterly Journal of Economics*, Vol. 63, pp. 507–31.

Dean, J. (1936) Statistical determination of costs with special reference to marginal costs, *Studies in Business Administration*, Vol. 7.

Dean, J. (1941a) *The relation of cost to output for a leather belt shop*, National Bureau of Economic Research, Technical Paper No. 2.

Dean, J. (1941b) Statistical cost functions of a hosiery mill, *Studies in Business Administration*, Vol. 14.

Dean, J. (1942) Department store cost functions, in O. Lange (ed.) *Studies in Mathematical Economics and Econometrics*, Cambridge University Press, pp. 222–54.

Dean, J. (1951) *Managerial Economics*, Prentice-Hall.

Dorward, N. (1985) Variance analysis: pitfalls of present costing techniques, *Accountancy*, November, pp. 204–6.

Eiteman, W. J. and Guthrie, G. E. (1952) The shape of the average cost curve, *American Economic Review*, Vol. 42, pp. 832–8.

Ferguson, A. R. (1951) An airline production function, *Econometrica*, Vol. 19, pp. 57–8.

Goldschmid, H. J. (1974) *Industrial Concentration: The New Learning*, Little Brown.

Goodlad, J. B. (1965) Industrial management, *Management Accounting*, UK, Vol. 43, January, pp. 16–22.

Hart, H. and Prusmann, D. F. (1963) *A Report of a Survey of Management Accounting Techniques in the S. E. Hants Coastal Region*, Department of Commerce and Accountancy, University of Southampton, December.

Horngren, C. T. (1982) *Cost Accounting: A Managerial Emphasis*, Prentice-Hall.

Howe, M. (1962) Marginal analysis in accounting, *Yorkshire Bulletin of Economic and Social Research*, Vol. 14, pp. 81–9.

Johnston, J. (1960) *Statistical Cost Functions*, McGraw-Hill.

Koutsoyiannis, A. (1979) *Modern Microeconomics*, Macmillan.

Middleton, K. A. (1980) A critical look at breakeven analysis, *The Australian Accountant*, May, pp. 264–8.

Sizer, J. (1965) Marginal cost: economists v. accountants, *Management Accounting*, UK, Vol. 43, April, pp. 138–42.

Sizer, J. (1966) The accountant's contribution to the pricing decision, *The Journal of Management Studies*, Vol. 3, pp. 129–49.

Sizer, J. (1971) Note on 'The determination of selling prices', *Journal of Industrial Economics*, Vol. 20, pp. 85–9.

Skinner, R. C. (1970) The determination of selling prices, *Journal of Industrial Economics*, Vol. 18, pp. 201–17.

Steele, R. and Gray, A. M. (1982) Statistical cost analysis: the hospital case, *Applied Economics*, Vol. 14, pp. 491–502.

Troughton, F. (1963) The teaching concerning costs of production in introductory economics, *Journal of Industrial Economics*, Vol. 11, pp. 96–115.

Walters, A. A. (1963) Production and cost functions: an econometric survey, *Econometrica*, Vol. 31, pp. 1–66.

Wylie, K. H. and Ezekiel, M. (1940) The cost curve for steel production, *Journal of Political Economy*, Vol. 48, pp. 777–821.

Yntema, T. O. (1940) Steel prices, volume and costs, *United States Corporation Temporary National Economic Committee Papers*, Vol. 2.

Zimmerman, J. L. (1979) The costs and benefits of cost allocations, *The Accounting Review*, Vol. 54, pp. 504–21.

5 The Allocation of Overheads and Joint Costs

THE COSTING BASE FOR THE PRICING DECISION

Despite the fact that almost all accountants working in business will, at some time or other, have been exposed to 'marginalist' management accounting, whether in their professional education or in reading the professional accounting literature, post-war empirical studies have shown the vast majority of businesses allocating overhead costs to product when making pricing decisions. Overheads are defined as indirect costs, including those of a fixed and variable nature.

The practice of allocating overheads is often referred to as full-cost pricing, by which a net profit margin is added to a costing base made up of direct costs plus overheads. Skinner (1970) found that 70 per cent of his respondents in Merseyside used it for some or all of their products and services. The British Institute of Management (1974) survey reported that 81 per cent of 273 UK group companies charged all or part of central expenses to product or service and that, of the 25 per cent of companies which had changed their accounting policy in the 'last five years', the majority had moved towards a greater allocation of overheads. Atkin and Skinner (1975), in their survey of marketing directors, found that of those using a cost-based approach to pricing, 63 per cent allocated overhead costs while 35 per cent used direct costs as the costing base. This pattern seems to be replicated over the English speaking world as will be shown in Chapter 9 which reviews the empirical evidence on pricing.

When the costing base is restricted to either direct costs or the accountant's version of marginal costs – direct materials, plus direct labour, plus direct expenses, plus indirect variable costs – it is known as the 'marginalist' or 'contribution' approach. All non-variable manufacturing overheads and the selling and administrative expenses are regarded as period costs and so are not allocated to product but are accumulated as incurred expenses and charged against sales revenue. The difference between direct or marginal cost and the selling price is known as the 'contribution margin'. With the contribution margin approach the aim is not to attempt marginal cost pricing in the sense that price equals marginal cost but to accept orders whenever the price exceeds direct or marginal cost so that a gross profit is made which can contribute to the recovery of overhead costs and net profit. This approach orients the firm towards accepting the best possible price in excess of variable cost, and can be associated with the objective of maximizing total contribution. The contribution margin approach forms the accountant's approximation to the pricing model of marginalist economics. However, as discussed in Chapter 4, marginal cost as measured in accounting practice is likely to deviate significantly from the economist's concept.

The most popular method of overhead allocation is known as 'absorption costing'. The absorption cost base adds all indirect manufacturing costs, fixed and variable, to direct costs. This is the normal approach when accounting for inventorial purposes. Consequently all factory overheads such as indirect labour, indirect materials, factory rent, depreciation, fuel and power are included in the inventorial costs. Effectively, all these indirect manufacturing costs are aggregated and divided by some overhead allocation base such as labour hours or machine hours. This gives a rate per hour which can then be applied to product as the rate per hour times the standard number of labour or machine hours required to manufacture the product. The resulting production cost per product then has a gross profit margin added which is planned to recover the selling and administrative expenses, plus making a net profit contribution. However, unlike the contribution margin, the absorption cost gross profit margin is budgeted as a fixed contribution and, as such, determines the price publicized in the price list. In contrast, the contribution margin is determined *ex post* as it depends on the eventual price agreed with the customer.

REASONS FOR ALLOCATING OVERHEADS TO PRODUCT

Given that a full cost base plus a predetermined, and fixed, profit margin seems to be a concept quite removed from the marginalist model, it is necessary to examine the reasons why management has been so keen to absorb all indirect costs and business expenses in product costs. The British Institute of Management (1974) survey gives some clues. Seventy-one per cent of those who absorbed central overhead costs considered that full costing helped to ascertain real unit profits; 67 per cent felt that it showed managers the 'true' cost of their operating departments; while 50 per cent claimed it helped to determine the cost and price of products and services. As Macdonald (1978) pointed out, the validity of this reasoning is in doubt. Profits are determined *ex post* by the interaction of market price and unit cost so that a 'realistic' profit margin fixed in advance implies a high level of knowledge of the demand function. Yet the argument for full-cost pricing is based on the argument that the demand function is unknown. Again the so called 'true' cost referred to in the survey is based on standard costing which, as applied in practice, has already been seen to be an unreliable predictor of the true-cost function. In that the allocation of overheads ignores market demand, full-cost pricing cannot be a 'helpful' device for price setting.

The only theoretically comprehensive rationale for overhead allocation was given by Zimmerman (1979). He suggested that in given situations the allocation of overheads could yield positive net benefits by controlling discretionary expenditure by divisional management, and by substituting for some hard to observe marginal costs of utilizing centrally provided services. One situation discussed was where the divisional managers had utility functions which resulted in the overconsumption of perquisites, such as the size and decor of their offices or the number of staff. Borrowing heavily from Williamson (1964), Zimmerman (1979) suggested that the allocation of central overhead costs to divisions could act as a lump-sum tax forcing divisional managers to reduce their expenditures on those factors they valued as perquisites causing factor inputs to adjust *towards* those required at the optimal output.

The effect of the allocation of overheads on perquisite expenditure is shown in Figure 5.1. Subject to other factor inputs being held constant, reported profits *abcd* rise up to a maximum at *b*, when expenditure on factors valued as perquisites equals E^*. However, divisional management has a utility function based both on divisional profits and on perquisite expenditure. Consequently, the management indifference curves are shown as I and I^1, which are convex to the origin. As a result, management will maximize its utility by spending an amount, E, on perquisites, where the indifference curve I is tangential to the profit curve at *c*. By levying a fixed overhead on the division, reported profits will fall from *abcd* to *a' b' c' d'* and managerial utility will now be maximized with a profit of *c'* and perquisite expenditure equal to E'. As perquisite expenditure E' is less

Figure 5.1   Overhead as a lump-sum tax on discretionary spending (after Zimmerman, 1979)

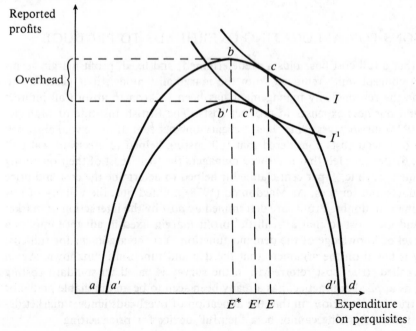

than E, the allocation of overheads has reduced the factor inputs towards the optimum at E^*. As a result, the profit contribution of the division has risen as c' reported profits plus the fixed overhead allocation is greater than the previous reported profit of c with no overhead allocation. However, the allocation of overheads does not necessarily ensure an efficient solution. That would only be possible if the overhead allocation 'taxed' all the divisional profits.

The second situation analysed by Zimmerman (1979) was where cost allocations could substitute for those opportunity costs caused by divisional users competing for a central service, such as delay costs frequently incurred in batch operated computer systems; degradation of service because supervisors become overstretched; and the purchase of relatively more expensive services external to the firm in order to avoid internal queues. Although these items would have increasing true marginal or incremental costs, Zimmerman (1979) claimed that the cost of measurement could prove excessive. Thus, a fixed allocation of overheads would somewhat crudely account for these increasing marginal costs. Furthermore, a full-cost allocation could provide an indication of the demand for the common service. If more than the total overhead was absorbed, it would suggest the need for an expansion of the service.

However, the effectiveness of the Zimmerman (1979) approach depends on the overhead allocation base being related to the divisional demand for central services. In his example, he used direct labour hours and so he must have assumed that the usage of service departments was a function of the time labour takes to complete the production of a unit of product. Therefore, the overhead allocation would encourage divisional management to economize on direct labour hours in order to minimize its liability for overheads. While this might be the case with the personnel function and labour supervision, it is most unlikely to occur with research and development and computing.

The full-cost allocation appears to be a rather crude and inaccurate measure of the opportunity costs of using central services and only improves central control when the central service is overutilized. Even then it does not cause the budgeted use of the service to move to the optimum. Consequently, it is not an efficient allocation in that it does not consistently shift the budget to an optimum solution.

ECONOMICS AND THE ALLOCATION OF OVERHEADS AND JOINT COSTS

The economic analysis of *ex ante* cost allocations is based on the premise that such allocations must be relevant for decision-making. Consequently, to the extent that direct manufacturing cost consists exclusively of the variable cost of materials and labour which are physically traceable to the finished product concerned, there is no problem in allocating cost to product. As Clark (1923, p. 219) said, 'Anyone who watches the [production] process can see that this labour and these materials are physically devoted to that product and no other.' Just as the physical composition of the product can be directly attributed to those directly applied factors of production, so the cost of the product can be allocated to those same factors in terms of units of value per kilogram or per labour hour. In this case, the operation of the production function is directly observable and the cost allocations which result are determined by that function. However, this determinacy is conditional on the finished product being produced separately from any other product.

When different products are simultaneously produced by the same process they are known as joint products and are only identified separately when they split off for further separate processing. During the stage of joint production, the products are technically inseparable. For example, paraffin, petrol, and lubricating oil only emerge as identifiable products when the basic refining process has been completed. The production function corresponding to the refining process cannot provide a solution as to how to break down the finished composition of the different products between the factors of production used during refining. No one, by either watching the refining process or by consulting the production function, can split the costs of refining between the several different outputs. In other words, 'Joint costs are usually inallocable on technical grounds alone, just as the physical product is inallocable between several factors of production.' (Wiles, 1956, p. 102.) As the division of the joint product costs is indeterminate in terms of the production function, any attempt to allocate them between the outputs must be on some arbitrary basis. With the production function being indeterminant on joint cost allocation, there can be no economic rationale for making such arbitrary allocations.

As Wiles (1956, p. 101) pointed out, 'By far the commonest joint costs are incurred by identical products – they are then called overheads.' Thus, just as joint costs are inallocable on technical grounds, so are all overheads, including variable and semi-variable indirect costs. The production function is silent on how much of the cost of electricity, watchmen, sales commissions, rent, depreciation, etc., should be charged to a given product within a given period. These items are not technically separable by product and can only be allocated by some arbitrary rule of thumb which would not accord with economic rationality.

Surprising to some, not all variable costs are allocable to products. Those non-allocable costs are the variable and semi-variable overheads and variable joint costs which should be consigned to a common joint cost category from which a marginal joint cost should be calculated and subsequently incorporated as a separate component in the profit function for the firm. Any attempt to allocate this marginal joint cost to individual products would be irrational and a denial of the essential jointness of the production process, as any such allocations could not be technically determined by the production function.

The resultant marginal joint cost must be added to the marginal separable costs for the different products to fix the profit-maximizing position for the firm. Obviously, the summation of the marginal joint and separate costs gives the difference in total cost for a change in the firm's total output. Although marginal joint costs must directly enter the profit function, they do so as a multi-product variable joint cost and not as the joint cost of product i or product j, for by their inherent jointness they cannot be rationally separated. This is the crux of Wiles's

(1956) argument when he erected his marginalist theory of joint costs and overheads. While this may solve the problem of variable overheads from a theoretical standpoint, it does not solve the practical problem of applying the discontinuous constant marginal joint costs that derive from the semi-variable stepped cost functions, the usual product of accounting data.

MODERN ACCOUNTING THEORIES OF ALLOCATION

The academic management accountant would accept the marginalist economics case, described above, against allocating overheads and joint costs when taking management decisions in respect of pricing or in judging the profit performance of products. However, this clear-cut theoretical stance on costing for decision-making has become clouded in recent years by the problem of motivating divisional management in multidivisional firms. The difficulties consequent upon the need to exert central control over decentralized organizational structures have introduced a major behavioural dimension into the process of cost planning and control which has become completely entangled with full-cost allocation procedures.

There is a widespread belief that the allocation of central overheads to divisions will have a beneficial effect on divisional management behaviour, yielding positive net benefits to the firm as discussed above. The result is that the accounting system is manipulated to induce the desired actions on the part of divisional management. Regrettably, concern over such manipulations tends to be concentrated on issues such as the equity or fairness of such allocations and their effect on profit motivation, largely ignoring the efficiency conditions for a firm-wide optimum.

The game theoretic approach

One area which has attracted considerable recent attention has been the efforts to apply game theory, as originally devised by Shapley (1953), to derive an equitable sharing of the overheads and joint variable costs arising from joint production in multidivisional firms. The Shapley scheme provides a unique solution for the allocation of joint costs using a co-operative n-person game, where the players can improve their payoffs by forming coalitions. The solution allocates the joint costs in a mutually satisfactory manner by taking account of all possible coalitions between the players. When applied to cost allocations, the solution ensures that the costs of joint production are fully allocated to the users.

Shubik (1962) applied Shapley's (1953) scheme to distribute the firm's profits net of joint costs between divisions and then allocated joint costs in accordance with these interdivisional profit distributions. Alternatively, Loehman and Whinston (1974) applied the Shapley scheme to derive a joint cost allocation based on the incremental costs of joint production instead of profits. Their charging formula for incremental joint costs reduces the information requirements over those of the Shubik (1962) procedure, for the latter involves detailed calculations of divisional profitability.

Although these allocation schemes allow for mutually satisfactory, or equitable, joint cost solutions between divisions and so encourage the exploitation of the motivational benefits flowing from decentralization by profit centre, they have been heavily criticized by Hughes and Scheiner (1980) for their failure to satisfy the efficiency conditions for a firm-wide optimum output solution. As Hughes and Scheiner (1980, p. 88) stated, these schemes do not take into account the competing demands of the user divisions for the joint products such that 'marginal profits before common cost allocations ... [to the] ... user divisions equal the marginal costs of supplying the common good'. Only a centrally imposed marginal cost-pricing scheme for the common service or joint product would ensure a firm-wide optimum output decision, but such a centrally imposed solution would undermine the rationale for decentralization.

The inefficiency of game theoretic solutions

Hughes and Scheiner (1980) illustrate their efficiency argument by considering the optimization problem for a firm with two user divisions of a joint facility produced by a third supplier division. Each user division is charged on the basis of an incremental costing scheme for the joint facility where the charges are functions of the demands of the other user. Each division optimizes where:

$$\text{Max } \pi_1(q_1) - C_1(q_1, \bar{q}_2) \hspace{4cm} 5.1$$

and

$$\text{Max } \pi_2(q_2) - C_2(\bar{q}_1, q_2) \hspace{4cm} 5.2$$

where in equilibrium

$$C_1(q_1, q_2) + C_2(q_1, q_2) = C(q_1 + q_2) \hspace{3cm} 5.3$$

$\pi_1(q_1)$ and $\pi_2(q_2)$ are the profits of the two user divisions before the allocation of joint costs and are given as functions of their respective outputs q_1 and q_2, $C_1(q_1, q_2)$ and $C_2(q_1, q_2)$ are the incremental charge formulae for the two user divisions. The full-costing function is assumed to have decreasing marginal costs.

Assuming Cournot-type behaviour (each user division assumes that the other's demand is constant), Hughes and Scheiner (1980) derive the first-order conditions where each user division acts as an independent profit centre. These are given as

$$\pi_1'(q_1) = \delta C_1(q_1, q_2)/\delta q_1 \hspace{4cm} 5.4$$

$$\pi_2'(q_2) = \delta C_2(q_1, q_2)/\delta q_2 \hspace{4cm} 5.5$$

Here the marginal profitability of each user division, before the allocation of joint costs, equals the marginal joint costs of meeting each division's joint product requirements. While these first-order conditions optimize the position of each user division, they are sub-optimal from the point of view of the firm as a whole. To the extent to which the requirements of the two divisions are different, reflecting the differences in their profit functions as given by $\pi_i'(q_i)$, they will respectively optimize at different marginal joint costs. Consequently, the marginal profitabilities $\pi_i'(q_i)$ will not equal $\delta C(q)/\delta q$, the marginal cost for the output at which the firm as a whole maximizes its profit. The firm-wide view can be ascertained by combining the objective functions of the two user divisions, equations 5.1 and 5.2, to form the firm-wide objective function. This is given as

$$\text{Max } \pi_1(q_1) + \pi_2(q_2) - C_1(q_1, q_2) - C_2(q_1, q_2) \qquad\qquad 5.6$$

The first-order conditions of equation 5.6 can be expressed as

$$\pi_1'(q_1) = \delta C_1(q_1, q_2)/\delta e_i + \delta C_2(q_1, q_2)/\delta e_i = \pi_2'(q_2) \qquad\qquad 5.7$$

As q equals $q_1 + q_2$, we get $\delta C(q_1, q_2)/\delta q_i = \delta C(q)/\delta q$, where $\delta C(q)/\delta q$ equals $\delta C(q)/\delta q_i$. Therefore

$$\pi_1'(q_1) = \delta C(e)/\delta q = \pi_2'(q_2) \qquad\qquad 5.8$$

This gives the firm-wide optimum as each division's marginal profitability, before the allocation of joint costs, equals the firm's marginal joint cost.

Of course, the Hughes–Scheiner (1980) thesis is nothing more than an echo of the economic analysis of overheads given in the previous section. With the charges to the user divisions being functions of either the complementary or competitive demands of other user divisions, all the joint costs are variable. This means that as one user division changes its demand for the joint product, then not only do its marginal joint costs change, as would be expected, but so do those of the other user division. If an increase in demand by the first division (perhaps as the result of an increase in demand for its final product) causes its marginal joint cost to fall, then, because of the inherent jointness of production, the marginal joint cost of the second division will also fall. This will cause the second division to increase its optimal output and demand for the joint product so in turn lowering the marginal joint costs of the first division, and so on. Consequently, the marginal joint costs faced by both divisions are a function of their *joint demands*. And so we cannot consider *independently* the optimal output of any one division. All divisions must be considered simultaneously.

The efficient allocation for a pure common input

Cohen and Loeb (1982) followed a public sector economics approach to examine the optimal full-cost allocation for a pure common input, one where the amount consumed by one division has no effect on the amount available for other divisions. In fact, once produced, a pure common input is freely available to all divisions. An example would be corporate image advertising where any division cannot be prevented from benefiting once the advertising has taken place.

Assuming that the costs of producing the pure common input are non-separable and that all divisions use the same amount of the input, equal to the quantity produced and given as X, the profit-maximizing level of input for the firm is given by the sum of the marginal profitabilities for the n divisions equalling the marginal joint cost of supplying X. The firm-wide optimal full-cost allocation (which follows that developed by Lindahl (1958) for a pure public good) is where 'each division should be charged that fraction of common input costs equal to the division's proportion of marginal profitability at the optimal level of the input' (Cohen and Loeb, 1982, p. 339). This means that the 'divisions are charged according to the marginal benefits they received from the common input' (Cohen and Loeb, 1982, p. 340).

The overwhelming difficulty of the Cohen and Loeb (1982) use of the Lindahl (1958) allocation is that the solution requires the headquarters to know the marginal profitabilities of the divisions and the collection of this information, an immense task in itself, would lead to the 'free-rider problem'. Free riding occurs when divisions deliberately understate their demands, or profits, to gain a very low full-cost allocation, yet still consume the larger amount given by their actual demand function. As with the game theory approach, efficiency is only possible by central intervention. Despite this, it is worth noting that the case of a pure common input is the only one where it is theoretically possible to have an *ex ante* allocation of full costs consistent with firm-wide efficiency. However, the narrowness of the theoretical concept of a pure common input will make it a rare case indeed for practical decision-making.

To the extent that the objective function is defined in terms of profit or wealth maximization, neither the game theoretic nor the Cohen and Loeb (1982) allocation procedures can be regarded as efficient as they do not unambiguously result in a firm-wide optimal price–output decision. Essentially, optimality requires the supplier division to charge a marginal cost price to the profit-maximizing user divisions, and this requires a relatively more centralized form of decision-making than is implied by the decentralization assumptions used in the full-cost allocation models.

METHODS OF OVERHEAD ALLOCATION IN PRACTICE

Despite the widespread acceptance of marginalist analysis by academic accountants, the practising accountant continues to allocate overheads and joint costs to product by a variety of rules of thumb, most of which have little logical connection with marginal profitability or marginal cost. Some insight into the methods of overhead allocation employed in the United Kingdom can be gleaned from a study of the costing data for 57 manufacturing firms as given in seven interview-based studies published by Hall and Hitch (1939; 33 firms), Edwards (1952; 1 firm), Pearce (1956; 1 firm), Pearce and Amey (1956–7; 1 firm), Balkin (1956; 1 firm), Barback (1964; 7 firms) and Hague (1971; 13 firms). Of these 57 firms, 42 gave sufficient details on costing for it to be possible to ascertain their methods of overhead allocation at the time of the survey.

Bases for cost allocation

The various methods of overhead allocation are comprehensively presented in Table 5.1. Several cost allocation bases seem to have been used for applying

Table 5.1 Methods of overhead allocation for 42 UK manufacturing companies

Allocation base	Assumed capacity utilization for applying overheads to base						Total responses by firms	
	Full or conventional or normal	Experience or last year's output	Actual or current output	Forecast sales or output	Last year's historical accounts	No information or not relevant or ambiguous	No.	(%)
% of direct cost	—	—	—	3	1	1	5	(12)
% of direct labour cost	—	—	1	3	2	4	10	(24)
% of direct wages	1	1	—	—	2	1	5	(12)
% of manhours or machine hours or materials	—	—	—	1*	1	—	2	(5)
Output or turnover	6†	2	3½‡	8½‡	—	—	20	(47)
Total responses by firm: No. (%)	7 (17)	3 (7)	4½ (11)	15½ (37)	6 (14)	6 (14)	42	(100)

* Firm allocated in proportion to either manhours or material content depending on which was greater.
† Only one response was for full capacity.
‡ Firm used the larger of actual or forecast output, hence response split between two categories.

overheads to product. The two essential characteristics of an allocation base are that it can be physically traced to the product and that it is directly related to the usage of the overhead facilities. Given the objective of allocating output cost per unit, the first characteristic is obvious. The second characteristic is required to convert a non-variable overhead into a variable which is a function of usage. For example, a reasonable allocation base for a fixed-overhead personnel department is one which is related to the number of employees and their level of usage, such as direct labour hours. It is important to realize that the allocation of overheads is essentially a mechanism which transforms a fixed cost into a variable cost which is then applied to product as a constant addition per unit, or per labour hour. A preferable allocation base is one which facilitates the transformation in such a way that those products making a relatively high use of the overhead (e.g. personnel department) because of the nature of their inputs (high labour hours) bear a relatively high share of the overhead cost.

Fifteen firms used either standard unit wages or direct labour cost as the allocation base. As these variable costs can be easily allocated to product by reference to the production function, they satisfy the first characteristic. Their satisfying of the second characteristic depends on indirect manufacturing overheads being labour related such as where the operational activity is predominantly manual. Seven firms used a variety of other bases including direct cost, direct labour hours, machine hours and direct materials. The little use of direct labour hours is surprising as this allocation base assumes that indirect costs vary in proportion to time, certainly most overhead costs are more related to time than to any other factor, e.g. depreciation, rent, taxes and insurance.

Budgeted output versus actual output

Of equal interest in Table 5.1 are the assumed capacity utilization levels used for budgeting costs for the production period. It is from these levels of capacity utilization or budgeted output that accountants derive their standard costs. They give the budgeted output figure at which overheads will be recovered and are used, therefore, for the estimation of the gross profit margin to be applied to the allocation base. By far the most popular capacity measure was forecast sales, or output, with sixteen firms applying it to their allocation base. The next most popular was the use of the traditional full, conventional or normal capacity measures. Six firms used the unit allocation calculated from last year's historical accounts which, by its dependence on a backward-looking perspective, is about as far away from marginalism as it is possible to get. Finally, only some four or five firms appeared to use actual, or current, output.

The prevailing view in accounting is that budgeted or forecast output is preferable to actual output as a method of allocation. (For example, see Horngren, 1982, pp. 507–8.) The budgeted quantity is that used to plan the use of available capacity such that each product is charged with the costs of providing that capacity corresponding to its budgeted output. The use of budgeted output 'avoids the short-run costs of a user department being affected by the fluctuations in the actual sales of the other user departments' (Horngren, 1982, p. 507). This means that a product whose actual output was less than budget would still be allocated the full costs of providing its budgeted capacity. The fear seems to be that if capacity costs were based on actual rather than budgeted output, falls in actual output would not result in a difference between actual and budgeted overheads. It is felt that the lack of such differences could disguise production inefficiencies which may have contributed to the lower than expected actual output.

Far from ensuring greater efficiency, allocating on the basis of budgeted output would be less efficient than allocating on the basis of actual or current output. It is preferable from the standpoint of economic efficiency to charge each product only with that proportion of overhead costs corresponding to the proportion, or operating time, of the plant used in its production. For example, if only 10 per cent of capacity was used to produce a given batch of product, that batch should be charged either the costs of specifically providing that segment of capacity or 10 per cent of the cost of providing total capacity. Any previously incurred costs of factors making up production capacity which were not brought into use during the production period would be accumulated and charged as losses. By charging each product only in relation to its actual use of production capacity, the allocation of overhead costs corresponds to the level of capacity utilization. This was the essential result of Noyes's (1941) theory of overhead allocation which would correspond to the marginalist result whenever direct variable costs were constant.

If we allocate the unit overhead and standard net income to product in direct proportion to the actual level of capacity utilization, the allocation is given as

$$K_i = \frac{M}{Q^*} \times \frac{Q_i}{Q^*} \qquad\qquad 5.9$$

where K_i is the per unit overhead allocation to the ith product, M is total overhead allocated to the production period, Q^* is efficient practical, or normal, capacity for the production period standardized by some common standard for all products produced, and Q_i is the actual output. The method of allocation will henceforth be referred to as the 'proportional allocation rule of thumb'. In simple terms it allocates at 50 per cent capacity utilization only 50 per cent of the unit allocation applicable at efficient practical, or normal, capacity. As capacity utilization rates (Q_i/Q^*) incorporate the effect of market demand, it means that where unit variable costs are constant the allocation is demand determined. When K_i is revised during the production period to correspond with changes in (Q_i/Q^*), the *ex ante* allocation method will shift in exactly the same way as the *ex post* marginalist profit contributions to overheads. As such it can provide efficient allocations (see Dorward, 1984, 1986, and Chapter 8).

Managerial discretion

The variety of methods used for allocating overheads shown in Table 5.1 is evidence of the wide discretion that management has over the allocation of overheads and joint costs. Given that such allocations are technically indeterminate *ex ante*, top management can manipulate them in ways considered necessary to retain budgetary control. All semi-variable and fixed overheads and joint costs (whether fixed or variable) can be regarded as discretionary costs. Management can decide whether to allocate them or not, in whole or in part. If none were allocated to product, we would have the contribution approach where the only items allocated to product would be variable manufacturing costs. If all overheads and joint costs were allocated to product, we would have the full-cost approach. Between those two limiting costing approaches there can be many variants for allocating overheads for decision-making purposes.

It follows that, if allocations can be made to meet given objectives at the same time as non-allocations to meet other objectives, a firm can also change from non-allocation to allocation and vice versa for decision-making purposes between production and pricing periods. This can occur without any significant change in either the amount or structure of semi-variable and fixed overheads. This gives costing with overhead allocation a much greater flexibility than would be assumed from reading the standard accounting literature.

REFERENCES AND FURTHER READING

Atkin, B. and Skinner, R. (1975) *How British Industry Prices*, Industrial Market Research Ltd.
Balkin, N. (1956) Prices in the clothing industry, *Journal of Industrial Economics*, Vol. 5, pp. 1–15.
Barback, R. H. (1964) *The Pricing of Manufactures*, Macmillan.
British Institute of Management (1974) *Profit Centre Accounting: The Absorption of Central Overhead Costs*, Survey Report No. 21, British Institute of Management.
Clark, J. M. (1923) *Studies in the Economics of Overhead Cost*, University of Chicago Press.
Cohen, S. I. and Loeb, M. (1982) Public goods, common inputs, and the efficiency of full cost allocations, *The Accounting Review*, Vol. 57, pp. 336–47.
Dorward, N. (1984) Pricing: formula to tame those wayward costs, *Accountancy*, Vol. 95, November, pp. 101–6.
Dorward, N. (1986) Overhead allocations and 'optimal' pricing rules of thumb in oligopolistic markets, *Accounting and Business Research*, Vol. 16, pp. 309–17.
Edwards, R. S. (1952) The pricing of manufactured products, *Economica*, Vol. 19, pp. 298–307.
Hague, D. C. (1971) *Pricing in Business*, George Allen & Unwin.
Hall, R. L. and Hitch, C. J. (1939) Price theory and business behaviour, *Oxford Economic Papers*, No. 2, pp. 12–45.
Horngren, C. T. (1982) *Cost Accounting: A Managerial Emphasis*, Prentice-Hall.
Hughes, J. S. and Scheiner, J. H. (1980) Efficiency properties of mutually satisfactory cost allocations, *The Accounting Review*, Vol. 55, pp. 85–95.
Lindahl, E. (1958) Just taxation – a positive solution, in R. A. Musgrave and A. T. Peacock (eds.) *Classics in the Theory of Public Finance*, Macmillan, pp. 168–76.
Loehman, E. and Whinston, A. (1974) An axiomatic approach to cost allocation for public investment, *Public Finance Quarterly*, April, pp. 236–51.
Macdonald, I. R. (1978) Nonsense is a nonsense, so why pretend otherwise, *Management Accounting*, UK, Vol. 56, January, pp. 18–19.

Noyes, C. R. (1941) Certain problems in the empirical study of costs, *American Economic Review*, Vol. 31, pp. 473–92.

Pearce, I. F. (1956) A study in price policy, *Economica*, Vol. 23, pp. 114–27.

Pearce, I. F. and Amey, L. R. (1956–7) Price policy with a branded product, *Review of Economic Studies*, Vol. 24, pp. 49–60.

Shapley, L. S. (1953) A value for *n*-person games, in H. W. Khun and A. W. Tucker (eds.) *Contributions to the Theory of Games*, Princeton University Press, pp. 307–17.

Shubik, M. (1962) Incentives, decentralised control, the assignment of joint costs and internal pricing, *Management Science*, Vol. 8, pp. 325–43.

Skinner, R. C. (1970) The determination of selling prices, *Journal of Industrial Economics*, Vol. 18, pp. 201–17.

Wiles, P. J. D. (1956) *Price, Cost and Output*, Blackwell.

Williamson, O. E. (1964) *The Economics of Discretionary Behaviour: Managerial Objectives in a Theory of the Firm*, Prentice-Hall.

Zimmerman, J. L. (1979) The costs and benefits of cost allocations, *The Accounting Review*, Vol. 54, pp. 504–21.

6 Marginalist Price Theory and Demand Estimation

DIFFICULTIES IN RELATING PRICE THEORY TO BUSINESS PRACTICE

In practice, the pricing decision tends to be the responsibility of the marketing manager who sets a price within the context of his overall market strategy. He seeks a practical solution to his problem of finding the 'right' price level at which to sell the goods or service. Fundamental economic principles such as charging a price at which marginal cost is equal to marginal revenue do not in practice enter his calculations. Frequently he is faced with the need to set a price for a product immediately having available only incomplete and outdated sets of cost and market data. Economic theory will not provide a formula for such an immediate and specific price decision. Instead, it will offer a body of principles, a toolkit for modelling market situations, which will enable him to understand better the complexities of his economic environment. As Nagle (1984, p. 4) stated recently, '[marketeers] are soon disillusioned if they look to economics for practical solutions to pricing problems' and 'the role of economics is not to price products, but to explain the economic principles to which successful pricing strategies will conform'.

The purpose of an economic theory of price is to provide an explanation of why a particular type of pricing decision is widespread and persistent, given a particular set of market conditions. What matters is that the implications of a theory in terms of its predictions are supported by the empirical evidence. As Friedman (1953, p. 15) stated in his essay on the methodology of positive economics, 'the relevant question to ask about the assumptions of a theory is not whether they are descriptively "realistic", for they never are, but whether they are sufficiently good approximations for the purpose in hand. And this question can be answered only by seeing whether it yields sufficiently accurate predictions.'

Unfortunately, it has proved difficult to select between theories on the criterion of predictive accuracy. The evidence on pricing is conflicting not only in terms of the observations produced by the different studies but also in terms of the interpretation of those observations. As a result most of the theoretical disputes concerning pricing policy remain unresolved.

There are several reasons to explain why it has proved difficult to relate business pricing practices to the underlying economic theory. The first difficulty concerns the apparent diversity of pricing strategies employed by firms. This is because the objectives guiding each pricing strategy are peculiar to the firm concerned. While some firms aim for prices which are expected to yield the highest profits, others may be more concerned with the matching of competitors' prices, maintaining market share, passing on increased operating costs, or meeting a target return on capital employed. The real difficulties begin when firms adopt a mix of pricing objectives incorporating short and long-run time perspectives. This will result in complex interactions between pricing, profit, sales growth and funding planned investment.

The second difficulty is that different economic/market environments are likely to require different pricing strategies. Thus, large multinational and multi-product companies like Du Pont will have different pricing policies to meet the different economic conditions encountered in its various markets. Alfred (1972) categorized six types of market situation which may require different pricing strategies, namely: type of product; the nature of the geographic market; the type of competitive market structure; the age of the product; the nature of production; and the level of production capacity in relation to expected market requirements. 'Most of these conditions can be combined with each other, so that the number of possible situations is very large, which accounts for the complex real situation already referred to' (Alfred, 1972, p. 6).

A third problem area concerns the definition of price. While for many products there is an easily recognizable price such as that for a sliced loaf from a supermarket, for others price is a very complex concept. In the USA Xerox and Kodak have thick pricing books for copying machines which incorporate complete quantity discount schedules so that the price is related to the rate of usage of the expected purchaser. In America the telephone companies employ non-linear price schedules. Health clubs, car rental companies, and the public utilities have the price in two parts incorporating a fixed charge and a usage rate. Antiques, oil leases, and some airline seats are sold by 'priority' pricing in which the pricing schedule relates to the ability of buyers to pay, with those electing to pay the highest price being served first (the auction method) and those electing to pay the lowest price either being served on a standby basis or not at all. Product 'bundling' by restaurants means that the same food is sold at lower prices in fixed-price meals than when ordered à la carte. Motor cars and many other consumer durables are sold with a 'trade-in' price, the amount of which depends on the state of trade and the age and quality of the item being traded in. Many products have published or scheduled prices which can vary quite substantially from the actual transaction price. When the transaction price results from haggling, secret discounts, and tendering, it can remain unknown to outside parties. All this complexity over the definition of price and the fact that so many different prices can be paid for physically identical products has made it difficult to be consistent when testing theoretical price predictions against actual prices paid.

Finally, all but the more recent economic models of pricing assume certainty, while the real economic environment is characterized by uncertainty. Real-world firms do not know with certainty the position and shape of their demand and cost curves. Often real exchange involves asymmetric information where the seller has more information on product attributes than the buyer. Some product attributes can only be evaluated after use, often over extended periods of time, so that buyers will only be well informed on a very few of the available substitutes (Nelson, 1970; Darby and Karni, 1973). Once incorporated into a theoretical model, the imperfect information assumption can result in significantly different behavioural implications. For example, when buyers can only get to know a few substitutes really well, any increase in the number of substitute products need not affect inter-brand price competition or the demand elasticity for any existing brand. Such a prediction is very different from that given by pricing models based on a perfect information assumption.

DEMAND FUNCTIONS AND DEMAND CURVES

The modern theory of demand is based on the formulation of demand functions which refer to the behaviour of all consumers as a group. Such functions are not derived directly from the traditional theories of the behaviour of individual consumers. The modern theory is pragmatic in approach. Demand is held to be a multivariational function determined by many variables and can be estimated directly from market data.

The demand function

The demand function specifies the relationship between the quantity demanded and the factors which determine this quantity. A function for consumer goods could be expressed as

$$Qd = f(P, Ps, Y, A, D, R, T) \qquad\qquad 6.1$$

where Qd is the quantity demanded, P is the price of the goods, Ps are the prices of substitutes, Y is consumer disposable income, A is the level of advertising, D is the size and age structure of the consuming population, R is the rate of interest (an important influence on the demand for consumer credit) and T is a trend factor for tastes. The variables included on the right-hand side of equation 6.1 will depend on the nature of the product, the market situation and on whether Qd is the demand for the product of the individual firm or for the entire market. Obviously in the latter case we would exclude variables representing the activities of competitors such as their prices and advertising levels.

Many other variables can be included when analysing particular market situations such as consumer expectations, operating costs, credit restrictions, the level of personal liquid assets and consumer confidence in the future. One set of variables which is becoming of increasing importance in analysing the demand for consumer goods is that relating to the characteristics of the family. Blattberg *et al.* (1978) found that certain family characteristics such as high levels of home and car ownership and few pre-school children made for a high family proneness to respond to special price deals.

For demand functions to be relevant to the formation of pricing strategies, management needs to know the *direction* and *extent* of influence of the variables determining demand. What is needed are estimates of the coefficients which state the explicit relationship between each of the independent variables and the quantity demanded. If the demand function given in equation 6.1 has a linear specification, it can be rewritten as

$$Qd = b_1P + b_2Ps + b_3Y + b_4A + b_5D + b_6R + b_7T \qquad\qquad 6.2$$

Demand functions such as equation 6.2 can be used by management to estimate the b_i coefficients. By relating the direction and extent of influence of each independent variable to the quantity demanded, each b_i gives a partial differentiation of Qd to each of the demand determinants. For example, b_1 is the price differential $\delta Qd/\delta P$, b_3 is the income differential $\delta Qd/\delta Y$, and b_4 is the advertising differential $\delta Qd/\delta A$.

The b_i coefficients or partial differentials show the effect on the quantity demanded of a unit change in each of the relevant variables. For example, if b_1 equals 2,000 then a $1 reduction in price would be expected to cause an increase in demand of 2,000. Estimated demand functions such as equation 6.2 provide information on the sensitivity of demand to changes in the independent variables determining demand. This information is especially important for those variables controlled by the firm such as price and advertising. The main measure of demand responsiveness is known as demand *elasticity* – the responsiveness of Qd to a change in an independent variable in the demand function.

The elasticity of demand for any independent variable can be defined as the percentage change in quantity demanded caused by a given percentage change in that variable. Three of the most commonly used elasticities are those for price, income and advertising. They can be calculated for a linear demand function such as equation 6.2 by multiplying the appropriate coefficient b_i by the corresponding values for Qd and the variable of interest.
This is given as follows:

(i)   own price elasticity $= b_1 \cdot \dfrac{P}{Q} = \dfrac{\delta Q}{\delta P} \cdot \dfrac{P}{Q}$

(ii) income elasticity $= b_3 \cdot \dfrac{Y}{Q} = \dfrac{\delta Q}{\delta Y} \cdot \dfrac{Y}{Q}$

(iii) advertising elasticity $= b_4 \cdot \dfrac{A}{Q} = \dfrac{\delta Q}{\delta A} \cdot \dfrac{A}{Q}$

With linear demand functions, the effect of each of the independent variables is assumed to be constant in an absolute sense throughout the function. Thus with b_i being constant, the variations in both the independent variable under consideration and the quantity demanded will cause elasticity to vary along the function. For example, at high prices and low volume the price elasticity will be high but it will fall continually as price is reduced. The constancy of the marginal effects of each variable, no matter what the value of that variable and the values of all the other variables in the function, has led to doubts being cast on the empirical validity of linear demand functions. The marginal effect of each variable as estimated from the b_i coefficients is likely to vary with the value of that variable. Consequently, much applied work has been undertaken with non-linear specifications.

Non-linear demand functions are normally specified in the *exponential* form

$$Qd = P^{\eta_1},\ Ps^{\eta_2},\ Y^{\eta_3},\ A^{\eta_4},\ D^{\eta_5},\ R^{\eta_6},\ T^{\eta_7} \qquad\qquad 6.3$$

In the exponential form the exponentials η_i are the elasticities of demand. These are assumed to remain constant. For this reason the exponential form is often referred to as the 'constant elasticity demand function'. In the exponential form the marginal effects of each variable are not constant as in the linear form.

In practice, the elasticities of exponential functions would be estimated by transforming the variables to logarithms. The demand function would then be expressed in the log–linear form as

$$\log Qd = \eta_1 \log P + \eta_2 \log Ps + \eta_3 \log Y + \eta_4 \log A$$
$$+ \eta_5 \log D + \eta_6 \log R + \eta_7 \log T \qquad\qquad 6.4$$

This transformation allows the elasticities to be estimated by linear regression.

It follows that management must first examine the nature of its market data in order to determine the appropriate specification of the estimating equation. Although the exponential form is the most commonly used, a large number of data sets have successfully been analysed with a linear specification.

The demand curve

The demand curve is derived from the demand function and expresses the relation between price and quantity demanded. All the other independent variables are assumed to remain constant. In this way we isolate the effect of price on the quantity demanded from that of any of the other determinants. The demand curve can be expressed as

$$Qd = -bP + Ps + Y + A + D + R + T$$
$$= (Ps + Y + A + D + R + T) - bP \qquad\qquad 6.5$$
$$= a - bP$$

Thus we arrive at the conventional notation for the demand curve.

The concept of the demand curve does not preclude changes in any of the other independent variab'es. All that happens is that the change is incorporated as an adjustment to the constant term of intercept. For example, an increase in advertising would be expected to increase demand by shifting the whole demand curve to the right. This would be expressed as

$$Qd = (a + \Delta A) - bP \qquad\qquad 6.6$$

Similar effects would be expected from increases in the prices of competing goods, disposable income, population, taste preference and a decrease in the rate of interest. The reverse of these changes would result in a leftward shift in the demand curve.

AN OPTIMAL PRICING POLICY

A pricing policy is only of direct concern to a firm which has scope to influence the price of its product. Such a firm is referred to as a *price maker* in that it has sufficient market power to set a price different from that of its market competitors. Firms who have to accept a given market price have little option but to follow the market leader and are known as *price takers*. Pricing policy has little relevance to such firms.

We will assume profit-maximizing behaviour, a downward-sloping demand curve giving management discretion over the price charged, and a linear variable cost function from which we can derive a constant marginal cost. It follows that the optimal price, P^*, is determined by the marginal equivalence rule where marginal revenue (MR) equals marginal cost (MC). This is illustrated in Figure 6.1 in terms of unit costs and revenues.

Marginal revenue and the price elasticity of demand

Given a linear demand curve, marginal revenue will be equal to the total revenue generated from the extra unit sold at the lower price minus the loss of revenue

Figure 6.1   The optimal price

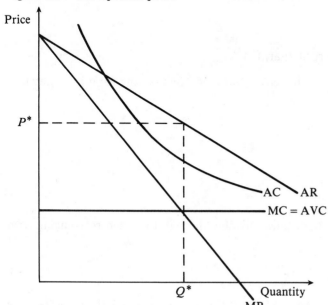

from selling all other units at the new lower price. Thus, MR can be given as

$$MR_{i+1} = P_{i+1} - (P_i - P_{i+1})Q_i \qquad 6.7$$

where P_i is the previous price corresponding to Q_i and P_{i+1} is the new price. It follows from equation 6.7 that MR is less than price so long as $(P_i - P_{i+1}) > 0$.

The relationship with the price elasticity of demand, η, is easily derived from equation 6.7 by showing the marginal change in revenue as follows

$$MR = \frac{\delta R}{\delta Q} = \frac{\delta(P \cdot Q)}{\delta Q} \qquad 6.8$$

Using the product rule of differentiation we get

$$MR = P \cdot \frac{\delta Q}{\delta Q} + Q \cdot \frac{\delta P}{\delta Q}$$

$$= P + Q \cdot \frac{\delta P}{\delta Q} \qquad 6.9$$

This can be re-expressed as

$$MR = P\left(1 + \frac{1}{\eta}\right) \qquad 6.10$$

(With η generally being negative the expression will be calculated as $P(1 - 1/\eta)$.)

Given this relationship between marginal revenue and the price elasticity of demand, managers can derive estimates of η from econometric estimates of their demand functions and use them to calculate their marginal revenue functions. Technically, the means exist for management to behave in a manner similar to that advocated by the marginal calculus.

Optimal price and profit margins

The optimal price is found by setting MR = MC and solving for price. Therefore, we get

$$P + Q \cdot \frac{\delta P}{\delta Q} = MC$$

and

$$P = MC - \left(Q \cdot \frac{\delta P}{\delta Q}\right) \qquad 6.11$$

Subtracting MC from both sides, dividing through by P and rearranging terms gives

$$\frac{P - MC}{P} = \frac{Q}{P} \cdot \frac{\delta P}{\delta Q} = (-)\frac{1}{\eta} \qquad 6.12$$

With a constant MC, we have AVC = MC and so $(P - AVC)/P = (-)(1/\eta)$. This gives $(P - \text{AVC})/P$ as the gross proportional profit margin, or mark-up, on price, Mp, as equal to the reciprocal of the own price elasticity of demand at the profit-maximizing price.

Alternatively, the gross profit margin can be expressed as a mark-up on cost. With MC = AVC,

$$\text{AVC} = P\left(1 + \frac{1}{\eta}\right)$$

From which we can derive the optimal price as

$$P = \text{AVC}\left(1 + \frac{1}{1 + \eta}\right)$$

and the optimal mark-up on cost as

$$\frac{P - \text{AVC}}{\text{AVC}} = (-)\frac{1}{1 + \eta} = \text{Mc} \qquad\qquad 6.13$$

The two expressions for mark-up, Mp and Mc, can be equated as $Mp = Mc/(1 + Mc)$ and $Mc = Mp(1 - Mp)$.

So long as management can estimate its own price elasticity of demand, it will be able to use equation 6.13 to calculate Mc, the optimal mark-up on variable cost. As we will see in the next section, the estimation of η is not as great as might appear at first sight. Only that part of the demand curve around current price is needed and this is the part about which most information is available. Subject to having sufficient data for estimating the demand function, econometric techniques can give a reasonably close approximation to the slope $\delta R/\delta Q$ and $\delta Q/\delta P$.

Optimal price and changing conditions of demand

First we will consider a change in the slope of the demand curve in the sense of pivoting it on the existing price and quantity. This is shown in Figure 6.2 by pivoting D_1 in a clockwise direction until it is identical with D_2. As the demand curve has steepened, $\delta P/\delta Q$ has become more negative, there will be a fall in MR at the old P. This will lead to a new and higher optimal price and a reduced output. Furthermore, as seen in equation 6.12, the increase in the slope $\delta P/\delta Q$ will reduce the elasticity of demand so increasing the value of the term, $1/\eta$, which increases the percentage mark-up, subject to a constant AVC. With non-linear AVC, the absolute mark-up $(P - \text{AVC})$ will rise, but the percentage change in the mark-up could be positive or negative depending upon the shape of the AVC curve.

Second, we consider the case where $\delta P/\delta Q$ remains unchanged, but P and Q both change. This gives a lateral and parallel shift in the demand curve. A rightward shift in the demand curve will raise both price and output, subject to a constant or positive MC. As seen from the analysis of equation 6.12, if Q/P rises while $\delta P/\delta Q$ remains constant, there must be a reduction in the own price elasticity of demand and so the value of the term $1/\eta$ will rise. The result is an

Figure 6.2   A clockwise rotation of the demand curve

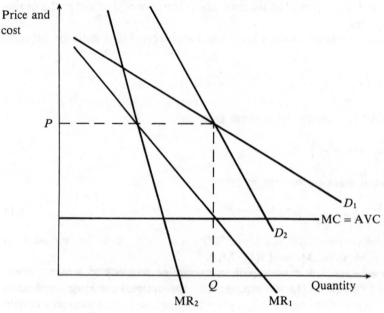

increase in the percentage mark-up, subject to constant AVC. With non-linear AVC, the absolute mark-ups can rise or fall depending upon the shape of AVC.

Consequently, with a constant MC an increase in the slope of the linear demand curve or an increase in demand will both lower the price elasticity and give rise to increases in the absolute and percentage mark-ups and in price. It should be noted that any increase in AVC will raise price and reduce both the proportional and absolute mark-ups.

ESTIMATING DEMAND FUNCTIONS

Demand estimation techniques

The most common technique has been the single equation regression model specified along the lines of equations 6.2 and 6.4. Regression analysis assumes that the direction of causation is one-way from the independent variables to the dependent variable, normally either the level of sales or percentage market share. Most regression estimates of the demand function are in the form of demand forecasting equations.

In many cases it has proved necessary to use an econometric approach, by which two or more equations are used to model the complex simultaneous inter-actions expected between dependent and one or more independent variables. An obvious example is the modelling of the advertising effect on sales, where sales levels also help to determine the level of advertising. The equations are solved simultaneously so that the coefficients are consistent across all the interactions modelled.

One of the most recent and conceptually difficult techniques is the Box–Jenkins (1976) approach to time series analysis. This permits the forecaster to search for the best specification of relationships within the time series data. One such usage is to gain an insight into the lag structure by which a change in an independent variable affects the dependent variable over one or more future time periods. It can be used to relate past values of disposable income and advertising to current levels of consumption. However, its use is limited to one-way causal relationships. It is not appropriate to use the Box–Jenkins (1976) approach when feedback effects from dependent to independent variables are present. However, procedures such as those developed by Haugh (1972) and Tiao and Box (1979) allow time series analysis to consider these feedback effects.

Examples of linear demand functions

One of the simplest estimates of demand elasticity, based on the assumption of a linear demand curve, is that of calculating the *arc* elasticity; the average elasticity over a restricted range of the demand function. This is calculated by dividing the percentage change in quantity demanded by the percentage change in the independent variable, usually price. It can be formally expressed as

$$\eta = \frac{\Delta Q}{\Delta P} \cdot \frac{(P_1 + P_2)}{(Q_1 + Q_2)} \qquad\qquad 6.14$$

This method of estimating elasticities would be appropriate where there was an appreciable change in price and where businessmen had insufficient data to differentiate the demand function. Its advantage is that it only requires a single pair of data points.

This technique was used by Simon (1966) to estimate the price elasticity of liquor in the United States. Its advantages in this case were that 'changes in taste occur with a vengeance in liquor consumption' (1966, p. 194) which made it inappropriate to apply time series regression analysis, and that price changes were relatively infrequent resulting in very few observations over a ten-year period. He examined the 'before' and 'after' sales of liquor within a given state in respect of a price increase of 2 per cent or more. Demand was measured by per capita consumption for twelve-month periods before and after, excluding the two months before and the four months after the price change as this is when speculative stocking-up and stock liquidation would disrupt the sales pattern.

The median of the price elasticity estimates for the twenty-three non-moonshine states was − 0.79. However, there was a considerable variation between states. Although the short-run demand for liquor was typically inelastic at state level, it would be elastic for the individual brands in normal circumstances. Marginalist prescriptions hold only under the condition that the firm is operating on the elastic portion of its demand curve.

Armstrong and Odling-Smee (1979) used a single equation regression model to estimate the demand for new cars in the UK. With over 90 per cent of buyers of new cars already being car owners, the major factor in determining the demand for new cars was the need to replace ageing cars. 'Past purchases of new cars are therefore an important determinant of replacement demand.' (Armstrong and Odling-Smee, 1979, p. 193.) However, replacement can be postponed or brought forward and so independent variables determining both replacement demand and the demand from first time buyers have to be included. The levels of these independent variables were held to determine normal demand, while changes in the levels were held to determine abnormal demand; that demand arising from buyers seeking to adjust their consumption from a sub-optimal position. The total demand for new cars in period t was expressed as q_t and was written as

$$q_t = \sum w_v q_{t-v} + n(z_t) + \alpha(z_t - z_{t-1}) \qquad\qquad 6.15$$

where the ws are a set of weights relating purchases to previous time periods, z is a vector of exogenous variables (variables whose future values are determined outside the model) and n and α are functions signifying normal and abnormal demand respectively. The first two terms measure normal demand and the last term abnormal demand. The regression equation was fitted to quarterly UK data over the 1963 to 1976 period

The Armstrong–Odling-Smee (1979) regression model is an example of the recent development of expressing demand functions in dynamic form. This is achieved by including lagged values of the quantity demanded, q_{t-v}, and other independent variables. In this way current sales are made a partial function of past events. Demand functions which include lagged values of demand and other variables are called *distributed-lag* models.

The best-fitting equation included the following explanatory variables:

0.02 PDI – 2.84 MIND – 1.91 HP – 0.49 RPD – 2.07 RC + 6.15 GDP + 1.53 LQ
(2.0)   (2.9)   (2.5)   (3.1)   (2.2)   (4.2)   (3.1)

They explained 90 per cent of the variation in the registrations of new cars, and satisfactorily predicted demand in 1977 (the t values are given in parentheses). The four exogenous variables explaining normal demand were PDI, the level of personal disposable income; MIND, the minimum hire-purchase deposit; RPD, the real difference between new and used car prices; and LQ, the liquidity ratio for the personal sector. The three rates of change exogenous variables explaining abnormal demand were HP, the change in the hire-purchase deposit; RC, the change in running costs; and GDP, the change in gross domestic product. All these exogenous variables were significant and of the expected sign. Therefore, the equation provided satisfactory estimates of the coefficients from which the demand elasticities could be calculated.

Examples of exponential demand functions

As already explained, exponential demand functions are the most commonly used in practice. One interesting application was that of Rea and Lage (1978) when estimating the demand elasticities for international telephone, telegraph and telex services in the United States. They constructed three separate demand equations to estimate the demand elasticities for the three international services where the dependent variable was measured as the total volume of outgoing messages from the United States.

In respect of the demand for international telephone services, a typical equation estimated from data for the 1969–73 period gave

$$\log TP = 6.61 + 0.06 \log TRADE - 1.72 \log PTP + 0.35 \log PTX$$
$$\quad (0.94) \ (0.11) \qquad\qquad (0.26) \qquad\qquad (0.19)$$

$$\quad - 1.42 \log PTG + 2.66 \log DISINC$$
$$\quad\ (0.42) \qquad\qquad (0.27)$$

the $\bar{R}^2$ was 0.96 and the standard errors are given in parentheses. The results show that telephone calls were strongly related to the prices of telephone calls (PTP) and telegrams (PTG) and to real household income (DISINC). The equation states that demand was price elastic at -1.72. There was also a high positive income elasticity of 2.66 where real household income was used as a proxy for demand from the household sector of the economy. Surprisingly, demand for telephone services did not seem to be significantly affected by the level of international trade (TRADE) which was included as a proxy for business sector demand.

One interesting result is that the equation gives direct readings on the cross-price elasticities. The cross-price elasticity shows the ratio of the percentage change in the sales of one product to the percentage change in the price of some other product and can be expressed as

$$\text{Cross-price elasticity} = \frac{\delta Qa}{\delta Pb} \cdot \frac{Pb}{Qa}$$

If the coefficient of cross-price elasticity is negative, as with the price of telegrams (PTG) in the telephone equation, it implies that the two products are complements. This means that as the price of telegrams falls the demand for telephone messages rises. In the case of the price of telex services (PTX) the positive sign indicates that telephone and telex services might have had a substitution effect. However, the elasticity coefficient was statistically insignificant which means that telex prices did not appear to have been a significant factor affecting the demand for telephone services.

The Rea and Lage (1978) analysis shows the number of interesting demand relationships that can be revealed by regression analysis. The high positive income elasticity of the demand for the use of the telephone suggested a growth market while the high negative price elasticity indicated that the exploitation of that growth required a sensitive pricing policy. Financing that future growth from revenue suggested the need for relatively lower than higher prices in the future.

Another investigation of price elasticities with interesting pricing policy implications was that undertaken by McElwain and Lifson (1983). They first used a single equation model with a log-linear specification to estimate the quantity of electricity used in each of the nine different time-of-day pricing periods by 278 households in a North Carolina pricing experiment, where each household was placed on one of nine time-of-day rates. The independent variables were the price in the given period and a number of socio-economic variables covering household income, house size and the capacity of household electrical appliances. The own price elasticities for the peak, intermediate, and off-peak periods together with the cross elasticities between periods were all insignificantly different from zero. This implied that the demand for electricity was perfectly inelastic, the elasticities all equalled zero so that 'changing the peak, intermediate, or base, period price of electricity has little impact on peak, intermediate, or base period usage' (McElwain and Lifson, 1983, p. 360).

Second, they estimated the partial price elasticities, those which measure the change in quantity demanded resulting from a change in the price of electricity both within the same period or between periods, when the total expenditure on electricity is held constant. Within this new equation the dependent variable is the budget share of total electricity expenditure in the ith period and the independent variable is the price of electricity in the jth period divided by total expenditure on electricity. Essentially, this estimation is investigating how consumers allocate their predetermined budget between the price periods. In this case, all the own price and cross elasticities were of the expected negative sign and all but one were statistically significant. This implies that different time-of-day prices of electricity affect the time of consumption but not the total expenditure, and so these differential prices have no revenue effect. However, by affecting the time of consumption they could be used to smooth out production and so reduce costs. The results also imply that consumers attempt to maximize their utility when subject to a budget constraint.

Cowling and Cubbin (1971) undertook an econometric modelling of the simultaneous relationship held to exist between advertising and market share for motor car brands in the UK. They used an exponential function to estimate the demand elasticities for explaining the market shares of UK motor manufacturers between 1957 and 1968. The dynamic version of the model is presented as follows:

$$\log S_{it} = -0.01 + 0.31 \log A_{it} - 1.92 \log \hat{P}_{it} + 0.66 \log S_{it-1}$$
$$(0.4)\quad (1.9) (3.3) (4.8)$$

$$\log A_{it} = 0.15 - 1.34 \log S_{it} + 1.54 \log S_{it-1} + 0.63 \log A_{it}$$
$$(2.0)\quad (1.8) (2.8) (3.62)$$

and assumes that advertising is partially determined by sales such that if sales increased sufficiently fast then advertising would be expected to increase. The t statistics are shown in parentheses. All the elasticities were significant with the exception of that for current market share (S_{it}) in the current advertising (A_{it}) equation.

In the current market share equation (S_{it}), the estimated market share function of the ith firm has a short-term advertising elasticity of only 0.31. However, by assuming a geometrically declining lag structure for the effect of past advertising on current sales, the long-term elasticity of past advertising can be calculated by dividing the short-term elasticity by (1 minus the elasticity of last period's market share, S_{it-1}). The elasticity coefficient for last period's market share is assumed to measure the strength of accumulated goodwill which is assumed to result only from past advertising. This gives a long-term advertising elasticity of $0.31/(1-0.66) = 0.914$. Consequently, the cumulative effect of previous advertising is shown to have a much greater effect on current market share than current levels of advertising. A similar calculation can be made to estimate the long-term price elasticity, where the price $(\hat{P}_{it})$ has been adjusted to account for quality differences between brands.

The validity of the long-term advertising and price elasticities depends on the appropriateness of the assumption of the distributed-lag conforming to a geometrically declining lag structure. Although this question will be considered in more detail in a later chapter – 'Pricing and Advertising Decisions' – it should be noted that geometrically declining lag structures normally have been assumed in the econometric modelling of past advertising effects.

Since Clarke's (1976) paper, the validity of the assumption is very much in doubt. Bass and Clarke (1972) stated that if the lag structure differs from the geometrically declining hypothesis then serious biases can occur in the results. This would undermine their usefulness in a price strategy context. Other lag structures have been used in recent years. For example, Ward (1976) examined a polynomial lag structure, while Mann (1975), Weiss, Houston and Windal (1978) and Bultez and Naert (1979) used a Pascal lag structure. However, they all imply a past advertising effect lasting through several purchasing periods.

An example of time series analysis

Aaker, Carmen and Jacobson (1982) considered that with several different lag structures available to choose from it was difficult to decide which would be appropriate for the particular market environment under consideration. Consequently, they argued that it was more appropriate to use time series analysis and allow the data to suggest the best lag structure. As the Box–Jenkins technique is not appropriate when there is a possibility of feedback, Aaker, Carmen and Jacobson (1982) used the Haugh (1972) procedure for identifying and estimating a variety of lag structures from data on the sales and advertising of six breakfast cereals in the USA over the 1956 to 1972 period.

The time series analysis revealed the absence of anything resembling a geometrically declining, polynomial or Pascal lag structure. The hypothesis of past advertising affecting sales was only supported in the case of Cornflakes and that of sales affecting advertising was only supported in the case of Rice Crispies. Neither hypothesis was supported by the other five brands. They also applied a geometrically declining lag structure to each of the six brands and estimated the effect of advertising on sales. They found the lagged sales effect to be significant for all six brands. However, the failure of the time series analysis to find any general causal effects between sales and lagged advertising must mean that the lagged sales variable in the geometrically declining lag structure equations was picking up past behavioural influences other than advertising. Therefore, the results in these latter equations were spurious. The specification of any lag structure to the breakfast cereal data would be erroneous and would lead to the estimated long-run elasticities incorporating serious bias.

The Aaker example demonstrates the value of applying time series analysis to data sets whenever distributed lag structures are expected before developing any specific lag structure model. This would ensure that the model specified is appropriate to the causal relationships expected in reality. A failure to do so could lead to inaccurate results which in a planning context would lead to harmful planning errors. Having said this, it has to be admitted that time series techniques are difficult to understand and so are not likely to be of immediate appeal to businessmen, most of whom have not yet come to terms with single equation regression analysis.

REFERENCES AND FURTHER READING

Aaker, D. A., Carmen, J. M. and Jacobson, R. (1982) Modelling advertising–sales relationships involving feedback: a time series analysis of six cereal brands, *Journal of Marketing Research*, Vol. 19, pp. 116–25.

Alfred, A. M. (1972) Company pricing policy, *Journal of Industrial Economics*, Vol. 21, pp. 1–16.

Armstrong, A. G. and Odling-Smee, J. C. (1979) The demand for new cars II – an empirical model for the UK, *Oxford Bulletin of Economics and Statistics*, Vol. 41, pp. 193–214.

Bass, F. M. and Clarke, D. G. (1972) Testing distributed lag models of advertising effect, *Journal of Marketing Research*, Vol. 9, pp. 298–308.

Blattberg, R., Buesing, T., Peacock, P. and Sen, S. (1978) Identifying the deal-prone segment, *Journal of Marketing Research*, Vol. 15, pp. 369–77.

Box, G. E. P. and Jenkins, G. M. (1976) *Time Series Analysis, Forecasting and Control*, Holden Day.

Bultez, A. V. and Naert, P. A. (1979) Does lag structure really matter in optimising advertising expenditures, *Management Science*, Vol. 25, pp. 454–65.

Clarke, D. G. (1976) Econometric measurement of the duration of advertising effect on sales, *Journal of Marketing Research*, Vol. 13, pp. 345–57.

Cowling, K. and Cubbin, J. (1971) Price, quality and advertising competition: an econometric investigation of the United Kingdom car market, *Economica*, Vol. 38, pp. 378–94.

Darby, M. R. and Karni, E. (1973) Free competition and the optimal amount of fraud, *Journal of Law and Economics*, Vol. 16, pp. 67–88.

Friedman, M. (1953) *Essays in Positive Economics*, University of Chicago Press.

Haugh, L. D. (1972) *The Identification of Time Series Interrelationships with Special Reference to Dynamic Regression*, unpublished Ph.D, Department of Statistics, University of Winsconsin–Madison.

Mann, D. H. (1975) Optimal theoretic advertising stock models: a generalisation incorporating the effects of delayed response from promotional expenditures, *Management Science*, Vol. 21, pp. 823–32.

McElwain, A. and Lifson, D. P. (1983) A comparison and reconciliation of full and partial price elasticities, *Applied Economics*, Vol. 15, pp. 353–62.

Nagle, T. (1984) Economic foundations for pricing, *Journal of Business*, Vol. 57, pp. 3–26.

Nelson, P. (1970) Information and consumer behaviour, *Journal of Political Economy*, Vol. 78, pp. 311–29.

Rea, J. D. and Lage, G. M. (1978) Estimates of demand elasticities for international telecommunications services, *Journal of Industrial Economics*, Vol. 26, pp. 363—81.

Simon, J. L. (1966) The price elasticity of liquor in the US and a simple method of determination, *Econometrica*, Vol. 34, pp. 193–205.

Tiao, G. C. and Box, G. E. P. (1979) *An Introduction to Applied Multiple Time Series Analysis*, Technical Report No. 582, Department of Statistics, University of Wisconsin–Madison.

Ward, R. W. (1976) Measuring advertising decay, *Journal of Advertising Research*, Vol. 16, pp. 37–41.

Weiss, D. L., Houston, F. S. and Windal, P. M. (1978) The periodic pain of Lydia Pinkham, *Journal of Business*, Vol. 51, pp. 91–101.

7 Pricing in a Competitive Environment

The purpose of this chapter is to develop the concept of a pricing strategy to incorporate the interactions between a firm and its competitive environment. The latter includes the structure of the market as well as the behavioural interactions between the established firms in the market, essentially whether they compete or co-operate, and the relationships between the established firms and potential new entrants to the market. This all forms the core matter of industrial economics and oligopolistic price theory and we shall be drawing quite heavily on both sources.

PRICE–COST MARGINS, MARKET SHARE AND COMPETITION

Until recently most of the empirical work by industrial economists tested the relationship between market performance and a number of relatively stable market structure characteristics, particularly the number and size distribution of sellers, the level of product differentiation and entry barriers, without basing their models on a well-defined theoretical construct. Recent theoretical work by Johnson and Helmberger (1967), McKean and Peterson (1973), Cubbin (1974 and 1983) and Cowling and Waterson (1976) has stressed the importance of the market price elasticity of demand in determining market performance. The omission of this variable from all but a very few models implies that demand elasticities do not vary across industries. Yet the evidence from econometric studies shows considerable differences in own price elasticities between industries (for example, see the work of Deaton (1975) in the UK). As we will now see, market demand elasticities are central to the development of theoretical models explaining price–cost margins and market performance.

The case of identical products

Following Cowling and Waterson (1976) we will assume an inverse market demand function $p = f(Q)$ where Q is the sum of the outputs of firms selling in the market, $Q = \sum_i q_i$. The profit function for the ith firm is given by

$$\pi_i = p(Q)q_i - C_i(q_i) \qquad\qquad 7.1$$

where C is the cost function of the ith firm and so allows for inter-firm cost differences. Maximizing profits we get

$$\frac{\delta\pi_i}{\delta q_i} = p + q_i \frac{\delta p}{\delta Q} \cdot \frac{\delta Q}{\delta q_i} - \frac{\delta C_i}{\delta q_i} = 0 \qquad\qquad 7.2$$

Of particular interest is the term $\delta Q/\delta q_i$ which shows the effect of a change in the ith firm's output on the outputs of the other firms. In order to maximize its profits each firm must make an assessment of, or conjecture about, the reaction of its competitors to a change in its output and so it must put a sign and a value on this term which is generally known as the *reaction function* or *conjectural variation*. We will assume for the present that it excludes the effect of expectations about the behaviour of potential competitors. The term can be expanded to read

$$\frac{\delta Q}{\delta q_i} = \frac{\delta q_i}{\delta q_i} + \frac{\delta Q_j}{\delta q_i} = 1 + \lambda_i$$

where Q_j is the sum of the outputs of the other firms, $j \neq i$. The anticipated competitive behaviour dimension is being captured by λ_i, with each of the i firms having their own expectations.

By rearranging equation 7.2 we can derive the expression for the price–cost margin in a competitive environment as

$$\frac{p - MC_i}{p} = -\frac{q_i}{Q} \cdot \frac{Q}{p} \cdot \frac{\delta p}{\delta Q} \cdot (1 + \lambda_i)$$

$$= (-)\frac{s_i(1 + \lambda_i)}{\eta} \qquad\qquad 7.3$$

where η is the market price elasticity of demand and s_i is the market share of the ith firm. Equation 7.3 shows that the ith firm's profit-maximizing price–cost margin is inversely related to the market price elasticity of demand and directly related to its market share and the anticipated reaction of rivals. If all the firms had equal market shares equation 7.3 could be written as

$$\frac{p - MC_i}{p} = (-)\frac{(1 + \lambda_i)}{\eta n} \qquad\qquad 7.4$$

where $i = 1, \ldots, n$.

The effects of competitive behaviour anticipated by the ith firm are encapsulated by λ_i. If the firm expects competitors to increase their outputs as a result of attempting to increase its own output, the value of λ_i will be positive and the firm will see itself facing a less elastic demand curve resulting in a higher price–cost margin. Alternatively, if competitors are conjectured as not altering their outputs in response to the firm raising its own output, λ_i will be zero and so competitive reactions will not be seen as affecting the price–cost margin. If competitors are conjectured as reducing their outputs in response to an increase in output by the firm, λ_i will take on a negative fractional value (greater than -1.0). This will increase the price elasticity of the firm's demand curve resulting in a lower equilibrium price–cost margin.

We can easily apply equations 7.3 and 7.4 to the conventional market structures of price theory when subject to identical products. In monopoly the market share variable becomes unity and λ_i will be zero. The price–cost margin simply reverts to being the inverse of the market elasticity of demand. In oligopoly the market share variable would become significant. However, the crucial variable will be λ_i as in oligopoly it is the reaction function which embodies the type of oligopolistic competition. We will return to this in the next section.

In conditions approaching perfect competition, the value of n in equation 7.4 will become very large causing an infinitely large own price elasticity of demand. With the firms being so numerous it is unlikely that there will be any inter-firm output reactions so λ_i will be zero.

The case of product differentiation

The case of product differentiation is much more complicated. Firms will be operating a number of decision variables apart from price, including advertising, product design, product characteristics and packaging. The differences between products will tend to give rise to market equilibriums characterized by multiple prices. In analysing such markets, the price refers to the firm's price and not to the market price. Consequently, unlike the case of identical products, one can no longer collectively relate the outputs of the n firms supplying the market to the one market demand curve. As such we cannot summate the firms' outputs to generate the reaction function $\delta Q/\delta q_i$.

Following Cubbin (1974 and 1983), we can approach the problem by maximizing profit with respect to price rather than output. Each firm has its own demand curve which because of product differentiation means that there is no assurance that the outputs of the firms automatically sum to market supply. The demand for the product of the ith firm is defined as

$$q_i = f_i(p_i, p_j), i \neq j$$

where p_j are the prices of the other $n - 1$ firms.

The ith firm's profit function is given as

$$\pi_i = p_i q_i - C_i(q_i)$$

Differentiating with respect to price we get

$$\frac{\delta \pi_i}{\delta p_i} = q_i + p_i \frac{\delta q_i}{\delta p_i} - \frac{\delta C_i}{\delta q_i} \cdot \frac{\delta q_i}{\delta p_i} = 0 \qquad\qquad 7.5$$

This can be rearranged to give

$$\frac{\delta \pi_i}{\delta p_i} = q_i \frac{(p_i - \mathrm{MC}_i)}{p_i} \cdot \frac{p_i}{q_i} \cdot \frac{\delta q_i}{\delta p_i} + q_i = 0 \qquad\qquad 7.6$$

It can be seen that $(p_i/q_i)(\delta q_i/\delta p_i)$ equals the price elasticity of demand for the ith firm's demand curve. The value of this elasticity, η_i, depends on the extent to which competitors respond to the firm's price changes. If the price change is matched by all the competitors, it implies that all firms face the same market demand curve and as they are all imitating the price behaviour of the ith firm, η_i is identical to that of the industry demand curve. On the other hand, if the price change is not followed, η_i is derived from the firm's own demand curve. In this case the concept of an identifiable market demand function has little meaning. Obviously, for such a lack of price reaction to occur there must be a high level of product differentiation.

From equation 7.6 Cubbin (1974) derived a price–cost margin for a product-differentiated industry as

$$\frac{p_i - MC_i}{p_i} = \frac{1}{\alpha\eta_I + (1 - \alpha)\eta_{fi}} \qquad 7.7$$

where η_I is the market elasticity of demand and η_{fi} is the elasticity of the firm's own demand curve. The term α is defined as the reaction function or the firm's expectations of rivals' pricing responses to its own price change. When it expects rivals to match its price cuts, α will take on a value of unity and the relevant elasticity will be that of the market demand curve. With the price–cost margin being equal to $-1/\eta_I$ it gives us the joint-monopoly result.

When the firm expects a zero price reaction α will take on the value of zero and η_{fi} will pertain. The value of α can vary between zero and unity so that by attaching probabilities to α the right-hand side of equation 7.7 could be formed from a combination of η_I and η_{fi} whenever the firm expected competitors to change their prices, but not by an identical amount. 'Thus $\hat{\alpha}$ is a convenient way of characterizing an oligopolistic outcome.' (Cubbin, 1983, p. 159.)

COMPETITORS' REACTIONS TO PRICE–QUANTITY CHANGES UNDER OLIGOPOLY

In oligopoly each firm makes its pricing decision with due regard to the anticipated reactions of competitors. Given the importance of these behavioural reactions to understanding oligopoly price behaviour and the large number of oligopoly theories which have derived from them, it is necessary to review briefly the main reaction functions.

The Cournot reaction function

Cournot (1938) postulated that each firm would select its profit-maximizing output on the assumption that competitors would not change their existing outputs. Therefore, each firm acts as if it is independent of its rivals. Consequently, it does not consider itself to be faced with a competitor reaction function. In terms

of equations 7.3 and 7.4, λ_i equals zero and so equation 7.3 reduces to
$(p - \mathrm{MC}_i/p) = s_i/\eta$.

As Friedman (1983) and Ruffin (1971) have shown, the Cournot (1938)
equilibrium is quasi-competitive in that the market price and the price–cost
margin both fall as the number of firms increase and market shares decrease.
However, so long as fixed costs are positive, the number of firms compatible with
equilibrium are strictly limited and, as a result, the Cournot solution will not
converge on the competitive equilibrium.

According to Friedman (1983), the significance of the Cournot (1938) zero
reaction function is that for a single period, with each firm *simultaneously*
making an output decision and collusion being prohibited, it provides the only
non-cooperative equilibrium which would not be worth breaking by any competitor. Yet it is the single-period characteristic that has raised the most controversy in terms of the usefulness of the theory. Critics claim that Cournot firms
are presumed to be incapable of learning from competitive behaviour. Over
several periods, the Cournot firm should realize that it cannot behave independently. In an oligopoly context all firms are interdependent and are more
likely to react to a reduction in market share than remain passive. However, if
each firm develops a profit-maximizing strategy based on its market experience
over several periods and assumes that its rivals will be thinking and planning in
the same way, then the optimal output decision will still be consistent with that
of Cournot. The point about the Cournot equilibrium is that it provides a solution to the oligopoly output problem which is best for all participants and for
which there is no other solution which is better and can be sustained in the long
run.

Collusion

Stigler (1964) argued that any profit-maximizing group of firms will always
attempt a collusive solution when given the chance. This is because collusion
allows the member firms to exploit a joint monopoly. Normally, in collusive
situations, the firm will expect competitors to attempt to maintain the ratio of
their market shares to its market share, $(1 - s_i)/s_i$. Consequently, we have a
collusive reaction function whereby each firm considers that its competitors will
act to maintain stable market shares and in terms of equations 7.3 and 7.4, λ_i will
be equal to $(1 - s_i)/s_i$. This reduces equation 7.3 to $(p - \mathrm{MC}_i/p) = 1/\eta_I$. In other
words, the price–cost margin is equal to the inverse of the price elasticity of the
market demand curve, the same as in monopoly.

Price leadership

Price leadership is a term used to characterize a set of practices by which a specific
firm, accepted as leader by the rest of the industry, announces changes in its
prices which are then followed by the other firms. The dominant firm price leader

is a single firm which dominates the market with all the other firms making up the competitive fringe. While the dominant firm will want to behave in a manner similar to a monopolist, it has to take into account the amount of output supplied by the fringe firms who react as pure competitors faced with a given market price. Therefore, the price–cost margin of the dominant firm will be inversely related not to the price elasticity of the market demand curve as was the pure monopolist but to the elasticity of its own demand curve; that which arises after allowing for the supply from the fringe firms.

Waterson (1984) defined the demand facing the dominant firm as

$$Q_d = Q(p) - Q_s(p) \qquad\qquad 7.8$$

where $Q_s(p)$ is the supply function of the competitive firms when relating their sales to market price, p. He determined the elasticity of the dominant firm's demand curve by differentiating equation 7.8 with respect to price. The result can be expressed in terms of the dominant firm's price–cost margin as

$$\frac{p - MC_d}{p} = \frac{s_d}{\eta_I + (1 - s_d)\eta_s}$$

where s_d is the market share of the dominant firm, $(1 - s_d)$ is the collective share of the fringe firms, MC_d is the marginal cost of the dominant firm, η_I is the market elasticity of demand and η_s is the elasticity of supply of the fringe firms. Consequently, the dominant firm's price–cost margin is directly related to its market share and inversely related to both the market elasticity of demand and the elasticity of supply of the fringe firms.

It is obvious that the key variable is the elasticity of supply of the fringe firms. As Waterson (1984) pointed out, where the fringe is a group of importers with a perfectly elastic supply at marginal cost (including tariffs and transport), the market price will be pushed down to this level. On the other hand, with a finite elasticity of supply and rising marginal costs, the price will exceed the marginal costs of the dominant firm.

Using data on the US coffee roasting industry Gollop and Roberts (1979) and Geroski (1982) both found that the dominant firm or price leadership reaction functions gave the best explanation of competitive behaviour. However, attempts at statistically estimating reaction functions from empirical data suffer from the drawback that it is difficult to interpret the results in terms of the traditional models of oligopoly.

The kinked demand curve

At almost the same time, and quite independently, Hall and Hitch (1939) and Sweezy (1939) proposed a theory to explain the price stability of oligopolistic markets. The theory is based on a pessimistic expectation as to the reaction of rivals to a price change initiated by the individual firm. The theory embraces two reaction functions: first, competitors are expected to match a reduction in price resulting in an equal market share price policy; and second, competitors are not

Figure 7.1   The kinked demand curve

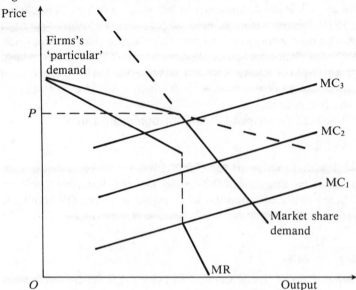

expected to follow a price rise. Consequently, the pessimistic oligopolist antici-
pates unfavourable responses to any price change it initiates.

In terms of the Cubbin (1974) solution for the optimal price–cost margin with
product differentiation, as given in equation 7.7, α will take on a value of unity
for a price reduction and a value of zero for a price rise. This asymmetric belief
about the reactions of others gives a kink in the firm's demand curve at the going
market price. Below this price the demand curve will have price elasticities equal
to those of the market demand curve, and η_I will apply. Above this price the
demand curve will be much more elastic, similar to a Cournot (1938) function
where rivals do not respond to price rises and η_{fi} will apply.

The kinked demand curve is illustrated in Figure 7.1. As a result of the kink,
we get a discontinuous marginal revenue curve, the relative range of the discontinuity being a function of the difference between the two elasticities, η_I and η_{fi}.
Depending on the size of the discontinuity, quite substantial changes in marginal
cost, for example a rise from MC_1 to MC_2 will have no impact on price. As the
discontinuity will still remain with an increase in demand, so variations in
demand are unlikely to affect price, although they will affect order books and
stock levels.

The kinked demand curve is likely to arise whenever market demand is relatively inelastic, where a price cut is not going to produce a worthwhile increase
in revenue, and whenever the competitors are few and have large market shares.
It predicts that prices will be rigid in the face of moderate cost and demand
changes. The theory has come under considerable criticism as being a theory of
price stability rather than of price determination.

Game theory

The game theoretic approach to the analysis of oligopolistic competition embraces some of the most recent developments. Although it does not provide mechanistic solutions for oligopoly pricing, it does offer insights into the pricing strategies that firms might adopt in given situations. Essentially, the firm is modelled as taking into account the various output or profit outcomes which could arise from its decision to raise, cut or maintain price when faced with competitors of equal market power. These outcomes are normally presented in the form of a payoff matrix.

The more interesting games for the understanding of oligopoly are those which are *non-constant sum* and *non-cooperative*. Non-constant sum means that the payoffs for adopting any given strategy do not have to sum to a predetermined figure. Non-cooperative means that the firms cannot make binding agreements to restrict competition. These conditions conform with those of the reaction functions already considered, with the exception of the collusive case.

We can easily model a non-constant sum, non-cooperative, game for two firms having both identical products and cost functions where each firm can choose one of three strategies, each firm choosing simultaneously. The three strategies are joint-monopoly (J-M), Cournot (C), and marginal cost pricing (MCP). These are shown in the payoff matrix, with firm A's payoffs given as the first term in parentheses.

Strategies		*Firm B*		
		J-M	C	MCP
Firm A	J-M	(5, 5)	(3, 6)	(2, 5)
	C	(6, 3)	(4, 4)	(1, 2)
	MCP	(5, 2)	(2, 1)	(0, 0)

Although joint-monopoly would be the mutually most satisfying solution, it is not likely to be sustainable in the absence of inter-firm co-operation and perfect information. Each firm could do better on an individual basis by assuming that the other firm will continue to follow a J-M strategy and, by increasing its own output at a lower price, adopt the Cournot strategy. If both firms simultaneously make the same decision, they will have equal payoffs of four. Having both adopted strategy C, there is no incentive for either firm to undertake further increases in output and move to the competitive solution. Mixed strategies of (C, MCP) always give lower payoffs for either firm than remaining at C. In this case strategy C is held to *dominate* strategy MCP as all firms would be better off moving to strategy C from strategy MCP. In other words, there is no incentive to price cut below the payoffs at C. It is also the case that there is no incentive to raise price, whenever the other firm is assumed to remain with strategy C. Given uncertainty over the other firms' reactions, the risk-averse profit maximizer will always choose the Cournot solution rather than the other two strategies.

The recent review of the application of game theory to oligopoly undertaken by Geroski, Phlips and Ulph (1985) shows that non-cooperative solutions are more likely the more imperfect the information available to the players. The collusive joint-monopoly solution has high information requirements in terms of either the output of each player or the total output of all players so that players can quickly make a response to cheating. The poorer the quality of this information on output the greater the incentive for players to cheat and the less sustainable is the collusive agreement. 'A series of experiments have suggested much the same answer ... that when information about competitors is limited, and in the absence of communication between players, ... with quantity decisions, the outcome is most often a non-cooperative Cournot–Nash equilibrium.' (Geroski, Phlips and Ulph, p. 372), where each firm assumes that the strategies of competitors are held fixed. Plott (1982) also considered that the Cournot (1938) solution became more likely as the number of competing firms increased.

Spence (1978) introduced uncertainty and imperfect information such as to make market signals, for example changes in market shares, the arguments of the reaction functions. Again, the signalling equilibria gave the Cournot–Nash solution as the most profitable whenever the firm took into account the probability of its cheating being detected. Also, Friedman (1977) showed that the Cournot–Nash equilibrium is the only type of equilibrium which will consistently emerge in non-collusive profit-maximizing oligopoly where all n firms can select an output or a price and can make their own conjectures. No other strategy will allow the firm the certainty of a higher payoff given that competitors can retaliate.

While the game theoretic approach has revealed the strategic strength of the Cournot (1938) reaction function despite the frequent criticisms of its naivety (although these are largely based on its non-dynamic or non-learning properties) this is not to suggest that real businessmen should or would adopt it as a strategy. Normally, businessmen employ strategies which in terms of their objectives are not internally consistent. This is not necessarily illogical, it simply reflects the complexities of real-world markets when both long-run and short-run factors have to be considered. However, this lack of consistency impedes attempts at more realistic modelling. What game theory has shown is that the Cournot–Nash equilibrium may be the best model for analysing and predicting competitive reactions in the absence of information to the contrary.

LIMIT PRICING AND POTENTIAL COMPETITION

In the preceding discussion we have made a number of references to barriers to entry and potential competition. It is now necessary to turn our attention to those pricing policies specifically directed at preventing the market entry of new competitors. The most important of these is *limit pricing* which is defined as the highest price that can be charged without attracting new entry.

Effectively impeded entry

Limit pricing is only a relevant policy where the barriers to new competition are not high enough to block profitable entry completely. If entry was completely blocked, the established firm(s) would have no motive to price with reference to potential competition. As defined by Bain (1956), *effectively impeded entry* is where some firms have cost advantages which provide barriers to entry, whose exploitation is more profitable over the long term by charging a limit price which is just low enough to deter entry but is not high enough for short-run profit maximization.

It would appear from the literature that the successful operation of limit pricing implies the following requirements:

(i)   that established firms and potential entrants maximize long-run profits;
(ii) a homogeneous product market so that a recognized limit price can be fixed;
(iii) either one or a few dominant firms able to agree and 'enforce' a limit price, which by implication means either collusion or price leadership;
(iv) significant cost differences between established firms and potential entrants, deriving either from absolute cost differences or from economies of scale.

The Sylos postulate

The main problem to be faced when determining the limit price is deciding how established firms are expected to react when potential competitors attempt to enter the market. Most economists settle for using the 'Sylos postulate' suggested by Sylos-Labini (1962). This assumes that potential entrants will expect the established firms to maintain their output levels when new entry occurs, and that the established firms know this to be the case. The effect of the Sylos postulate is to restrict new entrants to operating on that section of the demand curve below and to the right of the existing limit price–output; the new entrant can only serve the residual demand created by lowering price below the limit price.

Given the Sylos postulate, the determination of the limit price, P_L, is given in Figure 7.2 for the case of an absolute cost advantage. This arises when the established firm has lower production costs than the potential entrant at every comparable level of output. With AC_1 and AC_2 being the average costs of the established and potential entrants, respectively, the limit price is easily shown as being equal to AC_2. The demand curve faced by the new entrants is shown as dd' and represents that part of the market demand curve DD' to the right of the output Q_L produced by the established firms and sold at P_L. As AC_2 cuts the price intercept of dd', the new entrants can only sell at a loss. The established firms can collectively make excess profits equal to the difference between AC_1 and AC_2 multiplied by OQ_L, while at the same time effectively impeding entry. It should be noted that we are assuming that the joint profit-maximizing price is higher than P_L.

Modigliani (1958) demonstrated for the economies of scale condition that the

Figure 7.2 Limit price with an absolute cost advantage

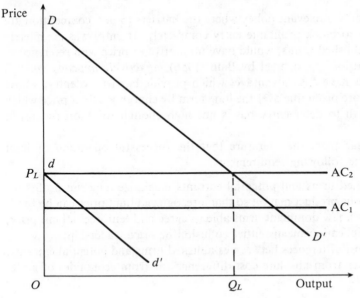

difference between the limit price and the competitive price, i.e. that price equal to constant marginal and average costs, was directly related to the importance of economies of scale and inversely related to the size of the market and to the price elasticity of market demand. These relationships can easily be derived in terms of the Modigliani (1958) model to demonstrate the full implications of limit pricing.

Modigliani (1958) assumed that the long-run average cost curve, LRAC, was L-shaped so that it became a horizontal straight line when the minimum efficient scale was reached (q in Figure 7.3). He also assumed that potential entrants would only enter at the minimum efficient scale, q. The market demand curve is linear, $p = a - bq$. The intersection of this demand curve with the horizontal section of LRAC determines the competitive output, Q_c, where long-run marginal cost, LRMC, equals the competitive price, p_c.

The established firms can determine the entry limiting output at Q_L which is less than Q_c by an amount just short of q, that output which can be produced optimally by a new entrant. This amount can be approximated by $Q_L = Q_c - q$, though strictly $Q_L + q$ must be just marginally greater than Q_c, so that any entrant will cause market price to fall below p_c. It is this economy of scale difference between Q_c and Q_L that provides the barrier to entry and protection for the corresponding limit price.

The above expression for Q_L can be rewritten as

$$Q_L = Q_c\left(1 - \frac{q}{Q_c}\right) \qquad 7.9$$

so that the minimum efficient scale is expressed relative to the competitive output.

Figure 7.3   Limit price and economies of scale

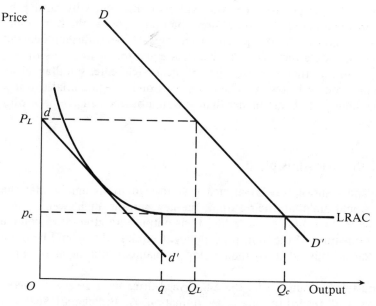

With both the competitive price and the limit price, P_L deriving from the same linear demand function, equation 7.9 can be expressed in terms of the limit price by substituting the right-hand side of the demand expression for the respective quantities Q_L and Q_c. This gives

$$P_L = a - (a - p_c)\left(1 - \frac{q}{Q_c}\right)$$

$$= p_c + \frac{q}{Q_c} \cdot \frac{\delta p_c}{\delta Q_c} \cdot Q_c$$

$$= p_c\left(1 + \frac{q}{\eta_c Q_c}\right) \qquad\qquad 7.10$$

where η_c is the modulus of the market elasticity of demand at Q_c.

From equation 7.10 we can easily derive the price–cost margin at the limit price

$$\frac{P_L - p_c}{p_c} = \frac{q}{\eta_c Q_c}$$

The price–cost margin will be higher, the larger the minimum efficient scale relative to the size of the competitive market, and the lower the market own price elasticity of demand.

One factor not taken into account by Modigliani's (1958) analysis is the effect of the number of potential entrants on the level of the limit price. Sherman and Willett (1967) and Omori and Yarrow (1982) have shown that limit pricing will have a tendency to be more profitable the larger the number of potential entrants, certainly when the number exceeds one. The argument is based on the proposition that the presence of other potential entrants will discourage entry by raising the probability of loss-making entry should more than one enter at the same time. While there might appear to the potential entrants to be sufficient demand available to accommodate one new firm at prices equal to, or in excess of, p_c, none might enter for fear that more than one of them might enter simultaneously and drive the price down below p_c. Therefore, two or more potential entrants may lead to the limit price being higher than it would otherwise have been with only one entrant.

Criticisms of the Sylos postulate

Fisher (1959) and Osborne (1973) argued that instead of assuming that the existing firms would maintain their output, the new entrant might well assume that it would be in their interests to reduce their output and attempt to collude with it in a continuation of the limit price policy. Certainly this would be more profitable to the established firms than trying to maintain output at the limit price.

The Sylos postulate assumes that the established firms have a very restricted range of options with regard to output determination. As Pashigian (1968) and Wenders (1971) pointed out, a more profitable policy for established firms would be to restrict output to the joint-monopoly level and threaten to increase output to the competitive level should entry ever take place. This would accord with a short-run profit-maximizing price policy. For the Sylos postulate to be a preferable assumption, the firms must either be operating at full capacity or face additional short-run costs in raising output from plants designed for efficient production at the smaller monopoly output.

Another problem with the Sylos postulate is the restrictive assumption of product homogeneity. Once product differentiation is possible then the competitive initiative can lie with the new entrant. By the use of research and development and advertising a new competitor can successfully gain entry to a market even to the point of supplanting the dominant firm(s). However, product differentiation introduces a new set of problems for the analysis of potential competition in that it is no longer possible to consider a single homogeneous market demand curve and so the concept of a limit price is no longer relevant.

Ineffectively impeded entry

With ineffectively impeded entry the dominant firms find it more profitable to price to control the rate of entry over time rather than to price for entry prevention. This puts the problem of potential competition in a more realistic dynamic context than the static analysis of limit pricing. It gives the firm freedom to select its pricing strategy anywhere from the range between the upper limit of short-run profit maximization and the lower limit of the limit price. It also allows the firm to alter its strategy over time to suit its interests.

The earliest theory was developed by Pashigian (1968). He restricted the dominant firms to a choice between two alternative pricing strategies, short-run profit maximization or limit pricing. He assumed that the dominant firms would begin by maximizing short-run profits and charging the joint monopoly price, p_m. The rate of entry is given as a function of the length of time during which p_m exceeds the limit price P_L, and so new entry continues to take place until the established firms decide to alter their strategy and reduce their collusive price to P_L. Notice that in this case entry is implied to occur sequentially over time and not simultaneously in a once-and-for-all lump.

The decision to move to P_L will be made on a comparison of the discounted flow of profits resulting from the alternative pricing strategies. If the firms were to switch to limit pricing at time t_1, the flow of discounted profits will equal the area under the thick line in Figure 7.4. Alternatively, if the firms continue to charge p_m after t_1 and allow new entry to continue until the market price drops to p_c, the flow of discounted profits will equal the area under the dotted line. If the area labelled A exceeds the area B, the established firms will be better off by maintaining price at p_m, otherwise it will pay them to switch to the limit price at t_1.

As with all the dynamic entry models, the decision is sensitive to the rate at which future profits are discounted. The higher that rate, the more the firms value present relative to future profits and the lower the probability of them switching to a limit pricing strategy.

Gaskins (1971) allowed established firms the choice of the full range of prices between limit pricing and short-run profit maximization. In this case the rate of new entry was proportional to the difference between the collusive price, p_t,

Figure 7.4 *Limit pricing v. short-run profit maximization*

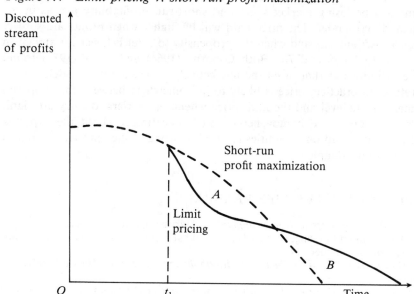

Figure 7.5   An optimal price path with new entry

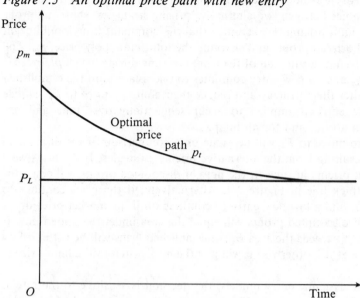

agreed at time *t* and the limit price. By charging high prices in the current period, current profits would be enlarged at the cost of a higher rate of new entry and lower profits in the future.

Compared to the Pashigian (1968) model, the greater price variation permitted to the dominant firms allows them to select a price path which maximizes long-run profits. A typical price path is shown in Figure 7.5 with an initial price some way below p_m falling at a decreasing rate over time to P_L. Throughout this period the firms will be losing market share and short-run profitability just as in the Pashigian (1968) model. The price path will be higher when profits are subject to a higher discount rate and when the propensity to enter is lower for any given difference between p_t and P_L. Both Osborne (1964) and Shaw (1974) found evidence of industries that fitted the ineffectively impeded entry model.

Therefore, in practice, price is likely to lie somewhere between the short-run profit-maximizing level and the limit price whenever barriers to entry are significant and products are homogeneous. Such uncertainty about the expected market price opens up opportunities to employ probabilistic approaches. Baron (1973) is a good example.

REFERENCES AND FURTHER READING

Bain, J. S. (1956) *Barriers to New Competition*, Harvard University Press.

Baron, D. (1973) Limit pricing, potential entry and barriers to entry, *American Economic Review*, Vol. 63, pp. 666–74.

Chamberlin, E. H. (1933) *The Theory of Monopolistic Competition*, Harvard University Press.

Cournot, A. A. (1938) *Researches into the Mathematical Principles of the Theory of Wealth*, Macmillan.

Cowling, K. G. and Waterson, M. (1976) Price cost margins and market structure, *Economica*, Vol. 43, pp. 267–74.

Cubbin, J. (1974) *A Measure of Apparent Collusion in Oligopoly*, University of Warwick Economic Research Paper No. 49.

Cubbin, J. (1983) Apparent collusion and conjectural variations in differentiated oligopoly, *International Journal of Industrial Organisation*, Vol. 1, pp. 155–63.

Deaton, A. (1975) *Models and Projections of Demand in Post-War Britain*, Chapman & Hall.

Fisher, F. M. (1959) New developments on the oligopoly front, *Journal of Political Economy*, Vol. 67, pp. 410–13.

Friedman, J. W. (1977) *Oligopoly and the Theory of Games*, North-Holland.

Friedman, J. W. (1983) *Oligopoly Theory*, Cambridge University Press.

Gaskins, D. W. (1971) Dynamic limit pricing: optimal pricing under the threat of entry, *Journal of Economic Theory*, Vol. 3, pp. 306–22.

Geroski, P. (1982) *The Empirical Analysis of Conjectural Variations in Oligopoly*, mimeo, Catholic University of Louvin.

Geroski, P., Phlips, L. and Ulph, A. (1985) Oligopoly, competition and welfare: some recent developments, *Journal of Industrial Economics*, Vol. 33, pp. 369–86.

Gollop, F. and Roberts, M. (1979) Firm interdependence in oligopolistic markets, *Journal of Econometrics*, Vol. 10, pp. 313–31.

Hall, R. L. and Hitch, C. J. (1939) Price theory and business behaviour, *Oxford Economic Papers*, No. 2, pp. 12–45.

Johnson, A. C. and Helmberger, P. (1967) Price elasticity of demand as an element of market structure, *American Economic Review*, Vol. 57, pp. 1218–21.

McKean, J. R. and Peterson, R. D. (1973) Demand elasticity, product differentiation and market structure, *Journal of Economic Theory*, Vol. 6, pp. 205–9.

Modigliani, F. (1958) New developments on the oligopoly front, *Journal of Political Economy*, Vol. 66, pp. 215–32.

Omori, T. and Yarrow, G. (1982) Product diversification, entry prevention and limit pricing, *Bell Journal*, Vol. 13, pp. 242–8.

Osborne, D. K. (1964) The role of entry in oligopoly theory, *Journal of Political Economy*, Vol. 72, pp. 396–402.

Osborne, D. K. (1973) On the rationality of limit pricing, *Journal of Industrial Economics*, Vol. 22, pp. 71–80.

Pashigian, P. (1968) Limit price and the market share of the leading firm, *Journal of Industrial Economics*, Vol. 16, pp. 165–77.

Plott, C. R. (1982) Industrial organisation theory and experimental economics, *Journal of Economic Literature*, Vol. 20, pp. 1485–1572.

Ruffin, R. J. (1971) Cournot oligopoly and competitive behaviour, *Review of Economic Studies*, Vol. 38, pp. 493–502.

Shaw, R. (1974) Price leadership and the effect of new entry on the UK petrol supply market, *Journal of Industrial Economics*, Vol. 23, pp. 65–79.

Sherman, R. and Willett, T. D. (1967) Potential entrants discourage entry, *Journal of Political Economy*, Vol. 75, pp. 400–3.

Shubik, M. (1959) *Strategy and Market Structure*, John Wiley.

Spence, A. M. (1978) Tacit coordination and imperfect information, *Canadian Journal of Economics*, Vol. 11, pp. 409–505.

Stigler, G. J. (1964) A theory of oligopoly, *Journal of Political Economy*, Vol. 72, pp. 44–61.

Sweezy, P. M. (1939) Demand under conditions of oligopoly, *Journal of Political Economy*, Vol. 47, pp. 568–73.

Sylos-Labini, P. (1962) *Oligopoly and Technical Progress*, Harvard University Press.

Telser, L. G. (1972) *Competition Collusion and Game Theory*, Macmillan.

Waterson, M. (1984) *Economic Theory of the Industry*, Cambridge University Press.

Wenders, J. T. (1971) Excess capacity as a barrier to entry, *Journal of Industrial Economics*, Vol. 20, pp. 14–19.

8 Marginalism versus Full-Cost Pricing

THE ANTI-MARGINALIST ATTACK

The analysis of the two previous chapters – 'Marginalist Price Theory and Demand Estimation' and 'Pricing in a Competitive Environment' – was based on the neo-classical theory of the firm and its widely accepted marginalist rules of behaviour. However, from 1939 until 1950 there appeared several economic papers which can be collectively characterized as an attack on marginalist principles as applied to the behaviour of real-world firms. This marginalist critique began with the empirical evidence on the actual behaviour of businessmen published by Hall and Hitch (1939) and was followed by attacks successively mounted by Lestor (1946), Oliver (1947), Gordon (1948) and Andrews (1949).

Although the academic discovery of the full-cost rule of thumb by Hall and Hitch (1939) is often seen as 'the first blast in the offensive against orthodox ... [marginalist] analysis' (Barback, 1964, p. 3), it was really an attack on the marginalist theory of imperfect competition which had its origins just a few years before in the works of Robinson (1933) and Chamberlin (1933). It was they who, by specifying a downward-sloping demand curve for the individual firm, provided a theory of the firm which allowed it to develop its own price strategy in a competitive environment. This theoretical development of oligopoly stimulated economists to test the theory against the behaviour of real-world price makers.

Hall and Hitch (1939) undertook the first major empirical study of pricing ever to be conducted in the United Kingdom. Of the thirty-eight firms investigated, thirty practised a full-cost pricing policy. This was generalized as 'prime (or "direct") cost per unit is taken as the base, a percentage addition is made to cover overheads ... and a further conventional addition (frequently 10 per cent) is made for profit' (Hall and Hitch, 1939, p. 19). The reasons given by firms for adhering to this policy varied but included considerations that it gave the 'right' or 'fair' price; that knowledge of the demand function was too sparse to attempt 'marginalist' pricing; that it minimized adverse competitor reactions and new entry; and that there were strong cost and behavioural factors which inhibited the frequent price changes that might be expected from pursuing a profit-maximizing objective.

Most inquiries into pricing behaviour have deliberately tried to find evidence of businessmen estimating marginal revenue and marginal cost, even if only implicitly. In this respect Hall and Hitch (1939) were no exception. Their feeling of justification in their attack on marginalism sprang from the failure of most businessmen interviewed to provide information regarding precise estimates of elasticity of demand or of the relation between price and marginal cost. This led them to cast doubt on any theory 'which places any weight on changes in the elasticity of demand in the short run as a factor influencing the price policy of entrepreneurs' (Hall and Hitch, 1939, p. 32).

The weakness of their approach to investigating the presence of marginalism is that it expects the constructs of the abstract model to be directly observed in actual business situations. The presence, or absence, of acceptable estimates of marginal revenue and marginal cost neither proves nor disproves the relevance of marginalist analysis. Marginalism is a valid positivist explanation of business pricing behaviour if it can predict, to an acceptable level of accuracy, the price levels and direction of price changes occurring in the business world. Hall and Hitch (1939), as well as others such as Barback (1964), seem to have fallen into the trap of equating marginalism with explicit textbook marginalist behaviour. This caused them to ignore, or at least play down, the ample evidence of implicit marginalism provided by their businessmen when departing from the full-cost price under pressure of market forces. This included shading the full-cost price and discounting for different, and changing, market circumstances; selecting a lower profit margin when competition became more intense; and adjusting the product composition of their sales by increasing the proportion of expensive lines at the expense of cheaper lines whenever business conditions were buoyant.

While Hague (1949) also found little evidence of explicit marginalist behaviour when interviewing twenty businessmen, he raised the interesting issue of managerial discretion over overhead allocation. He suggested that in multi-product firms cost accountants found it impossible to allocate costs between products with any degree of accuracy. Consequently, '[as] it is almost impossible to decide what the average cost of an individual product really is, ... [as] the firm cannot be sure how much of the overhead costs any one product should bear' (Hague, 1949, p. 146). As any cost allocation must be arbitrary, management can use its discretion in allocating overheads to take account of various market pressures. Indeed, the exercise of managerial discretion in overhead allocation could work to reconcile in part the application of full-cost pricing with marginalist principles. For example, if overhead allocations were adjusted between different products so as to correspond directly with such market pressures as unexpected shifts in demand, the full-cost model would result in pricing behaviour very similar to that predicted by the marginalist model when subject to constant marginal costs.

Seeking observations on actual price reactions to demand shifts is likely to be more fruitful in indicating marginalist behaviour than trying to discover firms who estimate marginal revenue or demand elasticity. As Gordon (1948) pointed out in his attack on marginalism, the uncertainty regarding future shifts in demand will be more important to the businessman than the shape of the demand curve at any particular moment in time. In this context he distinguished the full-cost pricer as strongly resistant to changing price in response to short-run demand shifts, while the marginalist would react by making continuous adjustments.

However, the price reactions of practical marginalism will not be as continuous as in Gordon's (1948) textbook marginalism, as account will be taken of the not inconsiderable information costs of adjusting prices in the short run. Unfortunately, Gordon (1948) tended to identify practice with full-cost pricing and theory with marginalism. Under the practice of implicit marginalism, price changes in response to significant demand shifts are expected to be a *normal* reaction. With a conventional full-cost pricing policy such price changes would be *abnormal*.

THEORIES OF FULL-COST PRICING

Andrews

The best-known full-cost price theory was that developed by Andrews (1949) which was presented in his book *Manufacturing Business* as an alternative to marginalism. On the basis of his empirical research and his experiences as a business consultant, he argued that businessmen normally quote a price which is determined by the average direct cost of the product. The difference between price and average direct cost he defined as the 'costing margin', 'the amount which he (the businessman) thinks he can take from the market without giving possible competitors an opportunity to cut into it (or his share of it) *in the long run*' (Andrews, 1949, p. 174). This policy is justified on the assumption that average direct costs will be relatively constant in the short run and correspond to an L-shaped slope in the long run.

Although his theory was presented as an attack on the marginalist price theory of Chamberlin (1933) and Robinson (1933), he also seems to have incorporated some marginalist features. Most of these concern the determination of the costing margin. His reason for presenting his theory as cost-determined was that he considered the costing margin to be stable over time. This was because it was derived from the experiences of businessmen as to what buyers would consider to be a 'fair' gross profit margin, and on their expectations regarding market demand and competition in the long run. As businessmen did not consider there to be a meaningful distinction between present price and future demand, the long-run demand curve was expected to be very elastic. Therefore, the costing margin was supposedly determined from a stable long-run perspective; short-run adjustments would undermine long-run market share.

Yet despite Andrew's (1949) presentation, the costing margin can be seen to be demand-determined, albeit by long-run forces determining market demand and competition. Marginalist demand features included different markets for the same product having different costing margins depending on their market circumstances (see Andrews, 1949, p. 159); relatively inefficient firms would be forced to accept lower margins (see Andrews, 1949, p. 169); and margins would be adjusted downwards to take account of depressed trade (see Andrews, 1949, p. 165) or more intense competition (see Andrews, 1949, p. 253). Given the fact that Andrews was primarily concerned with mature oligopolistic markets, there would seem to be little difference in terms of pricing outcomes between his theory and those of many profit-maximizing oligopoly models. The exception would be that concerning price leadership, for Andrewsian firms behave more as followers than leaders (Silberston, 1970).

Robinson (1950) in his critique of Andrews (1949) considered that the various competitive and market demand influences on the costing margin made it appear as the difference between unit direct cost and the price the firm estimates the market will bear. Furthermore, adjustments made to the costing margin were little more than a process of discovering a demand schedule. Therefore, the Andrewsian version of the full-cost model would appear to be very similar to what one would expect from applying a 'marginalist' profit contribution approach by which the costing margin is an attempt to approximate the unknown *ex post* gross profit contribution that would have resulted under profit maximization in a stable or mature oligopolistic market. Andrews (1949) seems to have inadvertently devised the first attempt at a contribution approach to full-cost pricing. As he did not find the distinction between overhead cost and the net profit margin to be useful for market price determination, his demand-determined costing margin can be thought of as transforming the conventional standard overhead allocation rate from a constant to a variable unit cost. To this extent, full-cost pricing looks like marginalism adapted to help cope with the problems posed by an unknown demand schedule.

While full costing can be regarded as a process of approximating points on an unknown demand schedule, it is also a behavioural response to the problem of imperfect cost information, particularly the inability of many firms to distinguish satisfactorily between fixed and variable costs. For example, Howe (1962), Skinner (1970) and Hague (1971) found the proportion of firms making such a distinction to be 73, 68 and 46 per cent respectively. Sizer (1971) remarked that making such a distinction did not necessarily imply marginal costing.

Noyes

Noyes (1941) tackled this problem by regarding all costs incurred in employing factors of production, whether incurred currently or previously, as costs of product. All costs of providing capacity (fixed overheads) would be accumulated until the capacity was actively applied to production when the accumulated costs would be allocated to a product in proportion to that part, or operating time, of the production capacity used in its production. For example, if only 10 per cent of capacity was used to produce a given batch of product, that batch would be

charged either the costs of specifically providing that capacity or 10 per cent of
the costs of providing total capacity for the time required to produce the batch.

Essentially, each product is being costed on its rate of usage of all factors
employed in its production, whether fixed or variable. Although the Noyes (1941)
approach transforms all costs into a variable form for allocation to product, it
still leaves unresolved the thorny problem of how to allocate joint costs or
overheads between different products. He regarded this as a technical problem.
Unfortunately, as we have already seen in Chapter 3, the production function
provides no help in terms of a technical solution to this problem.

Noyes (1941) regarded the costs of a product in terms of a systematic recovery
of all costs specifically incurred in production. He only considered marginal cost
concepts to be relevant when a non-earning investment was to be written off as
lost.

Eichner

A different type of investment approach was used by Eichner (1973) in his model
designed to explain the determination of the profit mark-up in oligopolistic
markets subject to free entry. The size of the mark-up was held to depend on the
demand for and supply of additional investment funds. Unlike the Andrewsian
oligopolist who appeared to be a follower, that of Eichner (1973) is a price leader
who uses market power to adjust the mark-up in the interests of inter-temporal
cash flows.

As the model is investment oriented it is based on a long-run theory of full-cost
pricing in which the industry price leader has to trade off the short-term gain of
a higher mark-up against the longer-term costs of consumers switching to
substitutes and an increased probability of new entry. The magnitudes of these
adverse events depend on the elasticity of demand and the probability of new
entry over *subsequent time periods*. The firm will raise the margin to the point
where the implicit rate of interest on these internally generated funds equals the
interest on external borrowings. The implied interest rate on the internally
generated funds rises directly relative to the mark-up as a consequence of the
increased probability of a long-term decline in cash flow caused by the twin
effects of product substitution and new entry. Possible direct government intervention was also introduced as a factor constraining relatively high mark-ups.

These theories of full-cost pricing are very much theories of long-run pricing.
Andrews (1949) argued that the businessman does not attempt to maximize short-
run profits with a complete disregard for long-run considerations. Noyes's (1941)
concern for the recovery of the costs of all factors used in production is really
based on the concept of a return on investment. Eichner's (1973) model is not
only clearly long run but could be interpreted as approximating one of long-run
profit maximization. Both Andrews (1949) and Eichner (1973) rely heavily on
concepts of highly elastic long-run demand curves. With long-run demand and
competitive factors dominating the pricing decision, successive short-run periods
cannot be independent and so conventional short-run profit maximization will

not ensure the maximization of long-run profits. Although the theories of long-run pricing were not presented in the form of long-run profit maximization models, the principal elements of such a paradigm are present in those of Andrews (1949) and Eichner (1973).

A RECONCILIATION OF MARGINALISM AND FULL-COST PRICING IN OLIGOPOLY

The full-cost model

Despite full costing generally being presented as a long-run theory, a reconciliation with traditional marginalist price theory is still possible within the framework of a single pricing period. The logic of this approach is based on the fact that businessmen appear to be primarily concerned with the current period and the immediate future when making pricing decisions (for example, see Gordon, 1948, and the empirical work of Barback, 1964, and Hague, 1971). Also oligopoly, as the only market structure considered by full-cost theorists, will give rise to a very uncertain long-term competitive environment making expected long-run profits the subject of a relatively high rate of time discount. Thus, matters concerning either the present or the next pricing period will tend to dominate pricing policy. The perspective adopted is essentially short run.

Under implicit marginalism, price will change in direct response to a substantial shift in demand, while full-cost theory predicts an invariant price in the short run. Therefore, it seems appropriate to focus any comparison of the profit performances of the two theories on the effects of unexpected changes in the rate of capacity utilization, using the latter as a proxy for substantial shifts in demand. Insubstantial shifts would be absorbed by adjusting stock levels or the lengths of order books.

In the following analysis, we will retain the engineering cost function adapted to the concept of efficient practical capacity as developed previously in Chapter 4 and illustrated in Figures 4.2 and 4.3 of that chapter. This gives a unit direct cost plus variable overhead which is constant up to efficient practical capacity, Q^*, and is shown by the continuous horizontal line b in Figure 8.1, which equals both average variable cost and marginal cost (MC_1). Outputs above Q^* will be subject to additional variable costs which, given the engineer's linear production function, will produce a rising and stepped marginal cost function (for example, MC_2). The effect of this cost function on average total costs plus standard net income is shown by the curve $ATC\pi$. This slopes downwards to Q^* and up to this point corresponds with Andrews's (1949) average direct cost plus costing margin. Beyond Q^*, it rises by a series of steps, each of which is the result of a new and steeper linear slope of the total variable cost curve (see Chapter 4, Figure 4.2).

All fixed overheads are denoted by M and are allocated to product at the rate of (M/Q^*). Standard net income is denoted by π and the planned gross profit, or costing, margin is given as $(M + \pi)/Q^*$. Finally, we will assume that full-cost pricers attempt to maximize short-run profits.

Full-cost pricing in competitive oligopoly

Under the profit-maximization assumption, full-cost pricing only makes sense when management has imperfect information on its product demand function. The full cost at the budgeted, or normal, output is used as the first estimate of price on an unknown demand schedule. In a competitive oligopoly the problems of estimating one's own product demand function are compounded by the unknown pricing and output reactions expected from competitors. When uncertainty is at its greatest (when the rationale for full-cost pricing is at its strongest), management will have little hard information to go on and is likely to assume that competitors will want to maintain, as far as possible, their budgeted level of output. Therefore, all it has to do is to estimate its own expected market share at the full-cost price. In doing this, management implicitly expects its own product demand curve to replicate that of market demand and to shift in a parallel manner with it. Given the poor quantity of available market information, it is likely to assume a linear demand curve. All this implies a Cournot–Nash solution which, as we saw in Chapter 7, gives the most likely, and most profitable, outcome whenever the information available is too poor to ensure the successful establishment and maintenance of collusive oligopoly.

Whenever management estimates that it can sell all its efficient practical capacity at full cost, as well as get the best possible net income, we get the full-cost price of P_1^*, as shown in Figure 8.1. Implicitly, the demand curve D_1, is being estimated as being tangential to ATCπ at Q^*. As this is the best price the market will bear it implies a marginalist solution with the implied marginal revenue,

Figure 8.1 Proportional allocated cost pricing with deviations from budgeted output

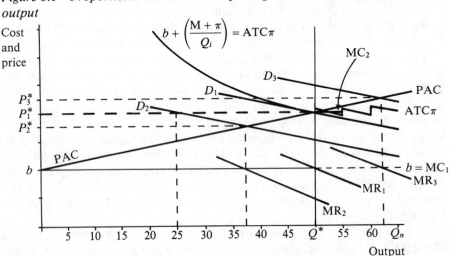

MR_1, intersecting MC_1, at Q^*. Therefore, given market uncertainty, the full cost gives the best estimate of the profit-maximizing price.

However, the profit-maximization problems of the full-cost price begin when demand turns out to be substantially different from that expected. For example, if an unanticipated drop in sales forces a reduction in production to only twenty-five units at the full-cost price of P_1^*, this would imply that demand had shifted to D_2. Assuming this were to be the case, the firm could have recouped more of its gross profit margin by reducing price to the profit-maximizing level of P_2^*. It would then have been operating at 75 per cent of the budgeted output of Q^* instead of at 50 per cent.

Therefore, a conventional full-cost pricing policy, where output rather than price is adjusted in response to short-run shifts in demand is incompatible with profit maximization in competitive oligopoly. It is also incompatible with the accounting full-cost objective of providing a systematic plan for the recovery of total outlay. More of the actually incurred costs would have been recovered under the direct marginalist solution of equating the implied MR_2 with MC_1.

The proportional allocation rule in competitive oligopoly

Although direct marginalist solutions would not be possible with imperfect information and uncertainty, as MR would not be known, an implied marginalist solution could be achieved. Recall from Chapter 5 that an efficient full-cost allocation would require the allocation of $(M + \pi)$ to be demand-determined. An appropriate allocation formula might allocate $(M + \pi)/Q^*$ to product in direct proportion to the rate of capacity utilization (Q_i/Q^*), where Q_i is the budgeted output prior to the commencement of the pricing period, and actual output once the period has commenced, $i = 1, \ldots, n$. Subject to a linear variable cost function and a Cournot reaction function, this method of allocation would yield actual gross profit margins approximating those resulting from the application of direct marginalism.

Under this proportional allocation rule, the optimal gross profit margin is given as

$$\frac{P_i^* - b}{b} = \left(\frac{1}{b}\right) \cdot \left(\frac{M + \pi}{Q^*}\right) \cdot \left(\frac{Q_i}{Q^*}\right) = \frac{1}{\eta_i + 1} \qquad 8.1$$

The full-cost allocation is modified to release overheads to product by the demand-determined adjustment factor (Q_i/Q^*). The resultant optimal prices, P_i^*, are given by the line PAC in Figure 8.1, which runs from the intercept of b in a positive linear slope intersecting the shifting Cournovian demand curves at their implied points of marginal equivalence. Therefore, with an implied demand shift from D_1 to D_2, PAC gives the optimal price of P_2^* at 75 per cent capacity utilization (the theoretical derivation of PAC is given in Dorward, 1986).

To achieve this 'marginalist' approach to full-cost allocation, all management needs to do is to estimate its average variable costs, b, and the best full-cost price it considers it can get at the budgeted output. The line PAC can then be inferred from these two estimates. In order to read new optimal prices from PAC, management has to find the optimal value for (Q_i/Q^*) appropriate to the new demand shift. This can be done easily for our earlier example by adding (Q_i/Q^*) at the full-cost budgeted output (1.0) to the resultant (Q_i/Q^*) from charging the full-cost price (0.5) and then multiplying the sum by 0.5. This gives the new inferred optimal rate of capacity utilization as 0.5 $(1 + 0.5)$ which equals 0.75. Relating this value to PAC gives the optimal price of P_2^*.

Consequently, the proportional allocation rule can be applied to estimate optimal prices in competitive oligopoly conditions where the demand function is unknown and subject to substantial shifts in the short run. The results are dependent on a Cournot-type demand function, independent short-run pricing periods, and constant marginal and variable costs.

The importance of the constant marginal cost assumption can be demonstrated in the case of demand shifts in excess of Q^*. When the firm discovers from a substantial unexpected rundown in the stocks of finished goods that its demand curve has shifted to the right of D_1, it will plan to increase production. If the true demand curve has shifted to D_3, the conventional full-cost pricer will continue to increase output from Q^* right up to maximum possible capacity at Q_n. However, the proportional allocation rule would suggest a slightly smaller output and a higher price of P_3^*. With $ATC\pi$ rising above the conventional full-cost price of P_1^* for some ranges of output (see Figure 8.1), the full-cost pricer cannot always expect to earn his planned net profit margin. The proportional allocation rule is again seen to yield higher profits than the conventional full-cost pricing policy (see Dorward, 1984, for a detailed comparison).

Yet neither the full-cost nor the proportional allocation rule will result in profit-maximizing decisions. Both decision rules have ignored the increase in marginal costs which arise from exceeding efficient practical capacity. The lowest level of marginal cost is MC_2 which is well above the implied marginal revenue curve for $D_3(MR_3)$. Thus, for an implied demand shift to D_3, the optimal price and output remain at P_1^* and Q^*, respectively. Therefore, the full-cost approach, even with demand-determined allocations, will not ensure optimal prices, whenever marginal cost is related to a changing volume of output.

Full-cost pricing in collusive oligopoly

Whenever the quantity and quality of information is sufficient for the successful establishment and monitoring of a market share agreement, members can act as joint monopolists. This implies that each member firm has a constant market share demand curve. Therefore, change in the level of market demand at any given full-cost price causes the constant market share demand curves to be redistributed by the adjustment factor (Q^*/Q_i). The result is a constant own price elasticity on any of a firm's demand curves at the full-cost price. In terms of equation 8.1, η_i will be constant and equal to that of the industry demand curve and so the optimum gross profit margin will also remain constant for all demand shifts. Effectively the capacity utilization variable in equation 8.1 is cancelled out

Figure 8.2   Collusive full-cost pricing with deviations from budgeted demand

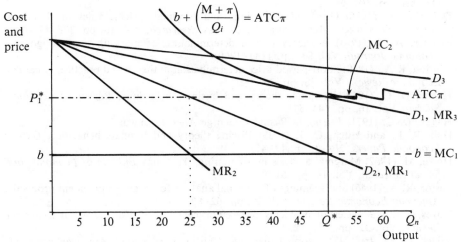

by applying the new demand shift adjustment factor (Q^*/Q_i). Therefore, subject to the full-cost price being the highest price that the market will bear, it will remain optimal for all demand shifts.

This result is illustrated in Figure 8.2. For a reduction in market demand of 50 per cent the adjustment factor is 2 so that the firm's new product demand curve D_2 will have twice the slope of D_1 and will be equal to MR_1. The new implied MR_2 intersects MC_1 at 50 per cent of capacity utilization and yields the same optimal price of P_1^*. However, as in the case of oligopolistic competition, the full-cost price will not be optimal for outputs greater than efficient practical capacity.

Consequently, when subject to constant marginal costs, full-cost pricing can be reconciled with marginalism so long as it is adapted to meet the relevant conditions of market demand. For optimal pricing, the allocation of overheads to product, or the Andrewsian costing margin, must be demand-determined in the short run. As we shall see when looking at the empirical evidence, there are frequent examples of full-cost pricing policies being adjusted for changes in demand and market competition. It was also no accident that full-cost pricing was frequently associated with minimum price agreements aimed at stabilizing market shares in the face of fluctuating demand (see Hall and Hitch, 1939; Barback, 1964). In fact a prolonged period of rigid full-cost pricing in association with fluctuating demand could be taken as one indicator of the existence of anti-competitive behaviour.

REFERENCES AND FURTHER READING

Andrews, P. W. S. (1949) *Manufacturing Business*, Macmillan.
Barback, R. H. (1964) *The Pricing of Manufactures*, Macmillan.
Chamberlin, E. H. (1933) *The Theory of Monopolistic Competition*, Harvard University Press.

Dorward, N. (1984) Pricing: a formula to tame those wayward costs, *Accountancy*, October, pp. 101–6.

Dorward, N. (1986) Overhead allocations and 'optimal' pricing rules of thumb in oligopolistic markets, *Accounting and Business Research*, Vol. 16, pp. 309–17.

Eichner, A. S. (1973) A theory of the determination of mark-up under oligopoly, *Economic Journal*, Vol. 83, pp. 1184–1200.

Gordon, R.A . (1948) Short-period price determination in theory and practice, *American Economic Review*, Vol. 38, pp. 265–88.

Hague, D. C. (1949) Economic theory and business behaviour, *Review of Economic Studies*, Vol. 16, pp. 144–57.

Hague, D. C. (1971) *Pricing in Business*, George Allen & Unwin.

Hall, R. L. and Hitch, C. J. (1939) Pricing theory and business behaviour, *Oxford Economic Papers*, No. 2, pp; 12–45.

Howe, M. (1962) Marginal analysis in accounting, *Yorkshire Bulletin of Economic and Social Research*, Vol. 14, pp. 81–9.

Lestor, R. A. (1946) Shortcomings of marginal analysis for wage–employment problems, *American Economic Review*, Vol. 36, pp. 62–82.

Noyes, C. R. (1941) Certain problems in the empirical study of costs, *American Economic Review*, Vol. 31, pp. 473–92.

Oliver, H. M. Jr (1947) Marginal theory and business behaviour, *American Economic Review*, Vol. 37, pp. 375–83.

Robinson, A. (1950) The pricing of manufactured products, *Economic Journal*, Vol. 60, pp. 771–80.

Robinson, J. (1933) *The Economics of Imperfect Competition*, Macmillan.

Silberston, A. (1970) Surveys of applied economics: price behaviour of firms, *Economic Journal*, Vol. 80, pp. 512–82.

Sizer, J. (1971) Note on 'The determination of selling prices', *Journal of Industrial Economics*, Vol. 20, pp. 85–9.

Skinner, R. C. (1970) The determination of selling prices, *Journal of Industrial Economics*, Vol. 18, pp. 201–17.

9 The Empirical Evidence on Pricing

The examination of the empirical evidence is organized into four sections. The first section covers those United Kingdom studies based primarily on either the intensive interview or case study approaches. Although some of these studies are by now rather historical, relating to business behaviour in the late 1930s and early post-war years, collectively they provide a detailed insight into the formulation of the pricing decision and its subsequent implementation.

The second section reviews the post-war surveys published in the economics and accounting literature which are based on the structured questionnaire. This is followed by a third section providing a brief synopsis of the results of the principal North American, European and Australian studies. The final section examines the evidence from the United Kingdom and North American econometric studies of pricing. These provide a particularly interesting set of results and, in the main, the studies are taken up with trying to assess the impact of market demand on pricing.

INVESTIGATIVE INTERVIEWS AND CASE STUDIES

The Hall and Hitch (1939) paper reported the results of interviews held with thirty-eight businessmen by the Oxford Economists' Research Group for the purpose of examining 'the way in which businessmen decided what price to charge for their products and what output to produce' (Hall and Hitch, 1939, p. 12). Of the 38 firms investigated, 12 claimed always to have practised a full-cost pricing policy and another 18 attempted to practise it in normal market circumstances or 'in principle'. In all, 79 per cent of the 38 manufacturers (30 firms) adhered to full-cost pricing. The behaviour of the remaining 8 firms did not fit the full-cost template, 5 of whom gave definite hints of adopting a marginalist response to demand changes, and in some cases even explicitly mentioned demand elasticity.

Just as important as the knowledge that full-cost pricing is the usual policy, are the occasions on which prices deviate from full cost. Hall and Hitch (1939) presented 33 responses from all 30 firms practising full-cost pricing, including the non-manufacturing firms, to the circumstances in which they would charge a price lower than full cost. Of these responses, 12 are related to depressed trading conditions, including price reductions to keep plant operating, and 9 specifically relate to competitors' price adjustments. It is also of interest that 5 responses related to capturing new markets or gaining large orders. Price increases over the full-cost price seemed to be a much rarer phenomenon, with only 5 responses covering 5 different reasons.

The number of occasions on which the alleged full-cost pricers were reported as being prepared to cut prices when market circumstances dictated has led to much argument over the interpretation of their results. This controversy has been fuelled by the reasons given for not charging a price different from that given by full costs. Of the 24 responses explaining why higher prices were not charged, 17 related to the fear of actual or potential competition. And of the 35 responses explaining why lower prices were not charged, 9 related to demand being unresponsive to price and 11 to competitors matching price cuts. As Machlup (1946) pointed out, these specific reasons for not departing from a full-cost pricing policy imply an estimate of demand elasticity 'which to the economist is equivalent to marginal revenue considerations' (Machlup, 1946, p. 546). The implicit marginalism contained in these reasons for adhering to a full-cost price, together with those given for departing from it, suggest a closer correspondence between conventional neo-classical price theory and the actual practice of full-cost pricing than Hall and Hitch (1939) either recognized or were prepared to acknowledge.

Edwards (1952) gave a clue to this close correspondence when he argued that the conventional view of the cost-based determinism of full-cost pricing ignored the informal process that took place between the preparation of the cost estimate and the actual setting of the price. These informal discussions would take into account 'the assumptions underlying the cost figures' (p. 299) and market conditions. This view was supported by statements made by a director of a firm of machinery manufacturers and by the chief accountant of a pottery manufacturer. The former explicitly took into account long-term considerations, detailed market forecasts, effects on other models in the range and competitors' prices.

Pearce (1956) and Pearce and Amey (1956) used a variety of research techniques to estimate the pricing behaviour of two firms as observed over several years. They first examined the cost estimates and compared them with actual prices charged. This was followed by an analysis of the *ex post* profit margins calculated from the annual trading accounts. Finally, senior executives were interviewed on a conversational basis to gain their views as to the pricing policy being followed by their respective companies.

The results were similar for both case studies. The accounting system estimated a selling price calculated on a conventional full-cost basis. Yet an analysis of the accounting data supported the view that the full-cost estimated selling price was used only as a guide and would invariably differ from actual price in the market transaction. They found no evidence to support fixed *ex ante* profit margins, the *ex post* margins derived from the final accounts moved in response to competitive pressure and there was no stability in the gross profit margin.

One very informative account of the pricing decision and its implementation within the clothing industry was given by Balkin (1956) when he described the pricing process within his own firm. In this industry in the early post-war period, the full-cost price was 'adopted' as the actual selling price 'in the majority of cases'. However, before this firm can be categorized as a full-cost pricer, consideration must be given to the 'occasions on which a different selling price is finally fixed'.

In the home market a price less than the costing price would be charged in recessions. Such reductions could be 'very substantial' when stocks of finished goods reached 'uncomfortably' high levels. Although periods of high demand would not see a reciprocal increase in prices, unless costs were also higher, there was a pricing–product differentiation response in that a few new styles would be introduced bearing margins higher than those given in the costing price. Therefore, changes in market demand would be associated within deviations from the full-cost price. Other reasons for charging prices lower than the full-cost price were to clear discontinued lines, tendering for a government contract when only about two-thirds of the normal overhead percentage would be allocated, and when a competitor offered a similar garment at a lower cost.

Barback (1964) was interested in finding explicit evidence of marginalist behaviour, but for the seven firms interviewed he found little justification for short-run profit maximization and only one firm showed a hint of explicit marginalism and even here there was a basic full-cost approach to pricing. The overall evidence reads very much as a post-war reaffirmation of the Hall and Hitch (1939) study. Four of the seven firms could be described as conventional full-cost pricers, although they were willing to cut prices and profit margins when trade was bad. However, all four took competition into account and were very conscious of competitors' potential for price cutting. This marginalist tinge has to be dampened somewhat as all the firms reported a very strong resistance to price changes. Barback (1964) concluded by rejecting a marginalist interpretation of behaviour and came out favouring the full-cost theory.

Finally, in what has undoubtedly been the most comprehensive study of pricing behaviour undertaken in the United Kingdom, Hague (1971) described the complete pricing decision process of thirteen manufacturing firms. A team of researchers looked at a wide range of pricing policy issues including the pricing objectives; the internal and external information on which pricing decisions were based; the way the data were analysed; who took the pricing decision; and the constraints placed on the decision-makers. A large number of research techniques were used including the interview, observation of intra-company meetings, and the examination of recorded price and cost data. The outcome is a number of excellent, detailed, case studies of the pricing process.

Although the thirteen firms used a variant of the full-cost formula as the first stage in pricing, in all but one case the costing price was modified to correspond with market conditions; ten firms took account of competitors' prices, at least four of whom varied the margins between products or customers by either discounting or differential pricing. While this might be taken to suggest that most firms in the Hague (1971) study were implicit marginalists, it should be recalled that seven firms did not separate fixed from variable costs in any systematic way.

An assessment of the investigative studies

This assessment is based on an analysis of the information on costing and pricing behaviour provided in the above-mentioned studies. They collectively provide data on fifty-seven manufacturing firms as reported in Hall and Hitch (1939) (their 33 manufacturing firms only), Edwards (1952) (the machinery manufacturer only), Pearce (1956), Pearce and Amey (1956), Balkin (1956), Barback (1964) and Hague (1971). Unfortunately, the use of seven different studies suffers from some inconsistency when reporting the pricing practices of the fifty-seven firms. The different researchers did not all have the same objectives, although they were overlapping and they reported at different levels of detail in non-standardized formats.

Despite these difficulties, it was considered that the reliability of the intra-study reporting and the wealth of detail across the studies, particularly for the post-war period, provided a unique and valuable set of observations on pricing worthy of further analysis. The analytical approach adopted is similar to that of Earley (1956) in seeking inferences as to marginalist business behaviour from the costing- and demand-related business practices reported.

Marginalist business practices

Evidence of marginalist behaviour is given in Table 9.1. The evidence is presented separately for the pre-war Hall and Hitch (1939) study and the six post-war studies, giving thirty-three and twenty-four firms in the respective groupings. This form of presentation is justified by the expectation, following Earley (1956), that modern marginalist methods of cost accounting would be more widely accepted by businessmen in the post-war period. Only clear and unambiguous references to costing and pricing practices were included in Table 9.1, making it a fairly conservative assessment of marginalist practices given the information available.

The most striking feature of Table 9.1 is that demand-related marginalist practices heavily outnumber those relating to costing by a ratio of 4:1 for the combined total. This is largely due to the fact that the Hall and Hitch (1939) survey provided little evidence of marginalist-type costing practices. With only five firms estimating marginal cost, the weight of available evidence on costing, even for the post-war firms, does not give much support to the explicitly marginalist behavioural hypothesis. In fact, the results are very similar to those of Howe (1962) who found only three of the twenty-eight firms he visited used marginal costing.

Of the post-war firms eighteen, or 75 per cent, took both competition and

Table 9.1   Evidence of marginalist behaviour

Business practice	Post-war studies by firm	Hall and Hitch (1939) by firm	Combined total
Cost related			
1 Use of marginal costs	5	0	5
2 Differential overhead allocation as a function of expected volume or capacity utilization	5	0	5
3 Partial absorption of overheads to obtain large orders at lower prices (government contracts)	5	2	7
4 Costs adjusted to a given market price	4	3	7
5 Cost increases absorbed in the short run	6	0	6
Total number of responses	25 (30)	5 (7)	30 (19)
Total number of firms with responses	15 (63)	5 (15)	20 (35)
Demand related			
6 Differential pricing and variable margins across products or markets	8	8	16
7 Awareness of demand elasticity or of buyer sensitivity to price changes	9	11	20
8 Considered general market conditions	12	8	20
9 Reduced prices in depressed markets	10	16	26
10 Reduced prices on large orders (exclusive of 3 above)	1	3	4
11 Considered actual or potential competition	19	20	39
Total number of responses	59 (70)	66 (93)	125 (81)
Total number of firms with responses	24 (100)	32 (97)	56 (98)
Cost and demand related			
Total number of responses	84 (100)	71 (100)	155 (100)
Total number of firms with responses (cost and demand)	15 (63)	5 (15)	20 (35)
Total number of firms	24	33	57

Percentages are given in parentheses.

either general market conditions or depressed markets into account when pricing and one other firm took competition into account while practising differential pricing. Of these, twelve had at least one marginalist-type costing practice. Another four firms considered general market conditions, price elasticity or applied differential margins, all four firms having at least two of these practices. *Therefore, twenty-three firms out of twenty-four demonstrated an important demand orientation when pricing.*

In the case of the Hall and Hitch (1939) study, fourteen firms took competition and either general market conditions or depressed markets into account in their pricing, and one other took competition into account while undertaking differential pricing. Also, five other firms considered general market conditions, demand elasticity, or had differential margins, each having at least two of these practices. *Therefore, twenty firms, or 61 per cent, had an important demand orientation in pricing.*

A classification of pricing policies

On the basis of the preceding analysis and information on the costing formulas for the fifty-seven firms, a classification of pricing policies has been compiled in Table 9.2. A comparison of Table 9.2 with the classifications made by some of the original surveys reveals several differences, particularly in the case of Hall and Hitch (1939). Only six firms were classed as determining their prices on the basis of costs alone. None of these firms had more than one marginalist pricing practice and in no case was it considered sufficiently significant to override the costing price. Also, three of the six firms were described by Hall and Hitch (1939) as being in price agreements.

As might be expected from the analysis of Table 9.1, forty-one firms, or 72 per cent, were classed as *modified full-cost pricers*. Their allocation of overheads and the size of the profit margin were ultimately demand-determined. Their response

Table 9.2   Pricing policies of 57 UK manufacturing firms

		Price policy		
Survey data	Full cost	Modified full cost	Contribution margin	Total
Barback (1964)	–	6	1	7
Hague (1971)	1	9	3	13
Edwards (1952)	–	1	–	1
Pearce (1956) and				
Pearce and Amey (1956)	–	2	–	2
Balkin (1956)	–	1	–	1
Post-war responses: No. (%)	1(4)	19(79)	4(17)	24(100)
Hall and Hitch (1939): No. (%)	5(15)	22(67)	6(18)	33(100)
All survey responses: No. (%)	6(10)	41(72)	10(18)	57(100)

to bad trading conditions was to write off part of their overheads as losses and in buoyant trading conditions they either reduced their discounts or increased the proportion of their product variants carrying higher net profit margins. Ten firms had characteristics resembling a contribution margin type of pricing policy. We, therefore, have only six firms with cost-based pricing policies and fifty-one, or 89 per cent, with demand-adjusted or demand-determined pricing policies. The differences between this classification and that of Hall and Hitch (1939) and Barback (1964) centre on the inferences drawn from information relating to the occasions on which the cost-based price is adjusted, statements concerning reactions to actual and potential competition, and references to demand elasticity and differential pricing.

POST-WAR SURVEYS BY QUESTIONNAIRE

The predominance of full costing as the initial stage of the pricing process was again confirmed by Skinner (1970) from his study of the determination of selling prices by a questionnaire sent to all members of the Merseyside Chamber of Commerce in 1968. Seventy per cent of 172 responses claimed to use cost-plus pricing, of whom 57 per cent used it for pricing all products. For the cost-plus pricers, 68 per cent applied a different percentage mark-up between products and orders, and of these, '81 per cent varied their mark-up according to the force of competition, 53 per cent according to the strength of demand, and 26 per cent to take account of other factors, mainly on the supply side (for example, the level of stocks or the existence of surplus capacity)' (Skinner, 1970, p. 205). It would seem, therefore, that as with the results of the interview studies the initial full-cost price is adjusted for market demand and competition to give the actual selling or contract price.

The Atkin and Skinner (1975) survey is somewhat unique in that the questionnaire was addressed to the marketing director rather than to the managing director or chief accountant. The survey generated 220 responses from medium to large manufacturing firms, marketing a wide range of industrial products. For those firms which determined price by cost-related methods, 63 per cent used full-cost pricing and 35 per cent used direct or marginal costing. In approximately 40 per cent of cases firms 'usually' or 'frequently' adjusted the cost-based price to take into account non-cost considerations. Only 14 per cent of respondents appeared to stick rigidly to the cost-based price. Furthermore, this pattern was 'broadly consistent regardless of the type of product sold'. Their most interesting finding was that 70 per cent of their respondents offered discounts on normal prices, with the proportion rising to 85 per cent for those firms publishing price lists. This led them to conclude that 'There is, therefore, some reason for believing that, in industrial selling, list prices often exist as a basis for discounting rather than as prices that customers in general are expected to pay' (Atkin and Skinner, 1975, p. 24). The single most important factor determining the discount was the category of customer.

With such large proportions of firms using marginal costs for pricing, adjusting the cost-based price to take account of non-cost considerations, applying widely different margins between products, and engaging in regular discounting, this study provides the strongest evidence yet against the conventional full-cost theory of pricing. In general, respondents were heavily oriented towards demand factors, even when employing full-cost practices.

These two questionnaire surveys support the hypothesis that implicit marginalism is the predominant business pricing behaviour. As businessmen do not, in general, have suitable information to make explicit marginalist pricing decisions, they practise an implicit form of marginalism, using direct standard costs as a low information cost surrogate for constant average variable cost, and allocating overheads and profit by a demand-influenced form of *ex ante* revenue recovery. Although such an approach to profit maximization will always be 'second best', it provides a practical alternative when faced with imperfect cost and demand information.

EMPIRICAL STUDIES IN NORTH AMERICA, EUROPE AND AUSTRALIA

One very interesting study of 'excellently managed' manufacturing companies, as rated by the American Institute of Management, was published by Earley (1956). Out of the 217 manufacturing companies listed he got 110 questionnaire returns. His main concern was to see to what extent the leading manufacturing companies had adopted the new marginalist accounting techniques previously presented in the management literature.

In response to his questions on pricing policy, Earley (1956) found that 73 per cent did not try to maintain equal price–full cost ratios among their products and markets; 84 per cent modified the price–cost ratios for differences in expected competitive pressures; 77 per cent modified the ratios for differing buyer sensitivity to price; and 61 per cent modified the ratios for differing variable and fixed cost compositions. In addition, one-third of the responses did all four of the above and another third followed at least two of the above policies. Consequently, he concluded that the best-managed companies tend to 'differentiate cost–price ratios to reflect major factors recognized in marginalist analysis' (Earley, 1956, p. 56) and typically can be described as practising 'marginalism on the wing' rather than being either short or long-run profit maximizers.

Haynes's (1964) study of the pricing practices of small firms complements Earley's (1956) study of the larger firms. Of the 88 firms subject to intensive interview, only 28 were manufacturing firms, 6 were rigid full-cost pricers, while another 5 followed a full-cost pricing policy subject to the mark-up varying between products and/or markets. A further 20 firms used full-cost pricing but adjusted the mark-up according to circumstances, such as demand conditions and competition. Haynes's (1964) interpretation was that the full-cost estimate was a reference price, or a resistance point, below which the company would not permit price to fall.

In a recent survey of the financial vice-presidents of the Fortune 1000 industrial companies, Govindarajan and Anthony (1983), found that 83 per cent of the 501 respondents used full-cost pricing in arriving at a target selling price or price list. However, target prices and list or catalogue prices are not the same thing as transactions prices, those prices at which the sale is made. Stigler and Kindahl (1970) found that in the United States, transactions prices diverged from list prices, with the latter lagging during downturns. Price lists are only revised periodically, normally annually, while market conditions and transactions prices are usually changing frequently.

It is also the case that firms which use full-cost pricing as the basis for setting list prices for standard product lines may, at the same time, use marginal costing in special circumstances. This was the case for the eleven firms interviewed by Bruegelmann et al. (1985). Marginal cost pricing was used frequently when introducing new products to the market, entering new markets with an existing product, pricing products during the phase-out stage in their life cycle, special orders, and when making contract bids to public utilities and non-profit organizations. It seemed that in all these cases the price was arrived at by totalling variable unit costs and adding on a variable mark-up, the size of which depended on the particular market circumstances.

Unfortunately, there have been very few non-United Kingdom, European empirical studies in pricing. Fog (1960) investigated 139 firms in Denmark and while he found that full costing formed the dominant costing influence and determined the target price, most firms adjusted this initial price to take account of demand and competition. On the other hand, Langholm (1969) developed a marginalist model of price determination to incorporate multiple periods. In applying his model to Norwegian company data, he found that the best results came from applying a rule resembling the full-cost rule of thumb. This would go some way to supporting full-cost pricing as a policy of long-run profit maximization.

There have been two post-war empirical studies of pricing in Australia. The first study, by Cook and Jones in 1954, reported results which rejected both the marginalist and the full-cost pricing rules. The second study was published by Watson in 1978. He reported results of an investigation into the pricing policies of thirty-one companies. He found that most firms set predetermined profit margins for broad ranges of their activities, and then set individual prices within these general guidelines, taking due account of market factors. He also found that both temporary and permanent increases in demand would not lead to price changes unless there was a backlog of previously unrecovered cost increases. Firms generally preferred increased volume to increased prices. However, demand decreases acted generally to decrease prices, with cost increases being either absorbed or leading to extensive cost cutting exercises.

It would seem from this brief review that the type and distribution of pricing practices within the countries reported largely replicate those of the United Kingdom. The general pricing behaviour is implicitly marginalist, with both explicit marginalism and rigid full-cost pricing being minority practices.

ECONOMETRIC STUDIES OF PRICING

There have been several econometric investigations into the proximate determinants of United Kingdom prices published over the last two decades. Most of
the models used in these investigations have specified price as a function of costs
and excess demand. The two principal issues in modelling price have been:

(i) to determine whether prices react to actual costs or normal costs – normal
     costs are those that result if output sticks to its trend path and as such could
     be regarded as long-run costs; and
(ii) to determine whether demand has a direct effect on the mark-up.

These two issues have been the source of much controversy concerning both the
specification of the equations generating the normal cost data and the identification of the excess demand variable. Consequently, many of the studies have been
attacked on the grounds that their estimated price equations do not adequately
test their price hypothesis. As a result, it is difficult to make an assessment of the
extent to which the evidence either supports or refutes the hypothesis that
demand is a significant determinant of the mark-up.

The normal cost hypothesis, that price is determined by a fixed mark-up times
historical normal direct, or prime, cost independent of the conditions of demand,
was tested by Neild (1963) in the first published econometric study. His basic
equation gave the final price, p, as:

$$p_t = \alpha_o + \alpha_1\beta_i W_t + \alpha_1\beta_2 M_t \qquad\qquad 9.1$$

where α_o and α_1 are ≥ 1, W is the current wage, M the current price of materials
(including fuel) and other costs and profit are given by a multiple, α_1, of prime
costs plus an additional fixed charge per unit of output, α_o. Neild (1963) applied
a distributed-lag function to W and M, with the weights decreasing according to
a geometric progression. In order to test for normal costs as against actual costs
being the principal price determinant, he introduced a productivity measure into
the model. The actual cost hypothesis was incorporated by dividing actual hourly
earnings by current productivity. The normal cost hypothesis was incorporated
by dividing standard hourly earnings by the long-run trend in productivity,
expressed either as an assumed trend increasing by a compound rate of 2.5 per
cent a year or by an actual statistical estimate of the trend. Using quarterly data
for UK manufacturing industry, excluding food, drink and tobacco for 1950–61,
Neild (1963) found that normal costs gave better results than actual costs and that
the assumed productivity trend gave results superior to those given by the
statistically estimated trend. He concluded that prices were 'not sensitive to
cyclical fluctuations in productivity or to cyclical variations in the pressure of
demand' (Neild, 1963, p. 50). Thus, price levels were determined by normal costs
times a fixed mark-up.

Neild's (1963) work was strongly criticized by Rushdy and Lund (1967). They
argued that by dividing standard hourly earnings by an exogenously determined
trend in productivity, Neild had implicitly incorporated a demand element into
his cost-based equation. This is because the level of demand and productivity are

positively correlated over the cycle. When demand is high, output per manhour is also high and so actual unit labour costs will be lower than their trend level. This means that the actual mark-ups will be rising when demand is rising even though prices may remain unchanged. Consequently, the finding of a high correlation between prices and normal unit labour costs implies that prices remain stable which invalidates the constant mark-up assumption. Stable prices and variable actual unit labour productivity must result in variable actual mark-ups. Thus, they argued that Neild's (1963) interpretation of his results was wrong and that they did not support the full-cost hypothesis. They then adapted Neild's equation (9.1) to express the dependent variable as the change in price rather than the price level and added demand as an independent variable measuring either the current or lagged index of demand for labour. From 192 estimated regression equations, they found that, in general terms, recent demand pressure had some effect on prices. They concluded that 'the level of demand cannot be dismissed as being an insignificant factor in the explanation of the price changes of manufactured goods' (Rushdy and Lund, 1967, p. 371).

McCallum (1970), in criticizing the Rushdy and Lund (1967) approach, developed a model based on the conventional theoretical proposition that price changes are caused by excess demand alone. The influence of costs is assumed to be restricted to affecting supply, the changes in which would be embraced by the excess demand variable. Of course, the analysis assumes competitive markets. He regressed price changes on a distributed-lag function of excess demand using the excess demand for labour as a proxy variable. The independent demand variables and the lagged dependent variable were significant and the equation gave a high level of explanation. Sylos-Labini (1979) argued that McCallum's (1970) assumption that the response in the labour market occurs one period behind the corresponding conditions in the product market ignored rational expectations which could imply the opposite. Nevertheless, McCallum's (1970) estimating equation is consistent with his hypothesis and his results suggest that excess demand is a significant cause of price changes.

Godley and Nordhaus (1972) followed Neild (1963) in attempting to test the normal cost hypothesis that 'the mark-up of price over normal historical current average cost is independent of the conditions of demand in the factor and product markets and is independent of the deviations of actual cost from normal cost' (Godley and Nordhaus, 1972, p. 869). They used quarterly data of United Kingdom manufacturing industry excluding food, drink and tobacco for 1953–69.

In order to test the hypothesis, they developed a sophisticated normalizing technique to derive normal unit costs. Smith (1982) regarded their method of normalizing variables as 'the best currently available' (p. 213). Normal unit costs were derived by eliminating reversible cyclical elements from earnings, employment and output. This resulted in an estimate of average labour costs along a trend growth path of output. They regressed the logarithm of the proportional rate of change of actual prices on both the logarithms of the proportional change in prices predicted from applying the 1963 mark-up as a constant to normal historical unit costs, and the absolute change in an output measure of current capacity utilization. While the explanatory power of the model was weak, the predicted price series based on normal cost was a significant predictor of actual price. With the coefficient of the capacity utilization, or current demand, variable being insignificant, the normal cost hypothesis was vindicated. Unfortunately, they did not introduce time lags into the relationship of actual price changes to excess demand, so making it difficult to relate their results to those from earlier work.

A more recent study of the normal cost hypothesis, but this time at the industry level, was that of Coutts, Godley and Nordhaus (1978). Using the same model as the 1972 study, they undertook 252 regressions in total for the seven industries. The results were broadly the same as for the earlier study with the coefficient for the index of demand pressure, with and without lags, being small and insignificant in the vast majority of cases.

However, these results, together with those of Godley and Nordhaus (1972), have been thrown into question as a valid test of the normal cost hypothesis by the recent work of Smith (1982). Using the Godley and Nordhaus approach to normalization, subject to a respecification of some of the equations used to generate normal costs, Smith provides evidence to refute the normal cost hypothesis.

Assuming that the 1963 mark-up was a constant, Smith (1982) tested the normal cost hypothesis for 1957–69 with price changes as the dependent variable. The lagged capacity utilization, or demand, variable was found to be significant and positive with the most appropriate lag being one quarter. This result occurred irrespective of the specification of the distributed lag applied to historical costs. Also the predicted price-change coefficients, summated for the normal cost variables, were significantly less than unity. This was also the case with the Godley and Nordhaus (1972) results, and in Coutts, Godley and Nordhaus (1978) only one of their seven industries had the predicted price-change coefficient approximating unity. A significant departure of this coefficient from unity refutes the strict interpretation of the normal cost hypothesis where observed price is a function of normal cost alone. When it is recalled that Rushdy and Lund (1967) by reworking Neild's (1963) data also refuted the normal cost hypothesis, there remains not one United Kingdom study in support of the normal cost hypothesis which has not subsequently been refuted.

The results of the main North American studies largely seem to replicate those for the United Kingdom. In his study of the Canadian cotton textile industry, McFetridge (1973), used quarterly data for 1958–69 to regress the proportional change in price on the proportional change in normalized unit labour costs, the proportional change in actual unit material costs and two demand variables – the ratios of unfilled orders to sales and of the finished goods inventory to sales. The coefficients on all variables were significant from which one can infer that while price changes took account of changes in unit direct costs, the mark-ups were also adjusted in response to changed product market demand conditions. As with the Smith (1982) and Coutts, Godley and Nordhaus (1978) studies, the aggregated coefficients predicting price changes on the bases of cost changes alone were significantly less than unity, so rejecting the Hall and Hitch (1939) hypothesis.

The significance of demand as well as costs in price determination was also an important feature of the Eckstein and Fromm (1968) study of wholesale list prices. When regressing either price levels or quarterly price changes on a number of variables, including standard unit labour costs, material prices, the ratio of unfilled orders to sales, and the rate of capacity utilization for all manufacturing industry, the two demand-related variables were significant. However, for both types of dependent variable, the sum of the *beta* coefficients for the cost variables exceeded that for the demand variables. The same result was found by McFetridge (1973). Thus while the demand variables were significant, they would appear to have a lesser effect than costs on the determination of list prices. However, as we have already noted above, list prices are expected to lag slightly after transactions prices with revised price lists simply notifying preceding changes in transactions prices. Therefore econometric studies, being dependent on list price data, are likely to understate the influence of excess demand variables on actual pricing policy. Unfortunately, actual transactions data sets are unavailable on a scale sufficient to test this hypothesis across a representative sample of industries.

By way of conclusion, it would appear that the results derived from the interviews, questionnaire surveys and this econometric work, suggest a rejection of the conventional full-cost theory of pricing. Market demand factors, whether in the form of changing capacity utilization, fear of potential or actual competitors, changing implied price elasticities, or some index of excess demand, appear to play a significant and independent, although not easily identifiable, role in price setting.

The problem of identifying the effect of demand is epitomized in this brief review of recent econometric work. Appropriate demand variables, unlike costing factors, are generally unavailable in a data format ideally suitable for statistical estimation. Part of the problem is that the demand effect, although systematic, appears to be very fragmented and enters the pricing decision in many guises. While demand directly affects the mark-up factor, its precise influence is complex and not even complete for it can subsequently lead to a further shading of the resultant quoted, target, or list price. While cost enters the pricing formulas directly and forms the initial costing base for the price decision, demand enters indirectly and generally seems to act as the factor which adjusts the costing price to correspond with non-cost considerations. Thus cost is easily recognized in the costing procedure, while demand plays a nebulous, ill-defined role. Consequently, it is very difficult to model demand when undertaking econometric work. What often results is low coefficients on the demand variable which are sometimes found to be statistically insignificant and of the wrong sign. The appropriate identification of the demand effect is the source of much of the controversy surrounding the applied econometric work reviewed above.

REFERENCES AND FURTHER READING

Andrews, P. W. S. (1949) *Manufacturing Business*, Macmillan.
Atkin, B. and Skinner, R. (1975) *How British Industry Prices*, Industrial Market Research Ltd.

122   The Pricing Decision: Economic Theory and Business Practice

Balkin, N. (1956) Prices in the clothing industry, *Journal of Industrial Economics*, Vol. 5, pp. 1–15.

Barback, R. H. (1964) *The Pricing of Manufactures*, Macmillan.

Bruegelmann, T. M., Haessly, G., Wolfangel, C. P. and Schiff, M. (1985) How variable costing is used in pricing decisions, *Management Accounting*, USA, Vol. 66, April, pp. 58–65.

Cook, A. C. and Jones, E. W. (1954) *Full Cost Pricing in Western Australian Manufacturing Firms*, Paper presented to Section G of 30th ANZAAS Congress, Canberra.

Coutts, K., Godley, W. and Nordhaus, W. (1978) *Industrial Pricing in the United Kingdom*, Cambridge University Press.

Domberger, S. and Smith, G. W. (1982) Pricing behaviour – a survey, in M. J. Artis, C. J. Green, D. L. Leslie and G. W. Smith (eds.) *Demand Management, Supply Constraints and Inflation*, Manchester University Press, pp. 192–212.

Earley, J. S. (1956) Marginal policies of 'excellently managed' companies, *American Economic Review*, Vol. 46, pp. 44–70.

Eckstein, O. and Fromm, G. (1968) The price equation, *American Economic Review*, Vol. 58, pp. 1159–83.

Edwards, R. S. (1952) The pricing of manufactured products, *Economica*, Vol. 19, pp. 298–307.

Fog, B. (1960) *Industrial Pricing Policies*, North-Holland.

Godley, W. and Nordhaus, W. D. (1972) Pricing in the trade cycle, *Economic Journal*, Vol. 82, pp. 853–75.

Govindarajan, V. and Anthony, R. N. (1983) How firms use cost data in price decisions, *Management Accounting*, USA, Vol. 65, July, pp. 30–6.

Hague, D. C. (1949) Economic theory and business behaviour, *Review of Economic Studies*, Vol. 16, pp. 144–57.

Hague, D. C. (1971) *Pricing in Business*, George Allen & Unwin.

Hall, R. L. and Hitch, C. J. (1939) Price theory and business behaviour, *Oxford Economic Papers*, No. 2, pp. 12–45.

Haynes, W. W. (1964) Pricing practices in small firms, *Southern Economic Journal*, Vol. 30, pp. 315–24.

Howe, M. (1962) Marginal analysis in accounting, *Yorkshire Bulletin of Economic and Social Research*, Vol. 14, pp. 81–9.

Kaplan, A. D. H., Dirlam, J. B. and Lanzillotti, R. F. (1958) *Pricing in Big Business*, Brookings Institute, Washington DC.

Langholm, O. (1969) *Full Cost and Optimal Pricing*, Universitersforlayer, Norway.

Lanzillotti, R. F. (1958) Pricing objectives in large companies, *American Economic Review*, Vol. 48, pp. 921–40.

Machlup, F. (1946) Marginal analysis and empirical research, *American Economic Review*, Vol. 36, pp. 519–54.

McCallum, B. T. (1970) The effect of demand on prices in British manufacturing: another view, *Review of Economic Studies*, Vol. 37, pp. 147–56.

McFetridge, D. (1973) The determinants of price behaviour: a study of the Canadian cotton textile industry, *Journal of Industrial Economics*, Vol. 22, pp. 141–52.

Neild, R. R. (1963) *Pricing and Employment in the Trade Cycle*, Cambridge University Press.

Pearce, I. F. (1956) A study in price policy, *Economica*, Vol. 23, pp. 114–27.

Pearce, I. F. and Amey, L. R. (1956) Price policy with a branded product, *Review of Economic Studies*, Vol. 24, pp. 49–60.

Rushdy, F. and Lund, P. J. (1967) The effect of demand on prices in British manufacturing industry, *Review of Economic Studies*, Vol. 34, pp. 361–77.

Skinner, R. C. (1970) The determination of selling prices, *Journal of Industrial Economics*, Vol. 18, pp. 201–17.

Smith, G. W. (1982) The normal cost hypothesis: a reappraisal, in M. J. Artis, C. J.

Green, D. L. Leslie and G. W. Smith (eds.) *Demand Management, Supply Constraints and Inflation*, Manchester University Press, pp. 213–37.

Stigler, G. J. and Kindahl, J. (1970) *The Behaviour of Industrial Prices*, National Bureau of Economic Research, New York.

Sylos-Labini, P. (1979) Industrial pricing in the United Kingdom, *Cambridge Journal of Economics*, Vol. 3, pp. 153–63.

Watson, I. R. (1978) *Pricing and Scale in Australian Industry*, AIDA Research Centre, Melbourne.

10 Pricing in a Marketing Strategy

PRICING STRATEGY AND MARKETING STRATEGY

Price is only one of a number of marketing decision variables which are collectively referred to as the marketing mix. The other decision variables include: items physically related to the product such as its styling, packaging, labelling and branding; methods of distribution; and a group of communications variables such as advertising, sales promotion and merchandising. Price is one of the communications variables.

The decision variables included in any one marketing mix will tend to be inter-related. For example, a change in the level of advertising expenditure will have implications for pricing strategy. Eskin and Baron (1977) using test market data found the effect of an increase in advertising on sales to be greater when prices were lower. This would suggest a negative relationship between pricing and advertising. The interdependence between pricing and other marketing decision variables included within the marketing mix means that management, in selecting decision variables for inclusion, should try and ensure that they form a coherent and well-integrated set whose performance through time is consistent with its marketing objective(s). This is normally achieved by adopting an appropriate marketing strategy.

A marketing strategy is designed to adjust the marketing mix through time so as to develop systematically better links with the consumer. Its purpose is to develop the interrelationships existing between the functional characteristics of the firm's products and customer requirements such as to achieve better customer satisfaction. Consequently, a pricing strategy should be in harmony with the overall marketing strategy.

This means that the making of a pricing decision can be a very complex operation, particularly as most of its interactions with the other marketing decision variables are poorly specified. Unfortunately, pricing has been relatively neglected by marketing researchers. Consequently, much less is known about the effects of price on buyer behaviour than about other variables such as advertising and new product introductions. Indeed, many marketing managers regard pricing as a variable of lesser importance than, say, advertising or product promotion. This lack of information by which to develop trade-offs between price and the other marketing variables has hampered efforts at generating well-integrated pricing and marketing strategies. Most of the research into pricing has been left to the economist whose efforts in the area of market strategy have been largely restricted to the pricing–advertising interrelationship. And even here there have been very few intra-company studies on price formation. This has been largely due to the difficulties of acquiring suitable data.

The term strategy implies that the decision variables are operated with reference to the long-term development of the firm. Rao (1984) suggested a framework for pricing in which the pricing decision was in two parts. The first was the long-run pricing strategy which was concerned with setting the base price for the product. The second was a set of tactical pricing decisions involving policies such as discounts and special offers which related to one particular time period in the planning horizon (short-run). He further proposed that this second set of pricing decisions be subsumed into decisions concerning other non-price variables in the marketing mix such as sales promotion. He regarded the division of the time horizon into a series of independent pricing periods as a myopic strategy (as in short-run profit maximization).

However, the adoption of a pricing strategy in which the planned base price, or a set of base prices over the life of the product, would be *consistently* followed over the long run requires a strategic *precommitment* which would preclude any opportunistic switching between alternative future pricing options. The successful adoption of such consistent long-run strategies would require good quality information on cost behaviour and market dynamics as well as stable market environments. In addition, this strategy when applied to oligopolistic markets would require the support of defensively strategic moves designed to restrict the price–output choices of existing and potential competition (De Bondt, 1984). The high informational demands and the constrained competitive environments implied by such consistent long-run strategies suggest that their applicability is restricted to collusive competitive conditions.

APPLICATIONS OF MARKETING STRATEGY TO THE PRICING DECISION

New product pricing

There appear to be two alternative strategies for pricing new products: skimming pricing and penetration pricing. They both derive from the work of Dean (1950). Although presented as opposite extremes, many intermediate positions are possible.

A *skimming strategy* is one of high initial prices accompanied by high promotional expenditures. It is usually applied to new products which have certain unique characteristics that protect them from competition in the initial stages of market development. However, imitations and further product developments by competitors will sooner or later encroach into the market forcing reductions in price. Thus, a skimming price strategy is characterized by a price path which declines towards marginal cost over time. Dean (1950) recommended a skimming strategy when the three following conditions pertain:

(i)   Demand is relatively inelastic as a result of the product's novelty value. With few close rivals in the early stages of market development, the cross elasticity of demand will also be low. Thus profit maximization suggests a high gross profit margin. Also the buyer, with little information or product experience, is very sensitive to advertising and sales promotion.

(ii)   When little is known about the demand function. A behaviourally safe way to explore the demand curve is to start by charging high prices and then progressively reduce them until a maximum profit position is found. The alternative strategy of starting with a low price and gradually raising it could undermine consumer goodwill.

(iii)   When the market is made up of groups of buyers having different demand elasticities. This allows the firm to price-discriminate over time by charging the different groups different prices for what is essentially the same product. Over the long run the firm works its way through the different groups, starting with the group having the lowest demand elasticity and then sequentially reducing price to tap profit from groups having a progressively higher price elasticity.

A *penetration strategy* is one of starting out with a low price and where, subject to market circumstances being favourable, the price path may rise in the long run. It is regarded as the strategy most appropriate for developing a mass market. Dean (1950) recommended it whenever market demand was thought to be relatively elastic and where the lead time for competitors bringing out imitations was relatively short. He also suggested using it as a method of discouraging potential entrants and so, in this respect, it can be regarded as a limit price. However, with a limit price strategy being non-profit maximizing, we cannot automatically associate penetration pricing with profit-maximizing behaviour.

To the extent that the profit margin is adjusted over time to correspond with an implied, or firm perceived, changing elasticity of demand, the skimming and penetration price strategies can be seen as continuous profit maximization through time. However, empirical observations on a profit skimming strategy might be little different from one of using price reductions to control the rate of new entry (Gaskins, 1971). Although the pricing objectives would be different and the timing of the price reductions would not be synchronized, the price paths might look very similar. However, an abrupt switch from a skimming to a penetration strategy would be easily detected. Such a move could indicate a profit-maximizing strategy giving way to limit pricing as in the Pashigian (1968) model.

De Bondt (1984) suggests that where price skimming policies are not observed to be consistently followed through time, such as by periodic shifts to penetration strategies, they would be undermined by buyers acting on the basis of their rational expectations. This would be likely in the case of durable goods where purchasing decisions can be delayed. Buyers with relatively low elasticities could rationally plan to wait whenever they expect a drop in price, an expectation based on their past observations or experiences. In order to make the skimming strategy more effective, the firm will have to convince buyers that high prices will be maintained and only gradually reduced through time. One appropriate signal might be to reduce investment in plant and machinery so as to demonstrate that output would be limited in the future (Bulow, 1982). However, while this might convince buyers, it will have the opposite effect on potential entrants who will now see greater potential returns from market entry. Therefore, whenever buyers adopt rational expectations behaviour, short-run profit-maximizing firms will have to choose between applying a consistent price skimming strategy through time and a consistent penetration strategy. A Pashigian (1968) type of mixed strategy will be untenable.

Pricing over the product life cycle

Market strategies for pricing new products are very much tied up with the concept of the product life cycle. There are five stages in the conventional life cycle. The first stage is the *introductory* period where there is little buyer awareness and the marketing problem is one of persuading consumers to try the product. The marketing emphasis is on advertising and sales promotion in the form of introductory discounts and trial offers. If the product gains market acceptance, it enters the *growth* stage and the marketing emphasis will be more on advertising and the maintenance of product quality. In the *mature* stage new buyers will have relatively high price elasticities and competition from substitutes will be at its most intense. Price has become the most important marketing instrument. When the market reaches the *saturation* stage, sales are largely dependent on the replacement demand of loyal buyers, who are by now relatively well informed on price and quality. This tends to result in low profit margins and intense competition. Finally, in the *declining* stage the product is being phased out and so the emphasis will be on a low price and good service. Consequently, the price elasticity of demand progressively increases throughout the conventional life cycle so that the optimal price–cost margin will correspondingly decrease.

Reekie (1978) provided evidence to support the conventional life cycle from his study of the United States drug industry. He found new drugs with important therapeutic gains to be more highly priced than those which were largely imitative and entering the mature stage of market development. He also found that during the first four years of a drug life cycle both the statistical mean and the dispersion of prices were reduced mainly by decreases in high priced drugs. Furthermore, his estimates of the price elasticity of demand for new drugs over the 1958 to 1975 period showed it to be lowest in the first year of the product life cycle as well as being relatively lower for those drugs making important therapeutic gains. With the latter also tending to have the highest prices, these results are consistent with a skimming price strategy and the conventional life cycle hypothesis.

Simon (1979) in a study of West German data on sales and prices of three different consumer goods derived results which challenge the conventional price path through a product life cycle. Price elasticities were typically found to be relatively high in the introductory and growth stages, lower in maturity and increasing in the period of decline. Simon (1979) held that these results supported a penetration price strategy and short-run profit maximization. The most surprising contrast with the conventional model are the relatively higher profit margins attainable in maturity when competition from substitutes should be having its greatest effect. It is also of interest that penetration pricing in the early stages of the life cycle gives way to rising prices in maturity.

Recent attempts at modelling the price path over the product life cycle as reviewed by Rao (1984) and Clarke and Dolan (1984) have only added further confusion to these conflicting empirical results. Very few of the models yield generalizable predictions and the price paths are varied. However, one of the more comprehensive models of life cycle pricing dynamics was that of Jeuland and Dolan (1982). They modelled purchasing behaviour in terms of an innovative trial, an imitative trial and repeat buying both for durable and non-durable goods. The optimal price is derived as the short-run profit-maximizing price subject to adjustments caused by the dynamics of their demand model. They found that when long-run profits are not discounted, the optimal price path for frequently repeat-purchased non-durable goods is a low introductory price followed by continuous price increases. In the case of durable goods, the optimal path is the same as that of Simon (1979) when imitative effects are important and the same as the conventional life cycle skimming strategy when imitative effects are unimportant.

However, when progressively higher discount rates are applied to long-run profits, the adjustments for dynamic purchasing behaviour gradually lose their importance and the optimal strategy becomes that of myopic short-run profit maximizing. Research into the dynamics of pricing is still at an early stage of development, but the widely contrasting results arising from different model specifications and empirical analyses suggest the need for considerable caution in making a strategic precommitment to any one price path over a product life cycle. The uncertainty created by the effects of competition over time and the many possible price reactions which may be required seem to imply the need for flexible, or discretionary, behaviour on the part of those managements wishing to follow profit-maximizing pricing strategies. Dean's (1950) dictum that pricing is an art still rings true today.

Pricing as an index of quality

While economics has concentrated on the allocative role of pricing, consumer research literature has emphasized the informative role played by price whenever consumers make brand choices in markets subject to product quality differences.

The accepted marketing view is that when consumers have very little information on the product, they tend to regard price as an index of quality. In general, the perceived price–quality link would only operate with reference to new, or relatively new, products which have not yet been satisfactorily evaluated from user experience. In the case of complex products or services, it may take an extended period of use involving several purchases or trials before the consumer can make a sound judgement. This would certainly apply in the case of medical services and complex electronic equipment.

Practising marketers are very conscious of these behavioural aspects of pricing. For many food products there seems to be a conventional floor price below which most consumers would regard quality as unacceptably inferior. In the United Kingdom this has always applied in the case of sausages and several other pre-prepared meat products. An example from the United States was Turtle Wax car polish which was developed as a low-cost petroleum based derivative providing a shine which lasted far longer than competing products. As a result of its low unit cost it was priced at the bottom end of the market. Consumers associated the low price with inferior quality, disbelieved the advertisements, and relegated the new product to the minor brand category. After recognizing the price–quality link, the manufacturer relaunched Turtle Wax as the most expensive brand and it quickly become the market leader.

While this all supports the old adage 'you get what you pay for', there is still not a satisfactory theory of consumer behaviour to support the hypothesis of price as an indicator of quality (see Bowbrick, 1980). Most of the results of this type of consumer research are based on consumer experiments and the conclusions are by no means uniform. For example, Etgar and Malhotra (1981) found that there was little evidence from their experiments to support a general price–quality link.

This behavioural aspect of pricing really derives from the problem of asymmetric information whereby the seller knows more about the quality of his goods than the buyer. This makes it difficult for producers of above average quality to persuade the buyer to pay more than the average price. Without a reliable indicator of quality, sellers of superior quality products would be forced to accept average prices which are unlikely to cover the higher costs incurred in incorporating superior quality product characteristics. Consequently, all producers get dragged down to the average quality. In fact, as Klein and Leffler (1981) have shown, a producer of a superior quality product would not have an incentive to maintain that quality unless the transactions price exceeded his extra costs. If the price were just sufficient to cover the extra costs, he would have an incentive to cheat and reduce quality, so gaining additional profits until consumers had acquired sufficient experiential information to discover the truth. Therefore, the price of high quality goods must not only cover the increased production costs but also earn a monopoly rent derived from exploiting the ignorance of consumers.

As a result of the Klein and Leffler (1981) analysis, high quality producers are shown to have a profit incentive to maintain the quality of their product over time and that this incentive will be greater the higher the relative price of the product. The problem for the producer of a high quality product will be to convince buyers that the quality exists and will be maintained over time. The solution lies in product branding. The considerable marketing expenditure required to establish a high quality brand name, the products of which are sold at relatively high prices, suggests to consumers that the producer has a vested interest in reliably meeting his quality claims. Consequently, the economics of asymmetric information can be used to explain the existence of product branding. According to Klein and Leffler (1981), the consumer will be prepared to pay a larger price premium for a high quality brand the more he fears being cheated by any false claims made for lesser quality products and the smaller his expected number of repeat purchases over the life of the product.

With buyer behaviour in markets with asymmetrical information being influenced by a price–quality relationship, producers of new high quality brands will be constrained to charging a high initial price to which they must remain committed until the brand enters the declining phase of its product life cycle. This high price, or skimming, strategy must be followed consistently over time as consumers of the brand will infer that any price reduction is being accompanied by a reduction in quality. However, the quality differentiation between brands will result in low price cross-elasticities so that competitive price cutting will not be an effective market strategy. Also a high quality brand will be protected from any new entrant claiming to offer the same quality at a lower price as the claim will not appear credible to existing consumers who have learned to rely on the price–quality offering of the established brand.

Price as an instrument of sales promotion

The offering of reduced prices on selected products in the form of temporary price discounts is commonly used by retailers as a strategy for promoting sales. In this context, pricing is being subsumed as a sales promotion decision. There is a rich marketing literature in this area which has determined the conditions for the optimal amount of discount, its duration, its frequency and its long-term effects. The literature has been reviewed recently by Rao and Sabavala (1980) who also stress the need for differentiating between short and long-run price elasticity when making both regular and temporary price reductions.

The likelihood of an interdependence between short-run discounts and long-term sales makes price discounting part of a rather complex decision set. One problem in determining optimal discounts is the estimation of both the gain in sales during the discount period and the subsequent sales reductions when the discount is withdrawn. The issue is complicated by the behaviour of consumers in stocking up during the discount period. An obvious danger is the effect of the discount in causing sales fluctuations without adding significantly to aggregate sales over the year. Blattberg, Eppen and Lieberman (1981) proposed a model which considers the transfer of stockholding costs from the retailer to the consumer. While the retailer seeks to trade off lower stockholding costs against revenue loss from the discount, the consumer trades off increased stockholding costs against the price reduction.

The offering of discounts of a non-temporary kind seems to be a very common occurrence in manufacturing industry. In the United Kingdom, Atkin and

Skinner (1975) found 85 per cent of their manufacturing companies giving discounts on published list prices. An analysis of the discounts showed 57 per cent related to the category of customer; 46 per cent depended on the quantity sold on any one order; 39 per cent depended on the quantity sold over a fixed period, and 33 per cent were for cash payment. Obviously, the structure of discounting policies is complex, with firms discounting for several reasons for any one customer. The scale of discounting activity shows the predominance of marketing factors over cost factors in the determination of actual transactions prices. Unfortunately, there has been virtually no consideration of the role of competition in marketing literature concerned with modelling price discounting. This would appear to be an area offering considerable opportunities for further theoretical and empirical research.

Pricing in segmented markets with product bundling

In practice, marketing management is very concerned with dividing up product markets into separate segments on the basis of differences in demand specifications between groups of consumers. The possible bases are many and include:

(i)   demographic criteria such as age and sex;
(ii) socio-economic differences such as income, education and family characteristics;
(iii) geographical variables;
(iv) buyer usage rates;
(v)   buyer motivation such as status, quality or economy;
(vi) personality factors such as aestheticism, gregariousness, taste or fetish.

For example, watches can be segmented by value, the number of different timing characteristics, fashion content, sex, resistance to water, shock or breakage and method of wearing (pocket or wrist).

The pricing strategies which accompany the segmentation of markets are aimed at pricing differently within different segments. Essentially, segmentation is a price discriminating device whereby either buyers in different segments are charged different prices for the same product or the same prices are offered simultaneously to all buyers but the pricing structure is such that these prices vary by points in time (airlines segment by time of flight), places of purchase, or with different bundles of related products. An example of the first type would be a price skimming strategy where one price is charged in each time period but between time periods the price is progressively reduced as the price discriminator moves sequentially through segments of progressively increasing demand elasticity. One of the most widely used of the second types of price discrimination is product bundling. An example is the practice used by hotels in bundling together some of the hotel amenities, such as in-room films, built-in bar facilities, sauna and a swimming pool, all of which would be included in the price of the room at a lower aggregate valuation than when priced separately. Although price discrimination is the subject of the next chapter, we will consider product bundling now as it has become such an important feature of marketing strategy.

Stigler (1963) explained the price strategy of product bundling by the use of an actual example of film distributors forcing exhibitors to block-book more than one film. It would pay a distributor to bundle films if, say, *Gone with the Wind* (film X) is more valuable to exhibitor A than exhibitor B, while the reverse is true for *Getting Gertie's Garter* (film Y). In Stigler's (1963) example:

A would pay $8,000 for film X and $2,500 for film Y
B would pay $7,000 for film X and $3,000 for film Y

If the two films were booked separately, Y would be hired at $2,500 per buyer so as not to exclude A, and X at $7,000, so as not to exclude B. The distributor's revenue would total $19,000. However, by bundling the two films together with a hire charge of $10,000 (the lower of A and B's valuations for X and Y together), the distributor could boost his revenue to $20,000. The revenue gain for the distributor comes from A and B having an inverse relation in their relative valuations of the two films and from the fact that their separate valuations of both films together are not too far apart. In Stigler's (1963) example, A and B's valuations of the bundle differ by only $500.

Although Stigler's (1963) example demonstrates the advantages of *pure bundling* as against selling products separately, it is not really a segmentation strategy as buyers are not given a choice between bundling and non-bundling. Segmentation requires a *mixed bundling* strategy where buyers are offered a choice between buying the bundle and the individual products making up the bundle. An example of mixed bundling would be BMW's practice of bundling together a luxury pack of motor car optional extras incorporating an electric sunroof, electric windows, alloy wheels and central locking, the individual items of which are also offered separately, but at higher prices than their part-value of the bundle. Those who buy separately form different segments from those who buy the bundle, with the former suffering the price discrimination.

Schmalensee (1984) derived the formal conditions for profitable bundling for a monopolist offering two products with zero cross-elasticities. Bundling is more profitable than non-bundling whenever buyers place a high valuation on either one of the bundled products relative to its cost and whenever their relative valuations of the two products differ. While these differences in valuation do not have to be negatively correlated, the relative profitability of bundling will become greater as the relative difference in the valuations increases.

Mixed bundling is more profitable than pure bundling (Schmalensee, 1984; Adams and Yellen, 1976) whenever some buyers value one of the items in a bundle relatively highly but value the other(s) near to, or below, cost and whenever there is a group of buyers with relatively high valuations for both (all) items in the bundle. This reasoning can be illustrated by an extension of the Stigler (1963) example. Assume that there are four film exhibitors with the following valuations:

A values X at $8,000 and Y at $2,500 (as before)
B values X at $7,000 and Y at $3,000 (as before)
C values X at $5,500 and Y at $5,000
D values X at $5,000 and Y at $5,500

Under a pure bundling strategy, the distributor would offer the bundle of X and Y at £10,000 to all four exhibitors. If the marginal cost of supplying each film is the same at $4,000, then the distributor's profit is $40,000 − $32,000 = $8,000. Note that under pure bundling A and B hire film Y, even though its marginal cost exceeds their valuations.

Mixed bundling can be even more profitable. The distributor can offer to rent out film X for $7,000, film Y for $4,000 and to bundle both together at a hire charge of $10,500. As a result, A, C and D will hire the bundle and B will hire film X only as the costs both of the bundle and film Y exceed B's respective valuations. The distributor's profit will be $10,500 × 3 + $7,000 − ($4,000 × 7) = $10,500.

However, the position of A is interesting in that he might prefer to hire film X for $7,000 instead of the bundle as the extra cost of the bundle exceeds his valuation of film Y by $1,000. If A so chose to hire X separately, then the distributor's profits would rise to $11,000 as he does not have to supply A with Y which has a supply cost in excess of A and B's valuations.

The reason for the dominance of mixed bundling is that it is a most efficient means of exploiting price discrimination. Buyers are offered a pricing structure whereby they are charged higher prices for buying the items separately (X + Y = $11,000) than in a bundle (X + Y = $10,500). Mixed bundling works as a price discriminating device by, first, using the bundle to extract the most from those who value it most − C and D who placed relatively high valuations on both films − and, second, charging a relatively high separate price for that item in the bundle which is valued very highly by some buyers − A and B who value film X very highly. It should also be noted in this example that, with a marginal cost of $4,000, a *non-bundling* monopoly price policy would have resulted in a profit of only $6,500 whereby A, B and C were charged $5,500 for film X and C and D were charged $5,000 for film Y. The economics of price discrimination will be taken up in more detail in the next chapter.

The assumption underlying the economic analysis of bundling is that buyers evaluate the bundle by adding together their valuations of the individual items making up that bundle. Whenever the manufacturer's price of the bundle exceeds the buyer's valuation, the latter will reject the bundle and purchase separately only those items in the bundle which he values greater than their prices when sold separately.

The only empirical analysis of buyer preferences for bundles was undertaken by Goldberg, Green and Wind (1984). The analysed guests' valuations of hotel amenities. First, guests were asked to estimate whether or not they would pay a given amount of dollars for an extra amenity such as a poolside bar. Second, the average of all guests' valuations of these extra amenities were added together as a predictor of their preferences for bundles of amenities. Surprisingly, they found guests' valuations of separate amenities to be a poor predictor of their preferences for specified bundles of these amenities. As a result, the assumption of buyers evaluating bundles by adding together their separate valuations of the bundled items is not supported. Markham (1984) suggested that this may have been due to many of the amenities being either substitutes or complements. For example, the value placed on a tennis court may depend on whether or not a sauna (substitute or complement?) is included in the bundle. Schmalensee (1984) avoided this problem in his theoretical analysis by assuming zero cross-elasticity. Yet in practice, most bundles will be made up of products or services which are related in terms of either function or buyers' usage. Consequently, Schmalensee's (1984) results as summarized above may not be generally applicable in actual business situations.

REFERENCES AND FURTHER READING

Adams, W. J. and Yellen, J. T. (1976) Commodity bundling and the burden of monopoly, *Quarterly Journal of Economics*, Vol. 40, pp. 475–98.

Atkin, B. and Skinner, R. (1975) *How British Industry Prices*, Industrial Market Research Ltd.

Blattberg, R. C., Eppen, G. D. and Lieberman, J. (1981) A theoretical and empirical evaluation of price deals for consumer durables, *Journal of Marketing*, Vol. 45, pp. 116–29.

Bowbrick, P. (1980) Pseudo research in marketing: the case of price/perceived quality relationship, *European Journal of Marketing*, Vol. 14, pp. 466–70.

Bulow, J. I. (1982) Durable goods monopolists, *Journal of Political Economy*, Vol. 90, pp. 314–32.

Clarke, D. G. and Dolan, R. J. (1984) A simulation model for the evaluation of pricing strategies in a dynamic environment, *Journal of Business*, Vol. 57, pp. 179–99.

Dean, J. (1950) Pricing policies for new products, *Harvard Business Review*, November–December.

De Bondt, R. R. (1984) Strategies with potential competition, Paper presented at the EISM Conference on New Challenges for Management Research, Leuven, 23–24 May.

Eskin, G. J. and Baron, P. H. (1977) Effects of price and advertising in test market experiments, *Journal of Marketing Research*, Vol. 14, pp. 499–508.

Etgar, M. and Malhotra, N. K. (1981) Determinants of price dependency: personal and perceptual factors, *Journal of Consumer Research*, Vol. 8, pp. 217–22.

Gaskins, D. W. (1971) Dynamic limit pricing: optimal pricing under the threat of entry, *Journal of Economic Theory*, Vol. 3, pp. 306–22.

Goldberg, S. M., Green, P. E. and Wind, Y. (1984) Conjoint analysis of price premiums for hotel amenities, *Journal of Business*, Vol. 57, pp. 111–32.

Jeuland, A. P. and Dolan, R. J. (1982) An aspect of new product planning: dynamic pricing, in A. Zoltners (ed.) *Marketing Planning Models*, TIMS Studies in the Management Sciences, Vol. 18.

Klein, B. and Leffler, K. B. (1981) The role of market forces in assuring contractual performance, *Journal of Political Economy*, Vol. 89, pp. 615–42.

Markham, J. (1984) Discussion, *Journal of Business*, Vol. 57, pp. 257–63.

Pashigian, P. (1968) Limit price and the market share of the leading firm, *Journal of Industrial Economics*, Vol. 16, pp. 165–77.

Rao, V. R. (1984) Pricing research in marketing: the state of the art, *Journal of Business*, Vol. 57, pp. 39–59.

Rao, V. R. and Sabavala, D. J. (1980) Allocations of marketing resources: the role of price promotions, in R. L. Leone (ed.) *Proceedings of the Second Market Measurement Conference*, Providence R. I.: TIMS College of Marketing and the Institute of Management Sciences.

Reekie, W. D. (1978) Price and quality competition in the United States drug industry, *Journal of Industrial Economics*, Vol. 26, pp. 223–37.

Schmalensee, R. (1984) Gaussian demand and commodity bundling, *Journal of Business*, Vol. 57, pp. 211–30.

Simon, H. (1979) Dynamics of price elasticity and brand life cycles: an empirical study, *Journal of Marketing Research*, Vol. 16, pp. 439–52.

Stigler, G. J. (1963) United States v. Loew's Inc.: a note on block-booking, *Supreme Court Review*, pp. 152–7.

11 Price Discrimination

PRICE DISCRIMINATION IN THEORY

Price discrimination is usually defined as *a practice whereby identical products or services are offered at different prices to different buyers*. It requires buyers to be segmented on the basis of their different preferences, income, demographic characteristics, location, or usage characteristics, each segment having a different price elasticity. We have already seen, in Chapter 10, that price discrimination is central to the economics of price skimming and product bundling, both being dependent on the successful segmentation of markets. The theory is normally presented with the assumptions of a monopoly market structure and identical products. However, neither assumption is necessary. We have already seen, in the analysis of product bundling, how price discrimination can be associated with profit maximization both within a competitive market strategy and with product differentiation.

However, the price dispersion that accompanies product differentiation does not necessarily imply price discrimination. Each product variant will tend to have its own unique combination of product characteristics or attributes which serve to differentiate it from other variants. As a result, production and other costs are likely to differ between product variants so giving a dispersal of product prices. Price discrimination will occur only where the price difference between any two product variants does not fully correspond with the difference in product costs. This means that the above definition of price discrimination must be extended to embrace the special condition of product differentiation. Phlips (1983, p. 6) suggested the following: '*price discrimination should be defined as implying that two varieties of a commodity are sold* (by the same seller) *to two buyers at different net prices, the net price being the price* (paid by the buyer) *corrected for the cost associated with product differentiation*' (emphasis supplied).

Conditions for profitable price discrimination

There are three necessary conditions for the successful implementation of price discrimination. The first is that, although price discrimination is not exclusive to monopoly *per se*, it is only possible when the intending discriminator has market power. This implies a downward-sloping demand curve for the firm's product.

The second condition is that it is possible to segment the market into different groups of buyers, with the price elasticity of demand differing between groups, and that constraints exist to ensure that at least some buyers do not, or cannot, transfer their demand to the cheapest segment. Non-transferability is inherent in product differentiated markets and takes the form of differences in buyer taste or product quality.

The third necessary condition is that it must be possible to prevent buyers in low priced segments from reselling to those in high priced segments (this is normally referred to as arbitrage).

The price discrimination model

The traditional theory of price discrimination states that the monopolist can increase total revenue and profits by charging different prices in each market segment such that the respective marginal revenues all equal the one marginal cost and, therefore, equal each other. We will demonstrate the theory by assuming a monopolist who sells his product in three different market segments which are characterized by non-transferable demand and the absence of arbitrage.

The demand curves for the three segments are shown in Figure 11.1(a) by the three parallel lines d_1, d_2 and d_3 with the demand elasticity at any price being lowest for d_1 and highest for d_3. Marginal cost is constant and is shown as k. The

Figure 11.1 Monopolistic price discrimination

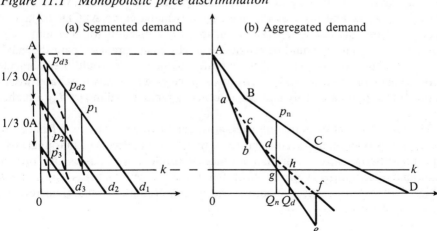

profit-maximizing rule for i market segments is given as:

$$MR_1 = MR_2 = MR_3 = MR_i = k$$

This results in the three discriminatory prices of p_1, p_2 and p_3. As the elasticities in the three segments are ranked $\eta_1 < \eta_2 < \eta_3$ so the profit-maximizing discriminatory prices are ranked $p_1 > p_2 > p_3$. This pricing policy also results in all three segments of the market being served.

The alternative non-discriminatory pricing policy can be illustrated with the aid of Figure 11.1(b). The aggregated demand for the three segments is shown by ABCD which represents the horizontal sum of d_1, d_2 and d_3. The marginal revenue corresponding to ABCD is given by the continuous zigzag line *abcef*. The intersection of this curve with marginal cost, k, gives the profit-maximizing non-discriminatory price p_n. Two things are worth noting about this price. First, not only does it not correspond with any of the three discriminatory prices, but it does not require the three segmental marginal revenues to equal marginal cost. Second, the price p_n exceeds the intercept of the d_3 demand curve so that no one in that segment will be served. The loss of sales to the most price elastic segment will contribute to a net loss of revenue and output compared with that resulting from price discrimination.

The difference between discriminatory and non-discriminatory pricing in terms of output and profit can be explained by comparing the effects of their respective aggregated marginal revenue curves. The discriminatory marginal revenue curve is given by the broken line *acdhf* and results from pricing differently on d_1, d_2 and d_3, rather than pricing uniformly on the aggregated demand curve ABCD. The intersection of *acdhf* with k gives a profit-maximizing output of Q_d (see Figure 11.1(b)) which is greater than the non-discriminatory output Q_n. So long as there are more than two segments, the quantity produced in the case of segmented linear gross demands will tend to be greater under monopoly price discrimination. This is because the effect of price discrimination is to cause the aggregated marginal revenue curve to shift to the right. Any increase in the number of possible market segments will cause the discriminatory marginal revenue curve to shift progressively to the right and so diverge away from the zigzag line *abcef* and towards the aggregated demand curve ABCD. In fact, if each purchaser became a separate segment with a demand for one unit only, perfect discrimination would be possible whereby each purchaser paid the maximum price he is willing to pay. The marginal revenue curve would then coincide with the demand curve ABCD, as any lower price paid by a new purchaser would apply to that purchaser only and not to other purchasers willing to pay a higher price.

The loss in profits from not discriminating can be directly observed from comparing the two marginal revenue curves at their levels in excess of marginal cost. The non-discriminatory marginal revenue schedule *abcef* misses out on the additional discriminatory profit illustrated in the geometrical areas *abc* and *dgh* which lie between the discriminatory and non-discriminatory marginal revenue curves above k.

PRICE DISCRIMINATION IN SPATIAL MARKETS

Spatial price discrimination deserves special consideration as it is the most prevalent form of price discrimination. In the following analysis we will assume that buyers have identical *gross* demand curves, where prices are defined as delivered prices (inclusive of transport costs). The effect of deducting the cost of transport from gross demand is to give different *net* demands at different distances from the supplier, the intercepts successively decreasing with greater distance. The more distant purchaser can be expected to have to bear higher transport costs in fhe form of a higher delivered price and, as a consequence, will have a lower net demand than purchasers located nearer the supplier.

This assumption on the nature of spatial demand can be depicted in Figure 11.1(a), with demand curve d_1 representing gross demand for all purchasers, as well as the net demand for those purchasers at the supplier's location. Demand curves d_2 and d_3 are the net demands for purchasers located at a transport cost of 1/3 0A and 2/3 0A, respectively, from the supplier. (Note that the transport costs are deducted from the price intercept to arrive at net demand.) With purchasers located at different distances from the supplier, *spatial markets are naturally segmentable into different net demands at zero cost.* Also with the elasticity of demand increasing with greater distance, the equality of the marginal revenues of the different spatial demands with the marginal cost of the firm requires an inverse relationship between the net demand price and greater distance. This means that the firm must absorb an increasing amount of the transport cost for progressively more distant purchasers.

In Figure 11.1(a) the addition of transport costs 1/3 0A to p_2 and 2/3 0A to p_3, gives the delivered prices p_{d2} and p_{d3} respectively (as read from d_1). As before, these prices result from price discrimination. However, the differences between the delivered prices p_1, p_{d2} and p_{d3} are all less than the difference in transport costs, 1/3 0A (in fact as the demand curves are linear the delivered price difference is half the cost of transport, equal to 1/6 0A). This means that profit-maximizing price discrimination results in systematic freight absorption. For the relatively nearer purchasers on d_2, the rate of freight absorption is 1/6 0A; for those relatively further away on d_3, the rate of freight absorption is 1/3 0A.

Recalling our earlier definition of price discrimination in product differentiated markets, we can see that spatial price discrimination results in purchasers with different net demands paying different delivered prices and that these differences do not fully correspond with the differences in transport costs. It follows that under profit-maximizing price discrimination the absorption of some of the costs of transporting to more distant purchasers serves to boost revenue, output and profits (as previously demonstrated by the use of Figures 11.1(a) and 11.1(b)).

Competition leads to increased spatial price discrimination

The recent work of Greenhut and Greenhut (1975) and Norman (1981) has shown that an increase in competition between locationally separated firms will be associated with an increase in the degree of price discrimination. In the Greenhut and Greenhut (1975) model, they gave the profit-maximizing condition for any competitor in a spatial economy as the equalization of spatial net marginal revenue and marginal cost,

$$P_d\left(1 - \frac{1}{n\eta}\right) = \bar{k} + \bar{t} \qquad\qquad 11.1$$

where P_d is delivered price, η is the elasticity of market demand at price P_d, n is the number of competitors in any given spatial market, $\bar{k}$ is the average of the marginal costs of the n firms, and $\bar{t}$ is the average transport cost of selling in a given spatial market.

The gross market demand curve can be given as

$$P_d = \alpha - \beta q \qquad\qquad 11.2$$

with a market demand elasticity, η, equal to $P_d/(\alpha - P_d)$. If competitors assume a Cournot behavioural reaction function, we can substitute the market demand elasticity into equation 11.1 and solve for the discriminatory delivered price. The result is given as

$$P_d = \frac{1}{n+1}(\alpha + n\bar{k}) + \frac{n}{n+1}\bar{t} \qquad\qquad 11.3$$

The factory gate price is given by the first term, while the second term defines the slope of the delivered price schedule (DPS) as a function of t. Subject to the profit-maximizing condition (equation 11.1), the slope of DPS will be positive and less than unity as $\delta P_d/\delta t = n/(n + 1) < 1$. This means that profit maximization requires the delivered price to incorporate some freight absorption. In the absence of price discrimination the slope of DPS would equal unity and the customer would bear the full transport cost. Thus, profit-maximizing competition in the spatial economy always requires some price discrimination.

However, equation 11.3 does not consider spatially separated competitors as all n firms are assumed to be at a single location. Let us consider the Greenhut and Greenhut (1975) case of sellers located at only two centres at either end (A and B) of a linear market (for example, a railway line) of length L, where the firms at A and B (n_A and n_B respectively) can supply the whole of L. This is shown in Figure 11.2(a).

The average transport cost, $\bar{t}$, is given as

$$\bar{t} = \frac{1}{n_A + n_B}(n_A t + n_B(L - t)) \qquad\qquad 11.4$$

With $n = n_A + n_B$, substituting equation 11.4 into 11.3 gives the slope of DPS as $(n_A - n_B)/(n + 1)$. This means that the slope of DPS is determined by the relative number of firms at the two centres. If more firms are located at A than at B, the DPS will rise as a positive linear slope as shown in Figure 11.2(a). On the other hand, should $n_A < n_B$, then DPS will have a negative linear slope. The lowest point of these delivered price schedules is given as the factory gate price (the first term of equation 11.3) which always exceeds $\bar{k}$ as a Cournot reaction

Figure 11.2   Delivered price schedules

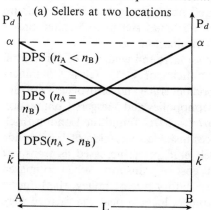

(a) Sellers at two locations

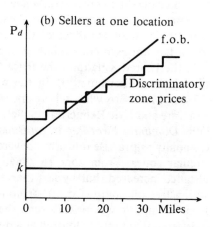

(b) Sellers at one location

function implies market power. The highest point is given by the price intercept α of the gross market demand curve (equal to 0A in Figure 11.1(a)).

One interesting result is where $n_A = n_B$ as DPS becomes horizontal and uniform delivered prices result. With the second term in equation 11.3 being zero, everyone pays the monopolist's factory gate price no matter where they are located. As the Greenhuts (1975, p. 410) stated, 'the more competitive the distant location...the greater will be the freight absorption rate of firms located at site A'.

Norman (1981) looked at other types of oligopolistic reaction functions applicable to spatial competition and again found that new entry at a distance resulted in increased competition and a greater absorption of transport costs. (The literature is summarized in Dorward, 1982.) We can conclude that when competitors are locationally separated, an increase in competition will lead to more, and not less, price discrimination.

The empirical evidence

Greenhut (1981) reported the results of a comparative survey of spatial pricing in the United States, West Germany and Japan. He found that 67 per cent of the 174 United States firms sampled adopted price discrimination when fixing delivered prices. The percentages were even higher in West Germany and Japan, 79 per cent of 34 firms and 82 per cent of 33 firms respectively. Of the overall sample, 24 per cent of the firms adopted uniform pricing only. Thus discriminatory pricing was the prevalent pricing practice. In a regression analysis explaining the level of freight absorption (price discrimination) he found the most important explanatory variables to be the location of competitors and the degree to which competition decreased or increased with distance. The more distant or dispersed were competitors and the more competition increased with distance, the greater was the level of price discrimination.

Greenhut (1981) also found that the intensity of price discrimination was greater in West Germany and Japan than in the United States. Unlike the former two countries, the United States gave no example of delivered prices being lower to more distant buyers than to those located nearby (negative DPS). This no doubt reflects the existence of the Robinson–Patman Act in the United States which has imposed constraints on price discrimination.

In the United Kingdom, the Price Commission found evidence of substantial spatial price discrimination in the pricing policies of U. G. Glass Containers (1978a), Metal Box when selling open-top food beverage and aerosol cans (1978b) and Tate and Lyle Refineries (1978c). The Monopolies and Mergers Commission in its *Dominant Firm Report on Building Bricks* (1976) found the London Brick Company to practise uniform delivered prices inside a succession of 5-mile-wide circular zones. From zone to zone, the delivered price increased as transport distance increased, but by less than the full cost of transport. When compared with a free on board (f.o.b.), or non-discriminatory pricing policy, the London Brick Company was pricing such that customers located near the factory were cross-subsidizing those located at a distance. A comparison of the delivered price schedules of the free on board with the London Brick Company's pricing policy is shown in Figure 11.2(b). The company's aim of using its zoning price policy to enlarge its market and so increase the consumption of bricks matches with the theoretical predictions of the monopoly price discrimination model outlined earlier in the chapter.

PRICE DISCRIMINATION THROUGH TIME

In Chapter 10, it was suggested that price skimming can be used as a method of price discrimination through time as it involves charging initially higher prices to those having high incomes and high time preferences (less willing to wait) and then progressively reducing the price to expand the market to those with lower incomes and lower time preferences. The problem for the price discriminator is one of determining the slope of the profit-maximizing temporal price schedule given that buyers have different valuations of the product depending upon their income and willingness to wait.

Phlips (1983) derived the profit-maximizing conditions for price skimming as a method of discriminating between buyers. The crucial assumptions are that buyers can be grouped into two or more income classes; and that higher income buyers are prepared to pay a higher price to acquire the product earlier. The seller has to determine a temporal price schedule such that those with the highest incomes purchase the goods as soon as they appear on the market and that the next highest income group enters the market when the price is next lowered and so on. The seller also has to ensure that higher income groups do not wait and transfer their demand to later periods when the price is expected to be lower.

The average valuation by income class i of one unit of the product delivered in period t can be expressed in terms of a reservation price R_t^i, where $i = 1, \ldots, n$ and $t = 1, \ldots, T$. The price charged to the highest income class n in the first period, given as p_1, should be the same as that charged under non-discrimination profit maximization. The actual price discrimination occurs in the relationship between the path of the future selling prices and the distribution of average reservation prices between the income classes. To persuade the highest income class

n to purchase in the first period and not wait until the price is lowered in the next period, the difference in selling price between periods $(p_1 - p_2)$ must equal the difference in the reservation prices of income class n $(R_1^n - R_2^n)$, where the subscripts indicate the time period. If the difference in the selling prices were greater than the differences in reservation prices, it would pay buyers in income class n to wait and purchase at the lower price p_2. On the other hand, if the difference in selling prices were smaller than the differences in reservation prices, the seller would miss out on some extra profit.

It follows that the temporal price schedule will be negative and its slope, $\delta p_t / \delta t$, will equal $\delta R_t / \delta t$ when marginal cost is constant. Thus the different prices charged correspond with differences in income classes (and a time preference positively related to income) and not with cost.

Many new durable goods, particularly those used in leisure activities, are subject to a price skimming strategy. Examples are television sets, video and stereo cassettes and home computers. Reekie (1978) found evidence of price skimming in the United States new drug market.

PRICE DISCRIMINATION BY PRODUCT BUNDLING, TIE-IN SALES AND METERING

We have already discussed product bundling as a form of price discrimination in Chapter 10. As part of that discussion we looked at pure bundling where the buyer is not permitted to purchase the items included in the bundle separately. Two special cases of pure bundling, which are exclusively price discriminatory in their objective, are briefly considered here. They are tie-in sales and metering.

The classic use of tie-in sales was by IBM in the United States before the practice was banned in 1936. The company exploited its monopoly in tabulating equipment by requiring all the customers renting the equipment to purchase their tabulating cards only from IBM. By pricing the cards well in excess of cost, IBM was able to price discriminate according to the number of cards used by different customers (discrimination by intensity of use). Customers using relatively more cards were forced to pay a higher net price for the bundle (equipment plus cards) than those customers using less cards – that is, after correcting for the production costs of the larger number of cards and the greater wear and tear of the machines.

Xerox in the early 1960s used a variant of tie-in sales by leasing its copying machines at a very low price and then metering their usage by charging a price per copy well in excess of marginal cost (Blackstone, 1975). The net price paid for the copying bundle and the contribution to Xerox's supernormal profit was higher for those customers using the machines more intensively.

REFERENCES AND FURTHER READING

Benson, B. L. (1984) On the ability of spatial competitors to price discriminate, *Journal of Industrial Economics*, Vol. 33, pp. 251–5.
Blackstone, E. A. (1975) Restrictive practices in the marketing of Electrofax copying

machines and supplies: the SCM Corporation case, *Journal of Industrial Economics*, Vol. 23, pp. 189–202.

Dorward, N. (1982) Recent developments in the analysis of spatial competition and their implications for industrial economics, *Journal of Industrial Economics*, Vol. 31, pp. 133–51.

Greenhut, J. and Greenhut, M. L. (1975) Spatial price discrimination, competition and locational effects, *Economica*, Vol. 42, pp. 401–19.

Greenhut, M. L., (1981) Spatial pricing in the United States, West Germany and Japan, *Economica*, Vol. 48, pp. 79–86.

Monopolies and Mergers Commission (1976) *Dominant Firm Report on Building Bricks*, HMSO.

Norman, G. (1981) Spatial competition and spatial price discrimination, *Review of Economic Studies*, Vol. 48, pp. 97–111.

Phlips, L. (1983) *The Economics of Price Discrimination*, Cambridge University Press.

Price Commission (1978a) *U. G. Glass Containers – Price of Glass Containers*, Report No. 5, House of Commons 170, HMSO.

Price Commission (1978b) *Metal Box Ltd – Open Top Food and Beverage and Aerosol Cans*, Report No. 3, House of Commons 135, HMSO.

Price Commission (1978c) *Tate and Lyle Refineries Ltd – Sugar and Syrup Products*, Report No. 6, House of Commons 224, HMSO.

Reekie, W. D. (1978) Price and quality competition in the United States drug industry, *Journal of Industrial Economics*, Vol. 26, pp. 223–37.

12   Transfer Pricing

DECENTRALIZATION AND THE PROBLEM OF TRANSFER PRICING

As firms get larger and increase their product ranges they tend to decentralize into semi-autonomous divisions or profit centres. The reason is that the semi-autonomous divisional managers are thought to be more effective than the centre in responding quickly to the specialized needs of 'local' markets and to information flows on new market opportunities. However, when the divisions are interdependent in terms of interdivisional transfers of goods and services, central management is faced with the problem of co-ordinating the output decisions of the different profit centres in the overall interests of the firm. Left to themselves, the divisions will tend to adopt monopolistic and monopsonistic patterns of behaviour so as to increase their own profits at the expense of the other divisions. This often results in a deterioration of overall corporate profitability. Consequently, the profit centre approach to decentralization requires central management to co-ordinate the divisions by determining a system of transfer prices which applies to the transfer of goods and services between the divisions.

Ideally, a transfer pricing system has two main objectives. The first is to permit central management to evaluate as accurately as possible the contribution of the separate divisions to overall corporate profitability. Usually, this is only possible when there are external markets providing perfectly competitive prices which can be adopted as the transfer prices. In this way, a profit centre can be evaluated as if it were a perfectly competitive independent firm. In the absence of such prices the interdependence existing between divisions means that any interdivisional allocation of profits will be arbitrary and, therefore, irrational. This aspect of transfer pricing is analogous to the related problem of trying to allocate overheads and joint costs between divisions and product groups (see Chapter 5). Optimal corporate profitability requires central management to determine the transfer price as equal to the marginal cost at the optimum level of output for the firm as a whole. Unfortunately, marginal cost transfer prices determined by the centre mean that the centre must also determine the optimum levels of output. Such interference by central management acts as a restrictive condition on divisional autonomy. Where interdivisional transfers form a high proportion of corporate added value, the benefits from decentralization must be largely outweighed by the complexities of trying to devise optimal transfer pricing systems.

The second objective of an optimal transfer pricing system is to motivate divisional management such that their efforts maximize total corporate profit. Certainly the marginal cost system of transfer pricing will not achieve this result whenever a division experiences constant marginal costs, as such a division cannot make any contribution to its own profit and so will be demotivated. Consequently, it will have little incentive to increase its efficiency, as lower marginal costs will result in a corresponding reduction in the transfer price received.

Therefore, in the absence of external competitive markets for the intermediate products, there are innate conflicts between the need for centrally dictated transfer prices and divisional autonomy. In such circumstances, transfer prices become the arbitrary outcome of a process of negotiation.

COMPETITIVE MARKET PRICES AS IDEAL TRANSFER PRICES

The existence of a perfectly competitive external market for an internally traded product provides the necessary condition for maximum divisional autonomy consistent with the corporate optimality. The only intervention necessary by central management is to ensure that the market price is used as the transfer price. This condition can be analysed by borrowing from Hirshleifer (1956). His model has a manufacturing division, M, producing an intermediate product which can be sold either to a perfectly competitive external market or to a distribution division, D. Likewise, D can buy either from M or from the external intermediate market.

The analysis of the optimal transfer pricing system is presented in Figure 12.1. The profit-maximizing position for M is to produce $0Q$ units of output where its marginal cost, MC_M, equals the external competitive market price and the transfer price, TP. It is indifferent whether it sells its output to the external market or to D. On the other hand, D will wish to purchase $0L$ units where its net marginal revenue curve, NMR, equals the marginal cost of purchase: the market price and the transfer price. NMR is derived by subtracting D's marginal cost, MC_D, of processing the intermediate product from the marginal revenue, MR, obtained from selling the final product. (Note that NMR plus MC_D equals MR which also equals MC_M plus MC_D at the equilibrium output for the firm.) D is also indifferent between trading internally or externally.

The output levels $0L$ and $0Q$ are optimal for the company as a whole as the company net marginal revenue schedule *abcd* intersects the intermediate marginal cost of production and external purchasing schedule *ecd* at Q. Therefore, the use of the perfectly competitive market price as the internal

Figure 12.1 External market prices as transfer prices

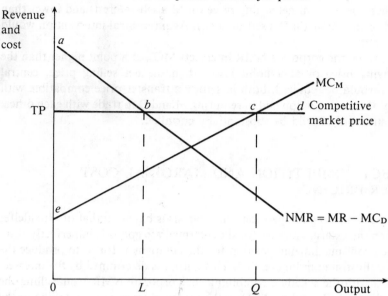

transfer price results in Solomons's (1965) ideal transfer price as the output Q and total company profit *abce* is the same as would occur if the two divisions M and D were centrally operated as a single profit centre. Under the competitive market price rule for transfer pricing, the separate profits of the divisions represent their real economic contribution to total company profits and so accurately measure their economic performance. The competitive market price rule also stimulates greater efficiency as divisional managers are subject to the same competitive pressures as if they were autonomous companies. Finally, efforts made by divisional management to improve their own divisional profitabilities will result in corresponding improvements in corporate profitability.

However, the use of a single competitive market price for pricing an internal transfer must inevitably be the exceptional case as in practice it will tend to be cheaper to purchase internally rather than externally. Internal transfers would not include the external market selling costs and, where the divisions are at adjacent locations, the transport costs would be saved. Therefore, one would expect a dual pricing situation with a higher external market price for purchasing in the intermediate market and a lower selling price for internal transactions. Divisions M and D would no longer be indifferent between trading internally and externally.

Gould (1964) investigated the optimality conditions for such a dual pricing situation. He found that an optimal transfer price which both maximized corporate profits and was freely negotiated between semi-autonomous divisions was only possible when the corporate NMR schedule intersected MC_M at a point somewhere between the higher external buying price and the lower internal net selling price. In this one case, both divisions would wish to deal exclusively with each other as the profit-maximizing price freely negotiated between them would be higher than the internal net selling price (in M's self-interest) and lower than the external buying price (in D's self-interest). Again, central intervention would not be required.

However, when the corporate NMR intersects MC_M at a point higher than the external buying price or at a point lower than the net selling price, central intervention would be required, both in setting a transfer price compatible with corporate profit maximization and in requiring M and D to trade with each other. Divisional autonomy would be substantially curtailed.

IMPERFECT COMPETITION AND MARGINAL COST TRANSFER PRICING

As in the case of perfect competition, the analysis is based on that of Hirshleifer (1956). When the external market for the intermediate goods is imperfectly competitive, the profit-maximizing position for the company is for M to produce the output Q, as illustrated in Figure 12.2. This output is determined by the intersection of MC_M with the schedule combining the corporate NMR from selling the final product with MR_M, where MR_M is the marginal revenue from selling to the imperfect external intermediate product market. This point of intersection gives the optimal transfer price TP. Therefore we have a marginal cost transfer price which can only be determined by the intervention of central management.

Division D will maximize its profits by purchasing Q' of M's output at TP, where its NMR will be equal to its marginal purchasing cost, TP. Division M will maximize its profits by selling Q'' (equals the difference between Q and Q') to the external market at a price of P_M, where MR_M equals the marginal cost of

Figure 12.2 *Imperfect external market and marginal cost transfer pricing*

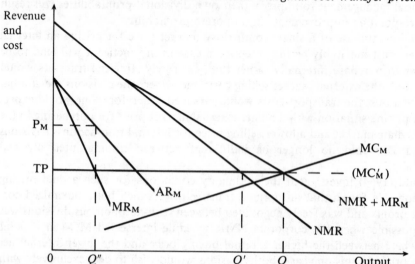

producing Q; and by selling Q' to D at the transfer price of TP (which equals MC_M at Q).

Notice that unlike the previous case of the perfectly competitive external intermediate product market, the imperfectly competitive external market price P_M is higher than the transfer price TP. The firm maximizes its profits by acting in the same way as a discriminating monopolist. Indeed, it is the monopoly element in imperfectly competitive market prices that precludes their usefulness as internal transfer prices.

However, the optimum position for the firm is dependent on it fixing a transfer price equal to its marginal production cost at the optimal output Q. Therefore, central management must first determine the budgeted outputs for the two divisions and then dictate the corresponding transfer price. Such central intervention has very high information demands in terms of divisional supply and demand functions.

In the case of marginal cost transfer prices, the monopolistic powers of M are severely curtailed. If M were assumed to have the same autonomy as an independent supplier, it would not produce the corporate optimum output of Q, where $NMR + MR_M$ equals MC_M. As the NMR schedule shows how much D would purchase at various transfer prices, M could perceive it as its demand curve, assuming it acts as a relatively autonomous monopolist. Division M would then derive its marginal revenue curve (for its internal sales) from NMR and proceed to maximize profits in the usual way. Obviously, its freely determined output would be considerably less than Q, as given in Figure 12.2. Yet by setting a transfer price on NMR (its perceived downward-sloping demand curve) higher than TP it could earn monopoly profits at the expense both of D and the company (whose output would be significantly reduced). Consequently, there is an inherent contradiction between semi-autonomous profit centres and the dictated marginal cost transfer prices required for overall corporate profit maximization, the latter undermining the former.

The problem of constant marginal costs

The analysis so far has assumed that marginal costs rise with increasing output. If, instead, marginal costs were assumed to be constant and central management fixed the transfer price equal to marginal cost at the profit-maximizing level of output, the manufacturing division would not make any profit on internal sales, neither would there be any contribution to its overheads. As a result, M would be motivated only to supply the external market.

This situation is illustrated in Figure 12.2 where marginal costs are given as MC'_M. The profit-maximizing position for the firm remains as before with Q as total output and a marginal cost transfer price of TP. As a result, division M will only just cover its variable costs on internal sales to D. All M's profits will derive from selling Q'' to the external market. Should there not be an external market, then M would not make any profit whatsoever and the logic for divisional profit centres would collapse.

Obviously, central management would be forced to instruct M to supply D at the transfer price of TP. The degree of autonomy allowed to M is restricted to its relations with the external market. For the internal market, central management specifies not only the transfer price and the quantity of M's total output, but also the amount it must allocate to division D. Given the widespread occurrence of standard unit costing, the problem that constant marginal costs presents to transfer pricing policy is non-trivial.

However, the above outcome for the case of constant marginal costs is not inevitable. Tomkins (1973) showed that when there were capacity constraints on the output levels of either M or D, which prevented output reaching that indicated by the intersection of the corporate marginal revenue and marginal cost curves, it was possible to devise transfer prices which would exceed M's constant marginal cost schedule and provide a company-wide optimal outcome. For example, if in Figure 12.2 M was technically unable to produce Q, the corporate optimal transfer price would be determined by the intersection of a vertical line drawn from M's constrained output up to the downward-sloping NMR plus MR_M curve. The resultant transfer price would exceed TP, so providing M with profits, and would give an optimal internal allocation of output to D. A similar result would occur should a constraint be operative on the amount D could purchase.

THE RONEN AND McKINNEY SOLUTION

In contrast to the Hirshleifer (1956) approach, Ronen and McKinney (1970) devised a transfer pricing system which allows the firm to profit-maximize with no more intervention than that required to exchange buying and selling information between the centre and the divisions. Central management would not make any price or output decisions but merely provide demand and supply curves to the divisions calculated from information supplied by the latter. There is no need for the Hirshleifer (1956) type restrictive instructions issued by central management. Also, their simple method of deriving transfer prices is the same whatever the state of market competition. Unlike the Hirshleifer (1956) approach, their method is not competition-specific.

Assuming the same two divisions as before, the method of calculating the transfer price is described as follows and is illustrated in Figure 12.3:

(i) Central management collects an MC_M schedule from M. An average cost schedule AC_M is derived from this data which is presented to D as its supply curve. This supply curve gives the transfer prices $P'(Q)$ that are charged to D for the various quantities supplied.

(ii) Central management likewise collects an NMR schedule from D from which it derives an average revenue curve AR_M. This is given to M as its demand curve as it shows the transfer prices $P^*(Q)$ offered to M for the various quantities supplied.

(iii) Division M calculates its MR_M schedule from AR_M and, in relating this to MC_M, determines its profit-maximizing output Q^*.

(iv) Division D calculates MC_M from AC_M and by equating $MC_D + MC_M$ to the

Figure 12.3   The dual transfer prices of Ronen and McKinney (1970)

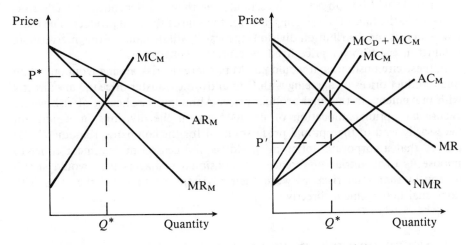

marginal revenue for the final product it purchases Q^* in order to profit-maximize.

Although both divisions independently determine the same profit-maximizing output Q^*, it would be most unlikely that the two transfer prices $P'(Q^*)$ and $P^*(Q^*)$ were equal. If $P^* > P'$, M is paid more than D is charged and the head office meets the difference with a subsidy. On the other hand, if $P' > P^*$, D pays more than M receives and the difference is collected by head office as a tax. It can also be seen from Figure 12.3 that NMR equals MC_M at Q^* level of output and so the optimal output for both divisions gives the profit-maximizing output for the firm.

So long as AR_M is downward-sloping, which requires that D does not simultaneously face a perfectly competitive final market and experience constant marginal distribution costs, the Ronen–McKinney (1970) method ensures that M can even earn profits if MC_M is constant. Therefore, they have overcome the zero profit problem that bedevilled the Hirshleifer (1956) approach to constant marginal costs. Consequently, by central management supplying demand and supply functions to its divisions, similar to those it would estimate from external intermediate markets, Ronen and McKinney (1970) offer a method which allows both divisional and corporate profit maximization while simulating the autonomy that divisions could enjoy as independent firms.

TRANSFER PRICING UNDER UNCERTAINTY

Kanodia (1979) extended the Hirshleifer (1956) analysis to consider the situation where the final product price would not be known when the production decision was taken. Many possible prices can be expected so that the simple profit-maximizing concept of a one equilibrium solution loses much of its meaning. If, under these circumstances, the transfer price is fixed by central management, then division M will regard it as a certainty. While the transfer price is certain, the sales by M to D will be subject to uncertainty, as they are dependent on D's risk-aversion in the face of uncertain prices for the sale of the final product. The more risk-averse is the distribution division, the less it will demand of the intermediate product at the transfer price fixed by central management.

In these circumstances, it would pay M to share the risk arising from uncertain final product prices by agreeing with D to allow the transfer price to vary directly with movements in the final product price. Although the sharing of risk would ensure an optimal allocation of profits between the divisions, it would not necessarily lead to the optimal profit solution for the company. Kanodia (1979) proved that a corporate optimum would require central management either to impose its own output preferences on divisional managers who would simultaneously share the risks between their divisions or to share the risks with divisional management directly.

TRANSFER PRICING IN PRACTICE

Surveys by the Centre for Business Research (1972), Tomkins (1973) and Emmanuel (1976) in the United Kingdom, and by Vancil (1979) in the United States, suggest that somewhere between 31 to 46 per cent of firms used the external market price of the intermediate product as the transfer price. Less than 6 per cent used variable or direct costs as the basis of transfer pricing. This suggests that the Hirshleifer (1956) marginal cost transfer pricing rule is not widely used. Between 25 and 56 per cent of firms used some form of full-cost pricing. About one-fifth of the surveyed firms used negotiated transfer pricing, the main form of which was cost plus a negotiated mark-up. Unfortunately, the empirical evidence is not available in a form suitable for evaluating whether the transfer pricing behaviour of the firms surveyed resulted in corporate optimality. Despite this, it is evident that a large majority of the firms were market-oriented to the extent that they used market prices, negotiated prices, or full-cost pricing with an emphasis on variable mark-ups. This provides some weak support to the neo-classical theory of profit maximization.

Transfer pricing involving the divisions of multinational companies gives rise to more complex decision-making than transfer pricing in the domestic economy. Many additional environmental variables have to be considered including tax legislation, customs duties and currency restrictions. Tang (1982) in a study of forty seven British multinationals found that the most important variable taken into account in transfer pricing decisions was company profit after tax. Other important variables were the competitive position of foreign subsidiaries, divisional performance evaluation, foreign restrictions on the repatriation of profits, and the maintenance of adequate cash flows in foreign subsidiaries. Transfer prices can be used to minimize tax liabilities by charging a high transfer price to a division operating in a country imposing high rates of profit tax. In a similar manner, high transfer prices can overcome restrictive profit repatriation legislation.

However, high transfer prices can also result in higher import duties being incurred. As a consequence of these complex issues, thirteen of the eighteen firms using transfer prices for international shipments between divisions surveyed by the Centre for Business Research (1972) claimed to use a different method of pricing international shipments than domestic shipments.

Yunker (1982) in her survey of fifty-two American multinational companies found that the most important perceived objective of transfer pricing was an increase in profit. The market price and the market price less selling costs were 'often used' as the transfer price by around half the firms surveyed and a quarter 'often used' negotiated prices. However, over half the firms also 'often used' full-cost pricing with a fixed mark-up. Notwithstanding this somewhat inconsistent behaviour, she found that firms which weighted profit heavily in performance evaluation also used market-oriented transfer pricing. Not surprisingly, she also found that a high degree of divisional autonomy was associated with a high utilization of market-oriented transfer pricing. This finding confirms the Hirshleifer (1956) expectation that the use of external market prices would minimize the need for intervention by central management. Overall, the market-oriented approach to the transfer pricing decision heavily outweighs the use of cost-based methods which confirms the evidence on pricing given in Chapter 9.

REFERENCES AND FURTHER READING

Centre for Business Research (1972) *Transfer Pricing: Management Control Project, No 3*, Manchester Business School.

Emmanuel, C. R. (1976) *Transfer Pricing in the Corporate Environment*, unpublished Ph.D thesis, University of Lancaster.

Gould, J. R. (1964) Internal pricing in firms when there are costs of using an outside market, *Journal of Business*, Vol. 37, pp. 61–7.

Hirshleifer, J. (1956) On the economics of transfer pricing, *Journal of Business*, Vol. 24, pp. 172–84.

Kanodia, C. (1979) Risk sharing and transfer price systems under uncertainty, *Journal of Accounting Research*, Vol. 17, pp. 74–98.

Ronen, J. and McKinney, G. (1970) Transfer pricing for divisional autonomy, *Journal of Accounting Research*, Vol. 8, pp. 99–112.

Solomons, D. (1965) *Divisional Performance, Measurement and Control*, Irwin.

Tang, R. Y. W. (1982) Environmental variables of multinational transfer pricing: a UK perspective, *Journal of Business Finance and Accounting*, Vol. 9. pp. 179–89.

Tomkins, C. (1973) *Financial Planning in Divisionalised Companies*, Accountancy Age Books.

Vancil, R. F. (1979) *Decentralisation: Ambiguity by Design*, Irwin.

Yunker, P. J. (1982) *Transfer Pricing and Performance Evaluation in Multinational Corporations*, Praeger.

13   Pricing and Advertising Decisions

THE ROLE OF ADVERTISING IN MODELLING DEMAND

Advertising forms one of the most important one-way communications links between the seller and a potential customer. Other communications links include sales calls, sales promotion, corporate public relations, and point-of-sale display. For the purposes of the following analysis, advertising will be used to denote all the various forms of selling and promotional expenses.

The role of advertising within a marketing strategy is to provide the customer with information about the advertiser, his product and services so as to 'develop attitudes and induce action beneficial to the advertiser' (Colley, 1961, p. 51) in the form of a positive move towards making a purchase. The marketing literature does not assume that advertising will necessarily result in an immediate purchase. Instead, the emphasis is on making the consumer aware of the product's existence, its characteristics and potential, so as to encourage a visit to the shop or showroom. The actual purchase may not occur until some time later. Consequently, an advertising message is seen as having dynamic properties in that it can affect sales over several future purchasing periods.

Informative versus persuasive advertising

Economists such as Telser (1964) have placed much importance on the distinction between the *informative* and *persuasive* content of the flow of advertising messages. While the former seeks to make the consumer aware of the existence of the product, its price, content and performance characteristics, and so assists choice on the basis of existing consumer preferences, the latter seeks to change consumer preferences by inducing a positive bias in favour of the advertised product. The usual economic assumption is that informative advertising increases the price elasticity of demand by making consumers better informed on the closeness of available substitutes. On the other hand, persuasive advertising reduces the price elasticity of demand by increasing the degree of product differentiation so that competing products are perceived as weaker substitutes. Therefore, the stronger the persuasive component in advertising messages relative to the information content, the more advertising will be expected to be associated with decreased competition and higher price–cost margins.

Doyle (1968) claimed that persuasive advertising will be more effective either when products are relatively cheap, as consumers will not expect to gain much financially from an extensive market search to check on the accuracy of the persuasive advertisements, or when it would be difficult for consumers to evaluate the product prior to purchase. Examples of this second case are complex consumer durables such as video recorders, washing machines or compact disc players. Doyle (1968) provided some empirical evidence to support both assertions.

However, Nelson (1975) took issue with the persuasive concept of advertising claiming that it was not supported by a theoretical explanation of how consumer preferences change. Consequently, there is no basis for making predictions on the effect of persuasive advertising. In contrast, Nelson (1975) modelled the effect of advertising on the demand function by assuming that it had an information function only. He also assumed that products were differentiated by branding, that all consumers had the same utility function, and that each consumer made the same quantity of purchases. As a result, his linear demand curve shows the relationship between the price per unit of utility and the number of consumers buying at each price. While consumers obviously wish to purchase units of utility at the lowest price possible, there is imperfect information on both the degree of price dispersal and the relationship between the prices and utilities of the different brands. This results in a demand curve of negative slope on which several prices prevail simultaneously.

The role of advertising in this model is to provide consumers with information at a lower cost to them than their searching from shop to shop, and so advertising by 'lowering the price of search increases the number of searches a consumer will undertake' (Nelson, 1975, p. 222). As a result, advertising increases the absolute value of the price elasticity at any given price. It also results in the lower priced brands gaining sales at the expense of those selling at a higher price per unit of utility, causing the most expensive brands either to withdraw progressively from the market or to reduce price. As cost of production provides a floor to the downward trend of prices, the result is a reduction in both the average price of the brands on sale and the dispersal of market prices. 'Since product differentiation must be defined in terms of the standard deviation of the price of a unit of utility, this analysis suggests that advertising reduces product differentiation' (Nelson, 1975, p. 225).

The profitability–advertising relationship

In the Nelson (1975) model, the lower priced brands will be pricing at points lower down his negatively sloped linear demand curve for units of utility and so will price at less elastic demands for their brands than brands charging higher prices. Consequently, they will enjoy relatively higher profit-maximizing price–cost margins which will permit larger advertising expenditures. Also, their lower production costs will mean they have more to gain from heavy advertising. As a result, there will be an observed positive relationship across the market between post-advertising profit rates and advertising expenditures which might imply that advertising caused higher profitability. To the contrary, by increasing the price elasticity of demand at any given price, advertising will have reduced price–cost margins at all prices. Advertising has not caused profitability to rise, it has simply shifted demand to the lower priced brands which happen to enjoy relatively higher (although absolutely declining) profit margins.

Economists have attached considerable significance to the profitability–advertising relationship since Bain (1968) and Comanor and Wilson (1971) claimed that persuasive advertising increases product differentiation making market entry by new brands more difficult. Consequently, evidence of a positive relationship between profitability and advertising is held to demonstrate that advertising acts as a barrier to entry. Unfortunately, there have been only a few theoretical studies of the effects of advertising on competitive behaviour. From these few studies, Schmalensee (1976) concluded, as did Nelson (1975), that it was profitability that gave rise to high advertising expenditure and not vice versa. It is the relatively efficient firms that can afford to spend more on advertising and so enjoy higher than average market shares. In a more recent study, Cubbin (1981) concluded that advertising intensity is a negative indicator of the presence of entry barriers and that any positive relationship found to exist between profitability and advertising must be due to monopoly power derived from sources other than advertising.

It seems that given the possible simultaneous nature of the profitability–advertising relationship and the frequently alleged ability of advertising to alter consumer preferences, advertising expenditure has a complex, and as yet not very well understood, role in demand analysis. This makes for immense problems when trying to model demand. Furthermore, as advertising is only one of a number of decision variables affecting sales it 'cannot be analysed independently of the other marketing instruments available to the firm' (Lambin, 1976, p. 16). Certainly, the effect of the pricing decision will have to be taken into account when determining the optimal advertising budget.

THE OPTIMAL ADVERTISING BUDGET

First, we will determine the optimal level of advertising expenditure when the full effect of advertising on sales is assumed to take place within the current purchasing period. The basic model used to determine the conditions for optimal advertising was developed by Dorfman and Steiner (1954) who consider the case of a monopolist having two decision variables, advertising and price. The demand function for such a firm can be expressed as:

$$q = q(p, a) \qquad 13.1$$

where q is the quantity demand, p is the price and a is the firm's current advertising expenditure. If total production costs are a function of output, $c[q]$, the profit function of the firm can be written as:

$$\pi = pq(p, a) - c[q(p, a)] - a \qquad \text{13.2}$$

By differentiating equation 13.2 with respect to advertising expenditure and price respectively, we can derive the first order conditions for profit maximization as:

$$\frac{\delta\pi}{\delta a} = \frac{\delta q}{\delta a}\left(p - \frac{\delta c}{\delta q}\right) - 1 = 0 \qquad \text{13.3}$$

and

$$\frac{\delta\pi}{\delta p} = \frac{\delta q}{\delta p}\left(p - \frac{\delta c}{\delta q}\right) + q = 0 \qquad \text{13.4}$$

Multiplying equation 13.3 by a and equation 13.4 by p, rearranging terms, and, finally dividing equation 13.3 by equation 13.4 gives the optimizing advertising condition for a monopolist as:

$$\frac{a}{pq} = \frac{(\delta q/\delta a)\,(a/q)}{-(\delta q/\delta p)\,(p/q)} = \frac{\eta_a}{\eta_p} \qquad \text{13.5}$$

Profit maximization requires the advertising to sales ratio (a/pq) to equal the ratio of the firm's advertising elasticity of demand to its price elasticity of demand.

One of the most significant relationships between the advertising and pricing decisions is that between advertising expenditures and the price elasticity of demand. Equation 13.5 shows that for any given price, the optimal level of advertising expenditure decreases as price elasticity increases. We have already seen that a similar inverse relationship exists between the price–cost margin and the price elasticity of demand. Consequently, we can rewrite equation 13.5 as:

$$\frac{a}{pq} = \eta_a \frac{(p - \delta c/\delta q)}{p} \qquad \text{13.6}$$

This can be interpreted as associating high advertising sales ratios with high price–cost margins in markets where sales are responsive to advertising expenditures. Therefore, with the price–cost margin being a measure of market power, it would appear that greater monopoly power will be associated with a higher level of profitable advertising. However, equation 13.6 assumes that the price is already fixed at the optimal short-run level before the optimal advertising budget is set. Consequently, it must remain as a special case, for equation 13.5 assumes that price and advertising levels are determined *simultaneously*, not sequentially.

The simultaneity problem is further complicated by interdependencies between pricing and advertising. In the previous section we have already discussed the effects of advertising on the price elasticity of demand. To the extent that advertising provides good quality information, it will increase the price elasticity of demand at any given price. This will serve to reduce both the price–cost margin and the level of advertising expenditure in the next period. Likewise, pricing may well have an effect on the advertising elasticity of demand. For example, Eskin and Baron (1977) found that the advertising elasticity was greater when prices were lower. There is, therefore, the possibility that pricing and advertising may have opposite effects on each other's elasticities of demand.

The effect of oligopolistic competition

The previous analysis, based on that of Dorfman and Steiner (1954), considered only the determination of the monopolist's advertising budget. However, the vast majority of firms have to compete and, consequently, have to take the possibility of rivals' reactions into account when making marketing decisions. As in the case of the price–cost margin, we need to formulate the advertising elasticity of demand in terms which account for the interaction of advertising decisions between firms. In order to simplify the presentation of the analysis, we will assume that all competitors charge the same price.

Given oligopolistic competition in advertising only, the demand function for the firm can be written as:

$$q = q(p, a, \bar{a},) \qquad\qquad 13.7$$

where $\bar{a}$ is advertising by rivals. We can then derive an expression for profits and differentiate with respect to the firm's own advertising as in equations 13.2 and 13.3. The oligopolist equivalent for η_a given in equation 13.5 can be derived as

$$\eta_a = \left(\frac{\delta q}{\delta a} + \frac{\delta \bar{a}}{\delta a} \cdot \frac{\delta q}{\delta \bar{a}} \right) \frac{a}{q} \qquad\qquad 13.8$$

This shows that the oligopolist's advertising elasticity is a function of two component terms, containing three advertising elasticities. The first component is the elasticity of the firm's sales with respect to its own advertising. The second component is the elasticity of rivals' advertising with respect to the firm's advertising *multiplied by* the elasticity of the firm's sales with respect to rivals' advertising. Of these three effects, $\delta q/\delta a$ is assumed to be >0; $\delta \bar{a}/\delta a$ could be either >0 or <0 depending on how the oligopolist conjectures rivals' responses; and $\delta q/\delta \bar{a}$ is assumed to be <0.

It follows from substituting the oligopolist's η_a into equation 13.5 that the oligopolist's profit-maximizing level of advertising is very dependent on its expectations of rivals' reactions. The optimal advertising to sales ratio will be larger, the smaller the *expected* positive reaction of rivals to a given change in the firm's level of advertising expenditure (with $\delta q/\delta \bar{a} < 0$, the second term in equation 13.8 will be negative whenever the advertising reaction function $\delta \bar{a}/\delta a > 0$). On the other hand, when the firm expects rivals to leave their advertising unchanged in response to a change in its own advertising – as in Cournot-type behaviour – the value of $\delta \bar{a}/\delta a$ will be zero and the second term will drop out of equation 13.8. This gives the same result as that of Dorfman and Steiner (1954).

When advertising is treated as a current input, we can conclude that the optimal advertising to sales ratio is determined by the reciprocal of the price elasticity of demand (or directly by the price–cost margin when prices are predetermined), the elasticity of demand with respect to the firm's own advertising and, in certain circumstances, the advertising reaction function of competitors. We now need to return to a concern of the marketing literature and consider the dynamic properties of advertising in affecting sales beyond the current purchasing period. This means analysing advertising as a capital input.

THE LAGGED EFFECTS OF ADVERTISING AND PRICING

Advertising can have an impact on sales in future periods as well as in the current period. There are several reasons to explain this cumulative, or lagged, effect. First, the consumer, having become aware of the product in the current period, may take several more periods to effect a purchase. For example, the timing of the advertising of consumer durables is unlikely to match the timing of consumers' expenditure. The consumer may first have to save, arrange credit, or even try and sell the currently owned model before making a purchase. Second, interdependencies between buyers, with some acting as 'trend setters' in the current period and others acting as 'following sheep' in future periods, will generate a lagged response to advertising new products. Third, it may take a series of advertisements either to make all consumers aware of the brand or to break down consumer loyalty to other brands. It follows that by having effects which persist beyond the accounting period in which the expenditure was made, advertising generates a *stock of goodwill* having the properties of an investment.

Nerlove and Arrow (1962) have determined the optimal stock of goodwill, g, as a dynamic version of the Dorfman–Steiner (1954) model:

$$\frac{g}{pq} = \frac{\eta_a}{\eta_p(r + w)} \qquad 13.9$$

where η_a is the elasticity of demand with respect to goodwill, r is the firm's discount rate, and w is the rate at which goodwill depreciates over time. This depreciation is caused by a number of factors including the fading of memory and the effect of new or revitalized advertising campaigns by competitors. It follows that current advertising expenditure should equal the depreciation of goodwill plus any intended net investment in goodwill. Then as the marginal change in goodwill will equal the marginal change in advertising, we can substitute a for g in equation 13.9 so as to express it in terms of a long-run advertising to sales ratio. The effect of taking the depreciation of goodwill into account will be to cause the long-run advertising to sales ratio to exceed that of the short run.

When the rate of depreciation is assumed to be at a constant proportional rate, a geometrically declining lag structure can be used to relate the effect of past advertising on current sales. Assuming also that the demand function is of an exponential form, we can estimate:

$$\log q_t = \alpha + \beta \sum_{i=o}^{\infty} \lambda^i \log a_{t-i} \qquad\qquad 13.10$$

where $0 < \lambda < 1$. The coefficient β directly estimates η_a, the short-run elasticity of sales with respect to advertising, λ estimates the cumulative effect of past advertising and $(1 - \lambda)$ provides an estimate of w, the rate of depreciation. Using these values we can derive $\beta/(1 - \lambda)$ as an estimate of the long-run elasticity of sales with respect to advertising (which is the sum to infinity of the coefficients on the lagged advertising variables a_{t-i}). So long as $\lambda > 0$, the long-run elasticity of the sales effect of advertising will exceed that of the short run. Therefore, by estimating equation 13.10, management can evaluate the rate of depreciation, and the short and long-run advertising elasticities. Using these values, together with estimated price elasticity, management can determine the rate of advertising expenditure which will maintain its optimal stock of goodwill.

The problem with the formulation of equations 13.9 and 13.10 is that they ignore any lagged effects of past pricing. Similar reasons to those explaining the cumulative effect of advertising may be used to support a lagged pricing effect. For instance, a strategy of charging low prices in the past may instil in consumers the belief that the brand concerned *always* gives value for money. Again, we have already observed in earlier chapters the dynamic effects of price skimming and limit price strategies.

When the geometrically declining lag structure is the same for price and advertising, we can derive the long-run price elasticity by dividing η_p by $(1 - \lambda)$. The optimal long-run advertising to sales ratio can now be written as:

$$\frac{a}{pq} = \frac{\eta_a(1 - \lambda)}{\eta_p(1 - \lambda)} = \frac{\eta_a}{\eta_p} \qquad\qquad 13.11$$

Thus, the long and short-run advertising to sales ratios are identical. In these circumstances, management can largely ignore the dynamic effects. However, the lag structure of pricing could well be different from that of advertising. In this case, the geometrically declining lag structure would be inappropriate as there would be different depreciation rates for advertising and price behaviour. While the different lag structure approach might appear to be more realistic, the practical estimation difficulties are immense and have yet to be resolved satisfactorily for practical implementation.

BUSINESS PRACTICE

Rules of thumb

In practice it is difficult, if not impossible, to achieve a simultaneous determination of advertising expenditure and price as required by the Dorfman–Steiner (1954) model and its dynamic extensions. Management is often faced with discrete and sometimes incomplete data preventing the estimation of the continuously differentiable functions needed to determine the optimal advertising budget. Even when past data are available, the basic relationships may be subject to unexpected change causing predictions to be subject to unacceptably high error variances. The typical management response is to treat advertising and price as independent decision variables and to adopt separate rules of thumb when determining their desired levels.

The most commonly used rule of thumb is to set the advertising budget at a predetermined and fixed percentage of sales revenue. There are several variants of this rule, all differing by the base used to calculate sales revenue. The most popular bases are last period's sales, average sales over several previous periods, and projected sales in the current period. The predetermined percentage is based on some 'historic' or 'behavioural' figure considered necessary to defend current market share. Dean (1951) suggested that the popularity of the rule might be due to the fact that it budgets for advertising expenditure to rise and fall in correspondence with the gross revenue necessary to fund it. Also, it is timed to occur when the tax effect is likely to be favourable.

Like many management rules of thumb, the fixed advertising to sales ratio may, at first sight, appear to lead to sub-optimal decision-making. It implies that current advertising expenditure is determined by either past or expected sales, while economic theory assumes that advertising helps to cause sales. However, spending a fixed percentage of sales revenue on advertising could be optimal if the demand function was expected to approximate an exponential form, as the pricing and advertising elasticities would be constant for all values of price and advertising. However, the problem still remains that the rule, as applied in practice, does not have any mechanism for determining the fixed optimal advertising to sales ratio in the first place.

Econometric studies

There have been many econometric estimates of short-run advertising and price elasticities. Lambin (1976) undertook one of the most comprehensive studies covering 107 brands, from 16 product classes in 8 different West European countries. Of his 40 significant and positive brand advertising elasticities, the highest was only 0.48 and the average was 0.1. These results suggest that the marginal effect of current advertising on current sales is very modest indeed. Similar results were reported by Cowling (1972) for his UK studies of cars, tractors, margarine, coffee and toothpaste; margarine was highest with an advertising elasticity of 0.59 and coffee was lowest with 0.14. Estimated elasticities of less than 1.0 suggest that all these brands were experiencing diminishing marginal returns to advertising.

On the other hand, price has been found to have a significant effect on demand, even in markets of high advertising intensity. Lambin (1976) estimated thirty-seven significant and negative brand price elasticities having an average value of −1.33 and so conforming with the greater than unity requirement of profit maximization. So many significant price elasticities suggest that intensive advertising had not eliminated consumers' price sensitivity. Lambin (1976) also provided evidence of significant advertising–price reaction elasticities showing that firms respond to rivals' advertising (pricing) activities by price (advertising) adjustments. The importance of these cross-variable reactions highlights the effectiveness of the marketing mix approach to market strategy outlined in Chapter 10.

Lambin (1976), Metwally (1975) and Cowling (1972) used their estimates of advertising and price elasticities to apply equation 13.5 in predicting the optimal current advertising to sales ratio for the relevant brands. These predictions were then compared with the actual. Metwally (1975) found the observed and predicted ratios for Australian brands of coffee, bottled beer, toilet soap and petrol to be sufficiently close to suggest short-run profit-maximizing behaviour. However, in the cases of cigarettes, washing powder and toothpaste, the actual ratios were excessively high. Cowling (1972) found his three non-durable products to be close to optimality but cars and tractors were considerably underadvertised. Half of the twelve brands Lambin (1976) examined appeared to conform to optimal advertising behaviour. Therefore, across these three studies, short-run profit-maximizing behaviour was indicated for just over half the brands.

Both Metwally (1975) and Lambin (1976) found evidence of reciprocal cancellation effects in competitive advertising. The cancellation effect is evident when the values of $\delta q/\delta a$ and $\delta q/\delta \bar{a}$ in equation 13.8 are of similar size, although of opposite sign. In this case, advertising is being used simply to protect market share by cancelling out the effect of rivals' advertising. It is interesting that the three brands in the Metwally (1975) study whose current advertising expenditures were in excess of the optimum – cigarettes, washing powder, and toothpaste – all exhibited evidence of reciprocal cancellation effects. This suggests that this defensive form of advertising may have an upward ratchet-like effect on expenditures. Both Lambin (1976) and Metwally (1975) found strong evidence to support the assumption that oligopolistic advertising reaction elasticities are positive.

Most of the econometric evidence suggests that advertising has a lagged effect on sales greatly exceeding the current effect. The cumulative effect in past advertising is estimated by λ, as given in equation 13.10. In his survey of sixty-nine published estimates of cumulative advertising, Clarke (1976) calculated an average value of 0.59; the highest was 0.99 and only eight estimates were below 0.3. This implies an average depreciation rate of 0.41 and a long-run advertising elasticity (estimated from equation 13.10 as $\beta/(1 - \lambda)$) of more than twice that of the short run. Metwally (1976) when substituting his estimates of the long-run advertising elasticity for three brands of washing powder into equation 13.9 found that the long-run optimal advertising to sales ratios were between three and four times greater than those estimated as optimal for the short run. However, the long-run optimal ratios were fairly close to the actual ratios, implying that these Australian brands were subject to a policy of long-run profit maximization.

REFERENCES AND FURTHER READING

Bain, J. S. (1968) *Industrial Organisation*, John Wiley.
Clarke, D. G. (1976) Econometric measurement of the duration of advertising effect on sales, *Journal of Marketing Research*, Vol. 13, pp. 345–57.

Colley, R. H. (1961) *Defining Advertising Goals for Measured Advertising Results*, Association of National Advertisers.

Comanor, W. S. and Wilson, T. A. (1971) Advertising market structure and performance, *Review of Economics and Statistics*, Vol. 49, pp. 423–40.

Cowling, K. (1972) Optimality in firms' advertising policies: an empirical analysis, in K. Cowling (ed.) *Market Structure and Corporate Behaviour*, Gray-Mills.

Cubbin, J. (1981) Advertising and the theory of entry barriers, *Economica*, Vol. 48, pp. 289–98.

Dean, J. (1951) *Managerial Economics*, Prentice-Hall.

Dorfman, R. and Steiner, P. O. (1954) Optimal advertising and optimal quality, *American Economic Review*, Vol. 44, pp. 826–36.

Doyle, P. (1968) Advertising expenditure and consumer demand, *Oxford Economic Papers*, Vol. 20, pp. 395–417.

Eskin, G. J. and Baron, P. H. (1977) Effects of price and advertising in test market experiments, *Journal of Marketing Research*, Vol. 14, pp. 499–508.

Lambin, J. J. (1976) *Advertising Competition and Market Conduct in Oligopoly Over Time*, North-Holland.

Metwally, M. M. (1975) Advertising and competitive behaviour of selected Australian firms, *Review of Economics and Statistics*, Vol. 47, pp. 417–27.

Metwally, M. M. (1976) Profitability of advertising in Australia: a case study, *Journal of Industrial Economics*, Vol. 24, pp. 221–31.

Nelson, P. (1975) The economic consequences of advertising, *Journal of Business*, Vol. 48, pp. 213–41.

Nerlove, M. and Arrow, K. J. (1962) Optimal advertising policy under dynamic conditions, *Economica*, Vol. 29, pp. 129–42.

Schmalensee R. (1976) Advertising and profitability: further implications of the null hypothesis, *Journal of Industrial Economics*, Vol. 25, pp. 45–54

Telser, L. G. (1964) Advertising and competition, *Journal of Political Economy*, Vol. 72, pp. 537–62.

14 Pricing and Investment Decisions

THE INTERDEPENDENCE OF PRICING AND INVESTMENT DECISIONS

In the context of the following analysis, investment can be defined as corporate expenditure on fixed assets used in production; examples would be new buildings, plant and machinery. Its main distinguishing characteristic is that of one or more periods of initial capital expenditure, or cash outflow, followed by several periods of positive earnings, or cash inflows (a stream of sales revenues minus a stream of variable production costs). As the earnings from investment are spread out over future years, an optimal investment decision must take account of the time value of money. This involves discounting future earnings so as to express them in terms of their present value; the present being the period in which the initial investment expenditure is incurred. In this way, the value of the stream of future earnings will be comparable with the investment expenditure from which they were generated.

One consequential problem is that the future earnings yielded by an investment cannot be known with certainty at the time the investment is made. This applies not just to their annual rate of flow but also to their expected lifetime. Therefore, predictions as to the amount of future earnings are subject to uncertainty; an uncertainty that tends to increase as the expected lifetime of an investment project increases.

The problem of predicting the additional earnings arising from a new investment is central to the interrelationship existing between the pricing and investment decisions. In neo-classical economic theory, a necessary condition for the firm having an optimal stock of investment capital is that the expenditure on a new investment equals the additional earnings it generates:

$$c\delta K = p\delta Q \qquad\qquad 14.1$$

where c is the implicit price of the services derived from the capital stock, K, and

p is the price of output, Q. From this we can derive the optimal stock of capital as a function both of output and the ratio of the price of output to the cost of capital ($p:c$). It follows that an investment decision has to be based on an assumption about future prices and the quantities to which they relate; in other words, a long-run demand function. Thus, an investment decision can only be made on the expectation that the assumed pricing decision will materialize.

However, from a management perspective, once the investment decision is made on the basis of an assumed sales price, the need to generate the predicted stream of earnings will influence all subsequent short-run pricing decisions. Lanzillotti (1958, p. 940) even went so far as to suggest that 'investment decisions in effect are themselves a form of pricing decision, and over time become an inherent part of pricing policy'. Certainly, the growing concern by management for establishing corporate planning and capital budgeting activities, as witnessed in the management literature over the last two decades, has led to a greater formal linkage between investment planning and price policy.

The interdependence between pricing and investment decisions is exhibited most clearly in the case of new products. New products selected for investment will be those having the greatest return on capital or highest net present value (the excess of discounted future earnings over the initial investment expenditure). However, these returns and net present values will be very much influenced by the selected pricing policy. A skimming price strategy (see Chapter 10) should provide higher earnings in the earlier years, resulting in a higher net present value for the first x years and a faster rate of recoupment of product development and other related investment expenditures. On the other hand, a penetration price strategy would be more likely to prolong the life of the investment by discouraging new competition, resulting in a longer period of earnings. When capital is relatively costly, the selection of new product investments will tend to be dominated by those with a potential for price skimming as this offers the possibility of a faster recoupment of capital. Thus, in certain circumstances, the capital supply conditions can determine company pricing policy.

One pricing policy which is directly determined by the investment decision is that of *target return* pricing, where the price is set to earn a target rate of return on capital. Lanzillotti (1958, p. 923) found that half of twenty companies interviewed in the US 'explicitly indicated that their pricing policies were based mainly upon the objective of realizing a particular rate of return on investment in a given year, over the long haul, or both'.

TARGET RETURN PRICING

As in the case of full-cost pricing, the planned gross profit margin is fixed in relation to the standard volume of output (expressed as efficient practical capacity, Q^*, in the full-cost pricing model presented in Chapter 8). The difference between full-cost and target return pricing is that the gross profit margin for the latter is specifically predetermined so as to yield the target rate of return on the capital investment at the standard volume of output. Therefore, unlike full-cost pricing, the cost of capital enters the price-determination formula as a variable in its own right.

If we assume that all budgeted costs are set in relation to the standard volume of output, the target return price can be expressed as:

$$p = \frac{\alpha K}{Q^*} + w + m \qquad\qquad 14.2$$

where α is the target rate of return, K is the capital investment, Q^* is the standard volume of output, w is the standard unit labour cost and m is the standard unit material cost. Equation 14.2 shows that the target return price is the sum of the standard unit gross return to capital, the standard unit labour cost and the standard unit material cost.

By differentiating price with respect to the target rate of return we get:

$$\frac{\delta p}{\delta \alpha} = \frac{K}{Q^*} \qquad\qquad 14.3$$

showing that the relationship between the selling price of the product and the rate of return on the capital investment (which facilitates its production) is determined by the capital–output ratio. The higher the capital–output ratio, the more responsive price will be to change in the target rate of return. Essentially, target return pricing places pricing policy at the heart of investment theory. Its main advantage is that it permits management to maintain consistency between its pricing and investment decisions. Eckstein and Fromm (1968) also suggested that it provides a mechanism for operating positions of price leadership; no doubt because the gross profit margin can be recognized by competitors as providing a satisfactory return on capital employed.

There are two major problems in trying to relate target return pricing to the profit-maximizing objective. First, traditional short-run profit maximization would require the firm to maximize its short-run gross return to capital. For this to happen, the planned unit gross return to capital would become an inverse function of the price elasticity of demand. If we express $(\alpha K/Q^*)$ from equation 14.2 as π and $(w + m)$ as b, the optimal gross return to capital can be expressed in terms of the more familiar gross profit margin as follows:

$$\frac{\pi}{b} = \frac{p - b}{b} = (-)\frac{1}{(\eta + 1)} \qquad\qquad 14.4$$

Therefore, the unit gross return to capital, π, must be inversely related to the price elasticity of demand, η. However, as we saw in Chapter 8 when discussing the closely related policy of full-cost pricing, this will require π to react to changes in the rate of capacity utilization. However, target return pricing 'is designed to prevent cyclical, or short-run, changes in volume or product mix from unduly affecting price' (Lanzillotti, 1958, p. 923). To the extent that target return pricing actually operates in this way, it would not appear to be compatible with short-run profit maximization.

While Lanzillotti (1958) reported from his interviews with US corporate executives that target return pricing was 'usually tied in with a long-run view of prices' (p. 928), he did not go so far as to suggest that this could be used as evidence for long-run profit maximization. The latter would require the firm to maximize the present value of its expected stream of future earnings by discounting with an appropriate time value of money (the discount rate).

This gives rise to the second problem of relating target return pricing to profit-maximization behaviour. When operating this pricing policy in practice, firms tend to apply α as an accounting rate of return. The latter does not take account of the time value of money and when applied to a single year it will not be a reliable measure of the economist's internal rate of return. Before considering further the compatibility of the accounting rate of return with long-run profit maximization, we need to return to a more detailed consideration of the investment decision.

INVESTMENT APPRAISAL

The long-term capital investment decision is normally analysed within a shareholder-wealth-maximizing framework, whereby the firm seeks to maximize the present value of its expected future net cash flows. Thus, when the firm selects investment projects offering the highest net present value, it will be aiming to maximize its market value to existing shareholders. This is analogous to long-run profit maximization. There are two methods of investment appraisal which can be used to achieve this objective; the internal rate of return and the net present value criterion. Throughout this section it is assumed that all cash flows are known with certainty.

The internal rate of return

The internal rate of return is that discount rate which makes the present value of the expected stream of future cash inflows equal to the initial investment expenditure. If the initial investment expenditure (a cash outflow) at the end of the year is expressed as I_o and the subsequent expected cash inflows at the end of each of the n years of the project are expressed as $x_1, x_2, \ldots x_n$, we can estimate the internal rate of return, r, directly from the equation:

$$\sum_{t=1}^{n} \frac{x_t}{(1+r)^t} - I_o = 0 \qquad\qquad 14.5$$

The left-hand side of equation 14.5 gives the net present value of the project – present value of expected cash inflows minus the initial investment outflow. Thus, the internal rate of return is that discount rate which makes the net present value equal to zero. As such, it represents the rate of return which an investment in the project is expected to return to the firm and so estimates the prospective yield. The value of r in equation 14.5 has to be estimated by trial and error.

In order to maximize the market value of the firm, management should continue to invest in projects having an internal rate of return greater than the market cost of capital. This applies so long as the projects are not mutually exclusive (where the acceptance of one project automatically precludes acceptance of the others). The optimal amount of investment occurs where the marginal internal rate of return equals the cost of capital.

So long as the cash flows are of the conventional type with a negative cash outflow followed by a consistent series of positive cash inflows, the internal rate of return method will provide a good comparative ranking of all possible projects for use in project selection. However, when the cash flows periodically interchange from positive to negative and vice versa over the life of a project, the method may either give multiple internal rates of return or no meaningful rate of return at all. Such a situation can occur whenever a project requires periodic injections of new investment expenditure, as in mining activities. While the occurrence of multiple rates of return does not invalidate the method, their successful interpretation will require additional information.

The net present value criterion

This approach discounts the expected stream of future cash inflows by the firm's cost of capital, denoted by i, so as to convert them to a present value and then deducts the initial investment expenditure from this sum to leave the net present value (NPV). The method can be expressed as:

$$NPV = \sum_{t=1}^{n} \frac{x_t}{(1+i)^t} - I_o \qquad\qquad 14.6$$

The firm will maximize shareholder wealth by investing in all projects where the net present value is positive or at least equal to zero (the optimal *level* of investment). If two or more projects are mutually exclusive, then the projects should be ranked and the one with the highest net present value should be chosen. Assuming perfect capital markets, the increase in the market value of the firm over a year will equal the sum of the NPVs of the investments made during that year.

Unlike the internal rate of return, the net present value will be influenced by the current cost of capital. The NPV will be at its highest when $i = o$ as it will simply be the sum of the undiscounted cash inflows less the initial investment expenditure. Progressively increasing i will cause the NPV to fall until it eventually reaches zero, at which point i will be equal to the internal rate of return of the project. Discounting by a value of i greater than the internal rate of return will result in negative NPVs and unacceptable or sub-optimal projects. Consequently, the internal rate of return is equivalent to the highest rate of discount that can be applied (making $NPV = 0$) without the investment project becoming sub-optimal in terms of wealth-maximizing behaviour.

However, the effect of different discount rates on the NPV will depend on the time profile of the cash inflows. If the cash inflows are concentrated into the early years, the NPV will not be as adversely affected by an increase in the discount rate than if they are bunched in later years. Therefore, projects having relatively fast paybacks (cash inflows concentrated into the early years) will tend to have relatively higher NPVs whenever the cost of capital is high. The one drawback to the NPV method is the practical one of determining the appropriate cost of capital (the opportunity cost of funds) to insert into equation 14.6.

The internal rate of return and net present value methods will result in identical investment decisions whenever the cash flows are of the conventional pattern and when the projects are not mutually exclusive. In the case of multiple internal rates of return or mutually exclusive investments, the NPV method is usually preferred as it always provides one unambiguous value and it directly accounts for differences in the cost of capital. However, the internal rate of return method can still be applied in these special circumstances (see Koutsoyiannis, 1982, ch. 4), although its use will require additional information either on the project with the highest NPV when the investment is mutually exclusive or on the average rate of return of existing assets when multiple internal rates of return are the problem. It is also the case that the NPV and internal rate of return methods will converge on the same ranking of mutually exclusive projects as the rate of discount rises towards the internal rate of return.

The accounting rate of return

This relates the expected annual net profit, after depreciation, to the investment expenditure or book value of assets at the beginning of the year. New investment is appraised by comparing this rate of return with the firm's cost of capital. Given the choice between several methods of calculating depreciation and asset values, there are a number of alternative accounting rates of return possible. However, they are all based on the accounting definition of profit which is subject to non-cash adjustments, such as depreciation charges, and so do not directly correspond to the cash flow concept used in determining the internal rate of return, or economic yield, of an investment. Also, as a non-discounting method of investment appraisal, the time value of earnings is ignored so implying an equal value to present and future earnings.

ACCOUNTING AND INTERNAL RATES OF RETURN COMPARED

Not surprisingly, Harcourt (1965) and Solomon (1966) found important discrepancies between the accounting rate of return and the internal rate of return. They claimed that these derived from the fact that the accountant's usual methods of depreciation are arbitrary and do not correspond with the economic pattern of depreciation as implied by discounting future receipts by the internal rate of return. The economic value of an asset should depreciate over a period by a sum equal to the present value of the receipts from that period.

However, Kay (1976), using continuous time instead of discrete time, and Peasnell (1982), using very short discrete time periods, have produced results which demonstrate that the accounting rate of return, measured over several time periods, will be a reliable proxy for the internal rate of return, irrespective of the amount and method of depreciation. It is when measured over a single year and applied to a single project that the former will be misleading. It is not generally misleading as claimed by Harcourt (1965) (see Luckett, 1984, for a survey of this literature).

Their work derives a set of useful relationships between the accounting and internal rates of return. First, when the former is constant over the life of a project, it will equal the latter. This would be directly applicable in the case of non-competitive government contracts, where it is normal practice to pay the supplier a constant target rate of return. Second, when accounting rates of return vary over time, their weighted average will equal the internal rate of return, subject to the weights being the discounted book values of assets. The weighting procedure is necessary to account for the fact that later accounting rates of return are of less value than those occurring in earlier periods. However, Peasnell (1982) showed that where 'the book value of the firm's assets grow through time at a constant rate equal to the [internal rate of return]' (p. 371), the weighting procedure is unnecessary and a simple arithmetic average of the accounting rates of return would ensure equality. Third, when the firm is in steady-state growth, the accounting and internal rates of return will be equal so long as either the firm is continuously reinvesting its profits, or if the accounting and economic asset valuations are the same. Finally, even when these three conditions cannot be met, there is a broad group of circumstances where the internal rate of return will be a linear function of the accounting rate of return, although subject to unbiased errors in the accounting valuations.

Given the fact that an analytical relationship exists between the accounting and internal rates of return, the adoption of target return pricing does not preclude long-run profit-maximizing behaviour. However, to be compatible, the accounting rate of return must relate the *expected future stream of net profits*, and not just a single year's profit, to the initial capital investment. It is only when the accounting rate of return forms a reliable proxy for the internal rate of return that we can be assured of conditions conducive to a correspondence between target return pricing and long-run profit maximization. The latter will occur when the firm continues to invest in those projects offering the highest rate of return up to the point where the marginal rate of return equals the cost of capital. For each project (product) accepted, the rate of return for target pricing should equal the internal rate of return (economic yield) expected from the investment.

BUSINESS PRACTICE

Uncertainty and the payback rule of thumb

In practice, virtually all investment decisions are made on the basis of uncertain estimates of future cash flows. Consequently, managers consider themselves to be personally at risk when making project investments (King, 1975), and those who are risk-averse tend to select projects whose cash inflows are either less subject to uncertainty (as with price leadership) or concentrated into the earlier years of a project's lifetime (as with price skimming). Although the usual techniques of investment appraisal can be adapted to evaluate risky projects either by calculating an expected value, or certainty equivalent, for cash inflows or by adding a risk factor to the discount rate, most firms seem to appraise risky projects by the simple payback rule of thumb. This defines the period it takes to recoup the initial investment expenditure from the subsequent cash inflows. The more management is risk-averse, the shorter the target payback period and the faster it seeks to recover its initial investment outlay. Although simple to apply, the payback rule is a rather crude form of investment appraisal in that it considers neither the time value of money nor the earnings that occur beyond the payback date.

All the survey evidence to date indicates payback as being the most popular method of investment appraisal. For example, Pike (1983) found 79 per cent of 150 of the largest UK companies using payback in 1980 compared with 54 per cent using NPV, 51 per cent using the accounting rate of return and 38 per cent using the internal rate of return. He also found an increased use of payback since 1975. This suggests that increased uncertainty over prices and profits during the mid-1970s might have encouraged a greater reliance on payback. Woods et al. (1985) found that firms investing in computer-aided design and manufacturing systems (high-risk technology) placed considerably more reliance on payback than other firms surveyed. Their most surprising result was that when investing in their first system, 37 per cent of the sample claimed not to use any formal appraisal technique. Perhaps these firms considered the uncertainty to be so great as to render cash flow predictions meaningless.

Target rate of return pricing

Lanzillotti (1958) reported that about half the twenty companies interviewed in his series of US case studies explicitly indicated that they followed this pricing policy. In the UK, Shipley (1981) found that 67 per cent of 728 respondent companies specified a profit target or required rate of return on capital employed as their principal pricing objective. Unfortunately, this result does not allow us to separate out target return pricing from other profit-motivated pricing policies. Shipley (1981) also found that nearly half his respondents attempted to maximize profits which, at least for some companies, puts target return pricing in a profit-maximizing context. It is of some interest that Pike (1983) found the accounting rate of return to be as popular as the NPV method of investment appraisal. The popularity of the accounting rate of return and target rate of return pricing could well be linked to the fact that the annual performance of many divisional managers in the UK is measured in terms of a rate of return on investment (Scapens, Sale and Tikkas, 1982).

Although the econometric work of Eckstein and Fromm (1968) found some weak support for the target return pricing hypothesis in the US between 1954 and

1965, they also found rates of capacity utilization and unfilled orders to be highly significant variables in explaining price levels and price changes. In the UK, Bain and Evans (1973) found that a distributed lag of capacity utilization significantly affected the mark-up on labour costs in manufacturing industry in the 1960s. This implies that target return pricing does not prevent cyclical or short-run changes in volume from affecting price–cost margins and that it is likely to be operated in the same way as the proportional allocation rule (see Chapter 8). This rather sparse amount of empirical research would suggest that target return pricing is operated largely in accordance with short-run profit maximization.

REFERENCES AND FURTHER READING

Bain, A. D. and Evans, J. D. (1973) Price formation and profits: explanatory and forecasting models of manufacturing industry profits in the UK, *Bulletin of Oxford University Institute of Economics and Statistics*, Vol. 35, pp. 295–308.

Eckstein, O. and Fromm, G. (1968) The price equation, *American Economic Review*, Vol. 58, pp. 1159–83.

Harcourt, G. C. (1965) The accountant in a golden age, *Oxford Economic Papers*, Vol. 17, pp. 66–80.

Kay, J. A. (1976) Accountants, too, could be happy in the golden age: the accountant's rate of profit and the internal rate of return, *Oxford Economic Papers*, Vol. 28, pp. 447–60.

King, P. (1975) Is the emphasis of capital budgeting theory misplaced?, *Journal of Business Finance and Accounting*, Vol. 2, pp. 69–82.

Koutsoyiannis, A. (1982) *Non-Price Decisions*, Macmillan.

Lanzillotti, R. F. (1958) Pricing objectives in large companies, *American Economic Review*, Vol. 48, pp. 921–40.

Luckett, P. F. (1984) ARR vs IRR: a review and analysis, *Journal of Business Finance and Accounting*, Vol. 11, pp. 213–31.

Peasnell, K. V. (1982) Some formal connections between economic values and yields and accounting numbers, *Journal of Business Finance and Accounting*, Vol. 9, pp. 361–81.

Pike, R. H. (1983) A review of recent trends in capital budgeting processes, *Accounting and Business Research*, Vol. 13, pp. 201–8.

Scapens, R. W., Sale, J. T. and Tikkas, P. A. (1982) *Financial Control of Divisional Capital Investment*, ICMA.

Shipley, D. D. (1981) Pricing objectives in British manufacturing industry, *Journal of Industrial Economics*, Vol. 29, pp. 429–43.

Solomon, E. (1966) Return on investment: relation of book yield to true yield, in R. K. Jaedicke, Y. Ijiri and O. Nielsen (eds.) *Research in Accounting Measurement*, American Accounting Association, pp. 232–44.

Woods, M., Pokorny, M., Lintner, V. and Blinkhorn, M. (1985) Appraising investment in new technology: the approach in practice, *Management Accounting*, UK, Vol. 63, October, pp. 42–3.

Author Index

Subject Index